CLASSICS OF STRATEGY AND COUNSEL

The Collected Translations of
Thomas Cleary

CLASSICS OF STRATEGY AND COUNSEL

CLASSICS OF STRATEGY AND COUNSEL

VOLUME THREE

The Art of Wealth
Living a Good Life
The Human Element
Back to Beginnings

SHAMBHALA
Boston & London
2000

Shambhala Publications, Inc.
Horticultural Hall
300 Massachusetts Avenue
Boston, MA 02115
www.shambhala.com

9 8 7 6 5 4 3 2 1

First Edition
Printed in the United States of America

⊗ This edition is printed on acid-free paper that meets the
American National Standards Institute z39.48 Standard.
Distributed in the United States by Random House, Inc.,
and in Canada by Random House of Canada Ltd

Library of Congress Cataloging-in-Publication Data
Classics of strategy and counsel: the collected translations of Thomas Cleary.
p.   cm.
Includes bibliographical references.
Contents: v. 1. The art of war—Mastering the art of war—The lost art of war—The
silver sparrow art of war—v. 2. Thunder in the sky—The Japanese art of war—The
book of five rings—Ways of warriors, codes of kings—v. 3. The art of wealth—
Living a good life—The human element—Back to beginnings.
ISBN 1-57062-750-9 (set) — ISBN 1-57062-727-4 (v. 1) — ISBN 1-57062-728-2 (v. 2)
— ISBN 1-57062-729-0 (v. 3)
1. Military art and science.   2. Strategy.   3. Management.
I. Cleary, Thomas F., 1949–
U104.C484   2000
355.02—dc21
00-030765

CONTENTS

PUBLISHER'S NOTE

The works contained in The Collected Translations of Thomas Cleary were published over a period of more than twenty years and originated from several publishing houses. As a result, the capitalization and romanization of Chinese words, and the treatment of the word 'Ali, vary occasionally from one text to another within the volumes, due to changes in stylistic preferences from year to year and from house to house. In all cases, terms are rendered consistently within each text.

THE ART OF WEALTH
Strategies for Success

INTRODUCTION

> Those who have not acquired wealth in youth ruminate like
> old herons on a pond with no fish.   —GAUTAMA BUDDHA

> Money talks, even in hell.   —JAPANESE PROVERB

More than two thousand years ago, a mysterious Indian philosopher
formulated a science of wealth and sovereignty, synthesizing social,
psychological, economic, and strategic principles into a comprehensive program.

Immortalizing this science in the Sanskrit language, an elegant
compound of poetry and logic, the philosopher taught his methods to
an obscure herdsman-soldier. Following the philosopher's advice, the
herdsman-soldier rose in the world and ultimately succeeded in
founding the greatest Indian empire in history.

The herdsman-turned-emperor was Chandragupta Maurya, founder
of the empire and dynasty named after him. Because he rose from
obscurity, it is not known when he was born. Referred to by the
Greeks as Sandracottus, Chandragupta flourished in the last quarter
of the fourth century B.C.E.

Uniting most of the Indian subcontinent for the first time under
one rule, Chandragupta went on to incorporate much of Kashmir and
Afghanistan, driving invading Greeks in Alexander's wake back as far
as Persia.

The Maurya dynasty ruled for nearly one and a half centuries, from
about 325 to 182 B.C.E. Emperor Ashoka, grandson of the founder,
who extended the empire by conquest and reigned from about 273 to
232 B.C.E., is particularly famous among the later Maurya rulers.

Eventually converting to Buddhism and renouncing warfare, Emperor Ashoka became a distinguished patron of culture. He convened
a historic Buddhist council and established an international Buddhist

mission spreading the wisdom of Buddha through the Indian subcontinent and west to Afghanistan, Persia, Greece, Egypt and beyond. The Edicts of Ashoka, pious exhortations inscribed on stone pillars throughout the empire, are one of the great monuments of the old world.

Through the Maurya conquests and cultural missions, Indo-Aryan civilization absorbed ancient Indian cultures on an unprecedented scale, and brought renewed contact with other branches of Aryan civilization—Greek, Latin and Celtic—each of which had in the meantime absorbed elements of numerous other ancient cultures in the course of migration and settlement in various regions.

While the ancient profusion of abstract philosophies makes the very idea of Indian thought seem exotic and rarefied to many people today, the fact is that nothing could be more concrete and practical than what we find in the classical Sanskrit *Art of Wealth*. Nevertheless, it cannot be considered a purely materialistic way of thought by any means because it is intimately connected with the psychological and moral condition of the individual and society.

Kauthilya, the thinker whose philosophy of wealth and sovereignty inspired and informed the remarkable success of the Maurya empire, has been called the Aristotle of India and the Machiavelli of India.

Because he integrates a broad spectrum of human concerns into his thinking, pursuing ethical principles with strategic sciences, Kauthilya's ideas naturally resemble other classical practical philosophies of both East and West. Some of the obvious parallels are illustrated here, to enrich the appreciation of Kauthilya's thought.

Common sense and ancient traditions both tell us that no formula for success in any domain can work like a magic charm, as it were, by mechanical application irrespective of the times, the circumstances and the people concerned. Perhaps the most interesting, creative and productive modern-day use of the perennial classics of great civilizations may be realized through the stimulus to thinking that the classics can provide when they are used freely and without bigotry or bias; employed for exercise rather than indoctrination; and considered rationally and reflectively rather than religiously and dogmatically.

The Art of Wealth

WITH COMMENTARY BY
THOMAS CLEARY

The root of happiness is justice; the root of justice is wealth. The root of wealth is sovereignty; the root of sovereignty is mastery of the faculties.

The root of happiness is justice because we can hardly be happy if we are constantly in conflict, constantly on guard, constantly worried, constantly scheming.

If we are so inconsiderate or so selfish that we habitually offend others and even transgress on their rights, we cannot possibly live a happy life, simply because of the friction and antagonism unjust behavior creates.

It is not possible to lead a happy life, moreover, if there is no sense of order or justice on which individuals and communities may draw in their dealings with one another, simply because of the insecurity and suspicion such conditions of mistrust will breed.

The root of justice is wealth because in conditions of overpowering want and need, instinct overpowers intelligence. Mencius, a Chinese sage who lived about the same era as the Indian philosopher Kauthilya, remarked that in his time fire and water were so plentiful that anyone would give them when asked; if only beans and wheat were that plentiful, the sage mused, no one would not be benevolent.

There is also another reason why justice is rooted in wealth. "Poverty gags the intelligent man," says the Sufi sage Hadrat Ali, "preventing him from making his case, and the pauper is a stranger in his own town." People who are not successful in the terms understood by their own societies are not respected, making it hard for them to obtain justice from the social system. Being unable to protect themselves, they are therefore unable to protect others. In this sense, a reasonable degree of affluence is a necessary accomplishment for anyone who bears social responsibility, especially responsibility for others.

It is a matter of daily experience, nevertheless, that material wealth alone is not all that is required for security and justice. Surely there are wealthy people who are still unsatisfied, ambitious and predatory. This is why, in the traditional Aryan social system, moral education precedes professional commitment.

The Sufi sage Hadrat Ali said, "There is no wealth like intelligence, and no poverty like ignorance." The intelligent one without material wealth may gain the materially necessary by application of that intelligence, while the wealthy one without intelligence is likely to lose existing advantages by failing to apply intelligence to his appreciation and employment.

So the root of wealth is not wealth itself, but that whereby wealth may be honestly secured and justly employed. The pundit says, therefore, that the root of wealth is sovereignty. This means more than a sphere of influence; it means the capacity to apply oneself and utilize one's resources autonomously, according to the dictates of intelligence, as best suited to the pursuit of well-being, justice and happiness.

Sovereignty begins with the self, with self-mastery, this sovereignty extending to the social and material environment in proportion to the inner development of the human faculties. Therefore the root of sovereignty, says the pundit, is control of the faculties. This has a two-fold meaning: self-control and self-application.

Mastery of the faculties as self-control is the root of sovereignty in that it enables the individual to work in the world with a buoyant heart, not subject to deviation by temporary attractions or diversions. The ancient Chinese strategists spoke of using desire and anger to manipulate opponents; those who have mastered their own faculties are to that degree winners, in that they cannot be ruined by such tactics.

Mastery of the faculties as self-application is also at the root of sovereignty, in that inner potential is useless unless it is mobilized. This mobilization of inner potential must correspond in some way, furthermore, to an existing outer potential. The ability to perceive, apprehend, and effectively employ this correspondence of possiblity and opportunity, moreover, is also an integral part of self-mastery, or master of the faculties.

From master of the senses, sovereignty; from sovereignty, wealth; from wealth, justice; and from justice, happiness—this, in sum, is the outline of the whole art and science of wealth. The aphorisms proceed from here, elucidating the process of moral and intellectual development through which one realizes self-mastery, sovereignty, wealth, justice and happiness.

The root of mastery of the faculties is guidance; the root of guidance is attendance upon elders. From attendance upon elders comes discernment; by means of discernment one may prosper.

The root of mastery of the faculties is guidance because it is impossible to attain control of one's faculties in an arbitrary manner. Not only is this impossible; moreover, the attempt is dangerous. Popularized versions of Eastern teachings sometimes suggest that mastery of the faculties can be attained just by some sort of meditation, concentration or yogic practice, but the well-documented fact is that oversimplified mental disciplines practiced in isolation for personalistic motives actually trigger psychological disturbances, harden fixations, and foster delusional thought and behavior.

No one could fairly deny that a certain degree of discipline and cultivation is necessary for life in the world, in the midst of society, where one is dealing with other people day in and day out. The inner life also can be cultivated, with beneficial effects on the outer life; but biased concentration on one facet of our being will inevitably produce an imbalanced or incomplete development.

Both the inner and outer life, as well as their interaction and interrelation in experience, respond adaptively to guidance in the process of their unfolding and their evolution. In the absence of conscious cultivation, that guidance may be no more than a series of more or less random impacts caused by happenstance and conditioned by historical and environmental accidents. The result is a personality without inner coherence, an individual without intrinsic autonomy. This is not a moral judgment so much as a description of bound energy.

The countermeasure to willy-nilly personal development is "attendance upon elders," or listening receptively to the voice of experience. As Ali, the Sufi sage, remarks, "There is no backup like consultation." Buddha said, "Just as the tongue discerns the taste of the soup, the intelligent one will realize the truth right away by associating with the wise for even a while." A Chan classic says, "Association with the good is like walking through dew and mist—although they do not soak you, in time your clothes become moist." Buddha said, "For those who are always courteous and respectful of elders, four things increase: life, beauty, happiness and strength."

The voice of experience comes to us in different forms. Sometimes the "elders" from whose company we gain discernment are experienced and knowledgeable people in our families, neighborhoods, and places of work and recreation. Sometimes the "elders are words of wisdom from our sacred traditions, our scriptures, our classics, our histories, our stories, our music, our art. Sometimes the "elders" are rocks, trees, rivers, hills and other features of nature, teaching us the lessons of their experiences and the natural laws of causality they must obey. As a Chinese thinker wrote, "Learning is an everyday affair, in which awareness should be exercised in each situation."

Discernment thus developed through observation, experience and actual practice becomes a permanent part of the personality, a permanent asset, a form of abstract wealth that can generate concrete prosperity by application to the potential of the times and circumstances in which one finds oneself. "That deed is well done," said Buddha, "that is not followed by regret, whose consequences are attended by joy and happiness." This appropriateness of action, the foundation of success, can be realized through the attainment and exercise of authentic discernment, seeing and knowing things as they have been, currently are and possibly can be.

The successful individual realizes self-mastery; one with self-mastery enjoys all riches.

Self-mastery enables the successful individual to enjoy all riches in a number of ways. To begin with, self-mastery underpins the patience and diligence needed to create wealth. In the process, self-mastery enables one to avoid being deviated from long-term goals by the seduction of short-term gains.

When success has been attained, furthermore, self-mastery prevents the successful individual from becoming complacent and squandering the fruits of honest effort.

There are many traditional expressions that address this issue. A Buddhist proverb says, "The spoils of war are used up in celebration." If we only labor to consume, and only consume whatever we earn, there is no further progress. The question of how we use the fruits of our labors beyond fulfilling the needs of our dependents is crucial to the perpetuation and progress of prosperity.

It might seem that nothing tries our souls like failure and defeat, but setbacks can actually stimulate determination and improvement. When we win some success, however, we are tempted to feel self-satisfied, and this can make us stagnate, or fill our heads with inflated ideas of our worth. Thus Ali said, "There is no test like fulfillment." So it is the one with self-mastery who can really enjoy all riches.

Attainment of wealth creates prosperity for the people; by virtue of the people's prosperity, even a leaderless domain will be orderly.

The ancient Chinese classic *I Ching* says, "Those above secure their homes by kindness to those below." One of the greatest enjoyments of wealth is in its sharing. Just as the successful individual who loses self-mastery squanders the wealth so painstakingly created, however, sharing wealth with squanderers achieves the same effect, with even greater rapidity. The generation and employment of wealth to create an ever widening circle of prosperity, in contrast, eliminates the consumptive effects of senseless consumption.

If people reasonably and conscientiously pursue occupations that generate wealth for themselves and others, the social fabric can be basically maintained by the shared sense of common interest, or the common sense of shared interest, the pragmatic perception that the good of individuals and the good of community are inextricably intertwined.

Seen from this point of view, religious commandments like "Love your neighbor as yourself" do not appear to be heroic ideals of self-abnegation, but practical appreciations of the fact that our neighbors are indeed a part of ourselves; our very subsistence, to say nothing of our happiness, depends in many ways upon our neighbors in the widest sense of this word.

The emergence of social order from mutual recognition as part of one another is a natural process, calling into play the reason and goodwill of all who consciously participate. When the activity of an individual, or of a coordinated body of individuals, generates wealth beyond immediate needs, the total profit does not consist solely of the wealth itself, but also of the creative redeployment of excess wealth, of the development of creative wealth. Whether in the life of the individual, of a family, of a corporation or of a nation, the function of wealth in the well-being of the whole body will ultimately determine the future state of the organization.

The wrath of the populace is the most serious anger of all.

The wrath of the populace is most serious because it undermines soli-darity and cooperation, and, furthermore, displaces energy from con-structive and creative activities to defensive or remedial measures. Whether in government, business or even social life, the opposition of rivals or enemies cannot compare with that of one's own people. Not only does internal disruption compromise the organism from within, it also creates increased vulnerability to pressures or threats from outside.

This idea is well represented in other traditions. The classical Chi-nese philosopher Mencius said that the basis of the state is not the government but the people. Confucious said that loss of trust is worse than death because "there has always been death, but without trust it is impossible to stand." Similarly, when the prophet Muhammad appointed a governor to Yemen, he warned him to "Beware the cry of the oppressed, for there is no screen between it and God."

The ancient *I Ching*, one of the major sourcebooks of both Confu-sian and Taoist tradition, also speaks to this point: "Cultivated people distribute blessings to reach those below them, while avoiding pre-sumption of virtue." Huanchu, Taoist thinker of the Ming dynasty, wrote, "If people who are lucky enough to obtain official positions and be well fed and house do not make it their concern to establish good education and do good works, even if they live a hundred years it is as if they had never lived at all."

Responsibility toward society is considered normal in classical tra-ditions, not only in view of the social nature of humankind and the need for cooperative order to secure material subsistence, but also in the sense of gratitude and appreciation for the amenities and comforts made possible by the collaboration of a multitude of individuals in many walks of life in a coherent and mutually satisfactory social structure.

It is better to have no master than to have an unruly master.

It is better to have no commitments than to be committed to an arbi-trary and erratic authority. Gautama Buddha said, "One who walks with fools will sorrow a long way." He also said, "It is better to walk alone; there is no companionship with a fool. Walk alone, like an

elephant in the forest." The more dedicated the effort, the more concentrated the mind, the more critical the question of whether or not
the dedication and concentration are rightly directed.

The Sung dynasty Confucian sage Cheng Yi, writing on the subject
of following leaders rightly and wrongly, defined "following downward" as "following those in error, abandoning understanding and
pursuing ignorance." Speaking of true leadership, the *I Ching* says,
"Leaders draw on limitless resources of education and thought to embrace and protect the people without bound." When there is no authentic leadership, however, the same classic says, "Cultivated
people can stand alone without fear."

*Having prepared oneself, one should seek accompanied; one with-
out allies has no certainty of counsel.*

These are the three basic requirements of effectiveness: self-prepara-
tion, sound advice and deliberate effort.

"Have prepared oneself" means that nothing can be done without
having first prepared oneself. In *The Art of War*, Sun Tzu says that
successful warriors are those who secure victory first, and only then
go into battle.

"One should seek accompanied" means that the knowledge, views
and ideas of others are an important resource in pursuing a constructive endeavor. Confucius said he could find teachers anywhere, by
objective observation, taking to the good and avoiding the bad. The *I
Ching* says, "Cultivated people form associations for discussion and
action."

A single wheel does not make it possible to move around.

Human beings are social creatures by nature, not only in the context
of our emotional and intellectual drives, but also in the context of
our productive and creative drives. Even when people are solitary and
alone, they are nonetheless still part of a totality without which nothing could be alive.

Privacy and companionship in due proportion, solitude and society
in appropriate measure, are equally necessary to individual health
and integrity, as the full significance of the integral individual unfolds
itself and inspires others in the midst of a rich and complex environ-

ment embracing many levels of experience in both mental and material dimensions.

An ally is one who is the same in happiness and misery.

Someone who cleaves to you in good times but vanishes in hard times is not really an ally, for hard times are when allies are needed most. Someone who is glad to share your gains but unwilling to share your losses is not much of a partner, as those who stand only to gain and have nothing to lose are missing half of normal motivation.

A Chan Buddhist proverb says, "My parents were the ones who gave birth to me; my companions were the ones who raised me." The issue of human associations has perennially been considered fundamental because it is in the nature of human beings to transmit impulses and attitudes simply through association. It was originally for this reason, more than for reasons of social or economic status, that knowledge was once most commonly concentrated and passed on in families, since the family was a natural center of human association.

The Sufi sage Ali counseled his own son on the subject of allies in these terms: "Do not befriend a fool, for he hurts you when he wants to help you. And do not befriend a stingy man, for he will distance himself from you when he is most needed." The *I Ching* says, "Cultivated people stand without changing places." Gautama Buddha said, "The sight of the noble is good, association with them is always happy. One who never sees fools will be happy forever."

The thinking individual should designate an adviser who is a fitting counterpart to oneself.

It might seem reasonable to choose someone quite different from yourself as an adviser, on the premise that this will provide you with different perspectives and different points of view. Advice that comes from a level of knowledge or a history of experience that is very different, however, may for that very reason prove to be impractical for the individual concerned.

For advice to be practical, it must be within the range of possibility. However good advice may be, if it is beyond one's ability to implement that advice, it is not really useful. Therefore an adviser needs to really understand an advisee well in order to provide advice that is sound in conception and practical in action. That is why it is recommended that one choose an adviser who is like oneself. The Taoist strategist Master of Demon Valley said, "Those with the same voice call to each other." Confucius said, "Those whose paths are not the same do not consult one another."

One who is unruly should not be made an adviser simply out of affection.

Personal feelings can distort our perceptions of others' character and cause us to misunderstand what they are communicating to us. We may like certain people, feel affection toward them and enjoy their company, but that does not mean that these are the people to whom we should turn for advice. The choice of advisers has to be more objective than subjective, as Confucius suggests: "See what they do, observe the how and the why, and examine their basic premises."

A Chan Buddhist dictum states that it is wise to see what is good about what one dislikes and to see what is bad about what one likes; the same is certainly true of people, whether acquaintances or strangers. When we understand the shortcomings and flaws of those toward whom we feel affection, and also can see the strengths and virtues of those whom we may not personally like, this balance makes it possible to work with people harmoniously under any conditions.

There is also an important principle to be observed here from the point of view of the adviser. When Confucius was asked how to work for a ruler, he said, "Don't deceive him, even if you have to offend him." Human feelings being what they are, just as personal affections might induce someone to choose the wrong adviser, personal affections might also inhibit a chosen adviser from giving the right advice for fear of causing emotional upset. As a Chan proverb says, "Sincere words may offend the ear."

In everyday life, we are ordinarily influenced by what we see and hear, even when (and sometimes especially when) we do not consciously register that influence. The sources of this influence naturally include the people around us, so to some degree we are more or less constantly exposed to the suggestions emanating from the social environment.

This is why classic traditions make so much of human associations in education and development. Buddha said, "If you find a prudent companion, a wise associate who leads a good life, having overcome all troubles, travel with that one, uplifted and aware."

One who is learned and innocent of pretense should be made a counselor.

It may go without saying that a counselor should be knowledgeable, but the fact of human psychology is that pride tends to go along with attainment, even to the point where it can be exaggerated into pretense, which then can outstrip reality. Ali said, "Many an intellectual has been killed by his ignorance, the knowledge he had with him failing to profit him."

This point is emphasized by many ancient sages. Confucius said, "Even if you have fine abilities, if you are arrogant and stingy, the rest is not worth considering." Huanchu said, "Those who make a show of morality are inevitably slandered on moral grounds; those who make a show of learning are always blamed on account of learning." Lao-tzu said, "To know unconsciously is best; to presume to know what you don't is sick. Only by recognizing the sickness of sickness is it possible not to be sick." The Taoist Master of the Hidden Storehouse said, "Those who are worthy of the name 'wise' do not call themselves wise."

All undertakings begin with counsel.

The master strategist Sun Tzu wrote, "Assess the advantages in taking advice, then structure your forces accordingly." A Chan proverb says, "Strategy at headquarters determines success abroad." Expending energy without direction drains people and renders them ineffective in the long run. The Taoist sage Lao-tzu said, "The journey of ten thousand miles begins with the first step." Without prudent planning, which includes seeking and taking advice from reliable and worthy sources, there is little chance of taking the first step in the right direction. As another Chan proverb says, "The crooked does not hide the straight." According to natural law, the result of an activity must be in conformity with the cause and conditions of its pursuit.

Misguided effort takes us further afield the harder we try. Diligence cannot compensate for misdirection. This is why counsel or guidance naturally includes a realistic assessment of one's situation and abilities. The Master of the Hidden Storehouse said, "The effectiveness of a mirror in showing a leader what he looks like is small compared to the effectiveness of educated people in showing a leader what he is like." The Master of Demon Valley said, "There is nothing to do but value wisdom. Wisdom employs what is unknown to most people, and can use what is invisible to most people. Once wisdom is in use, one acts on one's own by seeing what can be chosen and working on it; one acts for others by seeing what is unavoidable and working on that."

Fulfillment of what is to be done lies in keeping security of counsel; one who divulges advice ruins the task.

Keeping security of counsel protects plans from the interference of the interloper who aims to take advantage of others, from the attack of the spoiler who seeks the downfall of the able, from the impatience of the overeager one who seeks to profit right away and from the confusion of the controversialist who wants to argue and get his way.

There is, furthermore, also the logic of silence as space in which to act or maneuver. A master plan spoken too soon might become excessively rigidified in the minds of hearers, to the point where necessary flexibility could be lost. Strategic thinker Mei Yaochen wrote, "Insofar as you adapt and adjust accordingly in the face of opposition, how could you say what you are going to do beforehand?"

Through carelessness one will come under the control of enemies: counsel is to be kept guarded from all doors.

Inscrutability and impassivity, often thought to be character traits of certain peoples, are ordinarily results of training in the practice of reserve. Reserve, or discretion, is deliberately cultivated for the simple reason, articulated so concisely here by our pundit, that carelessness causes vulnerability. Those who misunderstand the nature of the strategy and take the products and effects of this training too personally inevitably lose out in both affective and competitive interaction with others.

When their brains can be easily picked and their inner thoughts revealed, or their emotions easily triggered and their private sensitivities exposed, people can be readily manipulated by those who seek to turn the frailties of the human condition to their own personal advantage. The Taoist Huainan Masters said, "When like and dislike began to have their says, order and chaos went their ways."

This principle is, quite naturally, emphasized very strongly in strategic literature. The Master of Demon Valley said, "In the use of tactical strategies, it is better to be private than public; and alliance is even better than mere privacy, alliance meaning a partnership that has no gaps."

It is in the state of "having no gaps" that the integrity of an individual, a relationship or a group is maintained. It is in this sense, more than in the sense of sinister secrecy, that the Master of Demon Valley said, "The Way of mastery is in concealment and covertness." Lao-tzu explains, "Is it empty talk, the old saying that tact keeps you whole? When truthfulness is complete, it still resorts to this."

By fulfillment of counsel, dominion grows; they say keeping counsel secret is of utmost importance.

Mastery develops through putting good advice into practice. Fulfillment of counsel demands first of all that one recognize what good advice is, how feasible it is, how valuable it is and what is necessary to its execution.

These preliminary discernments may be elementary, but they are not necessarily easy. Not only must one develop one's own perceptions, one must also cultivate the right company.

According to a Chinese Buddhist master of the Sung dynasty, writing at a time when religion and culture seemed to be flourishing, "It is hard to find anyone who will say that what is right is right and what is wrong is wrong, who is balanced, true and upright, free from hypocrisy."

Keeping counsel secret, or confidential, is not only important as a normal security measure; it is also important at an even earlier stage of planning, the stage of assessment of advice. Silently keeping one's peace while in the process of hearing counsel and evaluating it reduces random interference and fosters cool consideration.

The dual function of secrecy, for security and for privacy, is captured perfectly by the Taoist Master of Demon Valley, who explains that internal secrecy maintains the integrity of the group, while external secrecy maintains the integrity of the operation: "Those who are themselves on the inside but speak to outsiders are ostracized; those who are themselves outsiders but whose talk goes too deep are in danger."

Pursuing this line of thought, it can be seen how tactful reserve can enable one to avoid frustration by hostility and contention. The Master of Demon Valley said, "What people do not like should not be forced on them; what does not concern people should not be taught to them." Thus eventual success may be furthered by keeping things confidential until the one who is ultimately responsible has determined the needs and capacities, the mentalities and concerns, of those likely to be affected by a course of action.

Counsel is a lamp to one in the dark about what is to be done.

It is better to do nothing than to act at random and do something wrong. The advantage of gaining other perspectives may be there, but the fact remains that when one does not know what to do oneself, one will not necessarily recognize sound counsel simply by its presence. When in the dark, it is not enough just to follow direction; in order to tell whether it is worth following, one needs some sense of where this direction is to lead.

Following advice blindly when in the dark is to go from darkness to darkness. Authentic counsel, therefore, includes within it means of testing its probity. Proven character, intelligence and knowledge on the part of the person, perceptible logic, reason, and contextual feasibility in the advice—when these are all there, then counsel is a "lamp to one in the darkness" because it does not simply beckon enthusiasm or trust; it removes the darkness itself.

The faults of others are seen through the eyes of advisers; when advice is given, let there be no hostility.

Personal feelings or private debts of some kind may blind one to the shortcomings of associates in professional life. In such cases, the observations of objective advisers are of inestimable value, considering the loss and injury that can result from keeping the wrong company.

As long as emotional or other biases have indeed compromised one's ability to see people as they really are, one is not likely to be receptive to other points of view. According to a story in a Buddhist scripture, when a king once consulted a sage about which of his sons to designate as heir to the throne, the sage replied with withering criticisms of each and every one of the princes. This so enraged the king that he wanted to have the sage put to death. Now the sage laughingly bade the king to spare his life, for by such candor with a king had he not proven himself a fool, no sage at all, unworthy of a hearing?

While tact is surely needed in advisers, there is a limit to which truth can be covered without compromise. What is also needed is receptivity in those who seek counsel on account of the responsibilities of their positions. One who is impatient with anything but his own opinions has a hard time learning, even from experience.

People in positions of power have a correspondingly powerful need for the clarity to see beyond private feelings and evaluate others objectively. Yagyu Munenori, tutor to a shogun of seventeenth-century Japan, makes this point with great urgency in the context of political organization: "There are only a few people close to a ruler, perhaps five or ten. The majority of people are remote from rulers. When many people resent their ruler, they will express their feelings. When those who are close to the ruler have been after their own private interests all along, not acting in consideration of the leadership, they serve in such a way that the populace resents the ruler. Then when a crisis occurs, these very ones who are close to the ruler will be the first to set upon him!"

If one is not receptive to information or advice that would make it possible to see hidden treachery before it surfaces, there will always be pitfalls that remain imperceptible. Yagyu wrote, "If you do not see the dynamic of a situation, you may remain too long in company where you should not be, and get into trouble for no reason."

In *Forest of Wisdom*, a Chinese collection of Sung dynasty Chan extracts, it is explained that the best way to learn to take good advice is to learn how to recognize sincere advisers. As one thinker says, "Retain those who are more mature, and keep away opportunistic flatterers. The value in this is that there will be no slander of corruption, and no factionalist disruption."

Opportunistic flatterers may be the very ones to strangle off avenues of sincere advice, and their interference may in fact be perversely welcomed by those who secretly wish to be relieved of responsibility for hard choices and difficult decisions. In any case, however, those who get the reputation of listening to opportunistic flatterers will be abandoned by the intelligent and mired in the disputes and machinations of self-seeking "courtiers" vying for attention and influence.

Assent is when there is unanimity of three.

Two people may fool or flatter each other into believing themselves to be correct and then enjoy the illusion too much to pay any attention to another opinion. It is harder for a group of three (or more) to reach any sort of facile, uncritical unanimity, so as a result more questioning, thought and reflection go on before a decision or a determination is reached. Thus the process of advice and consent has a reduced margin of error.

This phenomenon is reflected in a popular Japanese proverb that says, "Three people together have the wisdom of a sage." The nature of everyday reality, moreover, is that of agreement, or convention, as illustrated by the Chinese proverb that says, "If three people call it a turtle, then it's a turtle." When there is "unanimity of three," this means that there is a practical agreement, a working convention, which can be used as a basis of coordinated undertakings and cooperative endeavors.

Advisers are those who see the true reason for what is to be done and what is not to be done.

An aim may be deemed desirable, and a plan conceived for its attainment, yet the enthusiasm and endeavor may turn out to be futile if the aim is unrealistic, the plan is unfeasible or perception of relevant conditions is unclear. The fact remains, however, that when desire produces enthusiasm and enthusiasm spawns effort, cold practicalities may be overlooked in the heat of the moment of inspiration.

Therefore consideration of reason and means is as important as generation of ideas and aspirations. When we truly understand why we are doing one thing or avoiding another, then we can reach the peak of effectiveness. If we only knew where we want to go but not how to get there, agitation to get going may delude us into thinking we will find our way as we go along.

Authentic advice, then, does not simply say what to do and what not to do, but makes this clear in the process of explaining why and why not. When causes and effects are understood, advice can be recognized without doubt and applied without distortion. The Master of Demon Valley said, "Strategic planning is the pivot of survival and destruction. If thinking is not fitting, then hearing is unclear and timing is inaccurate, resulting in mistakes in planning. Then intention is unreliable, vacuous and insubstantial."

Advice is betrayed by six ears.

Six ears means three people. There is an ancient Chinese saying that "Six ears do not have the same plans," meaning that it is difficult to maintain security when secrets are shared. The image is made more graphic by the use of the expression "six ears" instead of "three people" insofar as it alludes to "two ears" per person, suggesting that the mind of an individual may also be divided within itself. One ear may be hearing one thing, as it were, while the other ear hears another; one ear may be tuned to a private conference while the other ear may be receiving outside signals. The resulting complexity of differences in views, sources and interpretations then complicates the problem of security.

One whose affection remains sure in adversities is a friend.

It may go without saying that a "fair-weather friend," one who disappears in hard times, is in reality no friend at all, but there is neither wisdom nor consolation in realizing the truth after the fact. The Sufi sage Hadrat Ali counseled his son, "Do not befriend a stingy man, for he will distance himself from you when he is most needed; and do not befriend a profligate, as he will sell you for a trifle."

Although it is therefore desirable to recognize reality and falsehood in people before having anything to do with them, still one can hardly be comfortable in society if one is habitually suspicious and distrusting.

The appropriate balance is not necessarily easy to attain, particularly in a highly competitive society. Confucius said, "They are wise who do not anticipate deception and do not consider dishonesty, yet are aware of them from the start." This degree of serene clarity takes a lifetime of cultivation.

When there is more than individual responsibility involved in personal associations, when the total complex of official, professional, and social rights and duties is influenced by the company one keeps, after-the-fact recognition of fair-weather friends may be disastrous. For this reason, ways of testing people have been developed over the ages by practical thinkers in political, military, religious and professional fields.

Questionnaires and written tests do not necessarily do the job quite thoroughly enough. "The difficulty of knowing people troubles even sages," said a famous Chan Buddhist teacher of Sung dynasty China, explaining that "You cannot know their behavior for sure just from one answer or one question. Indeed, clever talkers cannot always be trusted in fact, while clumsy talkers may have irrefutable reason."

Strategists writing for political and military leaders have considered this issue one of crucial importance. The great Chinese leader K'ung Ming, whose exploits are immortalized in *The Romance of the Three Kingdoms*, wrote in his manual *The Way of the General*: "Hard though it be to know people, there are ways. First is to question them concerning right and wrong, to observe their ideas. Second is to exhaust all their arguments, to see how they change. Third is to consult with them about strategy, to see how perceptive they are. Fourth is to announce that there is trouble, to see how brave they are. Fifth is to get them intoxicated, to observe their inner nature. Sixth is to present them with the prospect of gain, to see how modest they are. Seventh is to give them a task to do within a specific time, to see how trustworthy they are."

The severity of the methods employed naturally depends on the nature of the situation, especially on the margin for error. The Greek philosopher Plato believed that the essence of whatever method used to evaluate people was to see whether they had greater taste for truth than for material comfort; he said, "You should test someone who resorts to you by deprivation and unjust treatment. If one patiently endures the deprivation but complains about the unjust treatment, you may attach him to yourself and treat him well. If one patiently endures unjust treatment and complains about deprivation, however, you may leave him and avoid him."

Power is attained by winning friends. The powerful one strives to gain what is lacking. Gaining what is lacking is not for the lazy.

The lazy one, moreover, cannot keep even what he has gotten. What is in the keeping of the lazy one, furthermore, does not grow; he does not direct employees. Gaining what has not been gained, maintaining it, developing it and employing it: these four are the essentials of sovereignty.

Cooperation, focus, determination and effort are all elements of attaining success. Attentiveness and diligence in consolidating gains and fostering growth, employing the fruits of success effectively, are all elements of maintaining success.

The Master of Demon Valley said, "Solidifying intent refers to formulation of mental energy into thought. The mind should be calm and quiet, thought should be deep and far-reaching. When the mind is calm and quiet, then brilliant measures are conceived; when thought is deep and far-reaching, then strategic plans are perfected. When brilliant measures are conceived, then the will cannot be disturbed. When strategic plans are perfected, then achievements cannot be blocked."

The course of practical philosophy depends on the essentials of sovereignty; system and arrangements are based on the essentials of sovereignty.

The Master of Demon Valley said, "Human leaders have a natural pivot, producing, growing, harvesting and storing, which is not to be opposed; those who oppose it inevitably decline, even if they flourish. This way of nature is the overall guideline for human leaders."

The system is dependent upon application in one's own sphere. Preparedness is focused on neighboring territories; neighboring territories are a source of alliance and discord.

To be successful, it is necessary to mind one's own business and do one's own task, but to enhance and to safeguard success, it is also necessary to consider what others are doing. It may be possible to make alliances, and it may be imperative to establish defenses. However one has mastered one's own sphere of action, it is not possible to control others as oneself; therefore it is essential to understand others and know whether they are likely sources of discord or suitable partners in alliance.

The Art of War says, "In ancient times, skillful warriors first made themselves invincible, and then watched for vulnerability in their opponents."

One who follows practical philosophy is sovereign.

Random action based upon the enthusiasm or ambition of the moment is not a secure path. A rational, intelligent, systematic approach to practical organization and tactical strategy enhances chances of success. The Master of Demon Valley said, "Without wisdom and knowledge, you cannot preserve your home with justice and cannot preserve your country with the Way."

An immediately neighboring population is a rival; one that is separated by an intermediate territory is a friend. Rivalry and friendship will be as such for a reason.

The Master of Demon Valley said, "If there is outward friendliness but inward estrangement, reconcile the inner relationship. If there is inward friendliness but outward estrangement, reconcile the outward relationship."

One who is in decline should make alliances. Power is the reason for uniting, for those who seek it. Metal does not unite with metal without being heated.

The Master of Demon Valley said, "The method of opposition and alliance demands that you gauge your own ability and intelligence, and assess your own strengths and weaknesses, seeing who does not compare among those far and near. Only then can you advance and withdraw freely and independently."

The strong should fight with the weak, not with a superior or an equal. Contention with the powerful is like battle with elephants; an unfired vessel is destroyed by collision with another unbaked one.

The Art of War says, "In ancient times, those known as good warriors prevailed when it was easy to prevail. Therefore the victories of good warriors are not noted for cleverness or bravery. So their victories in battle are not flukes. Their victories are not flukes because they position themselves where they will surely win, prevailing over those who have already lost. So it is that good warriors take their stand on ground where they cannot lose, and do not overlook conditions that make an opponent prone to defeat."

The action of enemies should be watched. Alliance is to be made on an individual basis. One should maintain one's own security from the wrath of the unfriendly.

The Master of Demon Valley said, "Those in ancient times who skillfully operated countries always measured the powers in the land and figured out the psychological conditions of local leaders. If measurement of powers is not thorough, you do not know the strong and the weak, the light and the heavy. If psychological conditions are not figured out thoroughly, you do not know the activities of hidden changes and developments."

Those of lesser capability must depend on the powerful. Reliance on the powerless brings misery. Let one go to a ruler as to a fire; one should not act in opposition to the ruler.

The Master of Demon Valley said, "In the relationship between ruler and minister, or between superior and subordinate, there may be those who are on friendly terms in spite of distance, and there may be those who are alienated in spite of closeness."

One should not wear exaggerated clothing. One should not act as if one of the gods. Double-dealing is done when there are two envious parties.

The Taoist Master of the Hidden Storehouse said, "When a country is going to perish, the officials at court are splendidly attired, their countenances are harmonious, their speech is flowery and genteel, their movements are careful and elegant. Although the administration of a moribund country may outwardly appear to be harmonious and obedient, inwardly the officials harbor suspicions and aversions, each pursuing his own personal aims, secretly plotting each other harm."

One who is extreme in addiction to some passion does not achieve what is to be done. Even with elephants, chariots, cavalry and infantry, someone controlled by the senses will perish.

The Master of the Hidden Storehouse said, "When fashions fan the flames of desire, the people are not faithful and pure; they are ashamed of simplicity and value ostentation."

No task is accomplished by one devoted to gambling. Virtue and wealth disappear from one addicted to hunting.

The *Tao Te Ching* says, "Colors blind people's eyes; sounds deafen their ears; flavors spoil people's palates; the chase and the hunt craze people's minds; goods hard to obtain make people's actions harmful."

Meaningful quest for wealth is not counted among the vices. One who is attached to lusts does not accomplish what is to be done.

The Master of the Hidden Storehouse said, "Things are means of nurturing life, but many deluded people today use their lives to nurture things. Thus they do not know their relative importance. Therefore, in matters of sound, color and flavor, sages take what is beneficial for life and reject what is harmful to life."

Violence of speech is worse than the burning of fire.

The Master of Demon Valley said, "The defense of insects with shells necessitates thickness and hardness in the shell; the action of poisonous insects necessitates a venomous sting. Thus birds and beasts know how to employ their strengths, while speakers know what is useful and use it."

By harshness in punishment one becomes odious to all people.

The Master of the Hidden Storehouse said, "The more insistent commands become, the more disorderly people become."

Prosperity abandons one who is satisfied by material wealth.

The *Tao Te Ching* says, "Which is more, your body or your possessions? Which is more destructive, gain or loss? Extreme fondness means great expense, and abundant possessions mean much loss."

Preparedness for the inimical is in the science of power. Practicing the science of power, one protects the people. Power leads to success. Without authority in power, there is no cabinet of ministers.

The Master of Demon Valley said, "In order to exclude or admit effectively, it is necessary to understand the logic of the Way, figure out coming events and settle any doubts that are sensed. Then there will be no miscalculation in the measures taken, which will then be successful and worthwhile. To direct a populace in productive work is called solidarity and inner cooperation. If the leadership is ignorant and cannot manage, those below get confused without even realizing it. Reverse this by solidarity."

People refrain from what they should not do on account of punishment.

The Taoist classic *Wen-tzu* says, "The nurturing of life does not force people to do what they cannot do, or stop them from doing what they cannot help doing." *The Way of the General* says, "First organize directives, then organize penalties."

Self-preservation depends on the science of power. With self-preservation, all becomes secure. Growth and decay depend on oneself. Power is to be guided by discernment.

The Master of Demon Valley said, "Focusing the mind's eye is for determining impending perils. Events have natural courses, people have successes and failures. It is imperative to examine movements signaling impending perils."

A ruler is not to be disrespected, even if weak; there is no weakness in fire.

The Taoist classic *Chuang-tzu* says, "Don't you know that tiger keepers don't dare to feed them live animals, because of the fury of the tigers killing the prey? And they will not give them whole carcasses either, for the fury of the tigers rending them. By gauging the timing of their hunger and satiety, they guide their furious tempers. Tigers are a different species than humans, but they are nice to their keepers as long as their keepers deal with them according to their nature.

Those whom tigers kill are those who deal with them in a manner contrary to their nature."

Action results from power. Acquisition of wealth is rooted in action. Justice and pleasure are rooted in wealth. The root of wealth is work. Work is accomplished with economy of effort.

Wen-tzu says, "The Way involves respect for what is small and subtle, acting without losing the right timing." The *Tao Te Ching* says, "Plan for difficulty when it is still easy, do the great while it is still small. The most difficult things in the world must be done while they are easy; the greatest things in the world must be done while they are small."

What is approached by expedient means will not be hard to do. Without expedient means, work is futile, even if it is done. Expedient means are the allies of those seeking to accomplish something.

Wen-tzu says, "To have many abilities means to be competent in both culture and defense, and to do precisely what is right in terms of your conduct in action and repose, in what you take up and what you put aside, what you dispense with and what you set up."

The aim of work is attained by human effort. Opportunity goes along with human effort. Without opportunity, even excessive effort will be fruitless.

Sufi master Ali said, "The man who gets the worse bargain and is the most unsuccessful in his endeavors is the one who wears out his body in seeking his wealth but is not assisted by destiny toward his aim." He also said, "Waste of an opportunity is torment."

The unfocused cannot act. Decide first, then set to work.

The Master of Demon Valley said, "The mind's eye is knowledge, focus is practical action."

When a task is ended, there should be no procrastination in what's next to be done.

The classic Chinese *I Ching* says, "Ideal people are consistent in their deeds." Sufi master Ali said, "Complacency hinders growth."

The unsteady one does not accomplish his task.

The *Tao Te Ching* says, "People's works are always spoiled on the verge of completion."

Work goes wrong from disrespect of what is obtained.

The *Tao Te Ching* says, "The most massive tree grows from a sprout; the highest building rises from a pile of earth; a journey of a thousand miles begins with a step."

Perfectly executed tasks are hard to find.

The *Tao Te Ching* says, "Be as careful of the end as of the beginning, and nothing will be spoiled."

A task that is an uninterrupted succession of difficulties should not be undertaken.

The *I Ching* says, "Coming and going, pitfall upon pitfall. In danger and dependent, one goes into a hole in a pit. Do not act this way."

One who knows the right timing will get the job done.

Sufi master Ali said, "Stupidity includes hurrying before the right time and waiting until the opportunity has passed."

Through the passage of time, time itself consumes the results. In all tasks, not even a moment of time is to be wasted.

Sufi master Ali said, "Everyone who is being overtaken by death asks for more time, while everyone who still has time makes excuses for procrastination."

One should begin a task after coming to know the particulars of the locality and the results. The expert in practical philosophy observes the place and time. Prosperity lasts for one who acts after observation. Prosperity forsakes even the fortunate one who acts without observation. Observation is to be done by means of knowledge and inference.

The Master of Demon Valley said, "All strategy has a way, which demands that you find the bases to discover the conditions. . . . People on a treasure hunt use a compass to avoid getting lost: measuring capacities, assessing abilities, and figuring out feelings and psychological conditions are the compass of business and political affairs."

All kinds of success are to be obtained by all kinds of means. Let one be devoted to whatever work one is good at. One who knows the appropriate means makes the difficult easy.

Wen-tzu says, "When sages initiate undertakings, they are always based on available resources, which they put to use. Those who are effective in one way are placed in one position; those who have one talent work on one task. When you have the strength for the responsibility, an undertaking is not burdensome; when you have the ability for a task, it is not difficult to perform. Because sages employ them all, people are not abandoned and things are not wasted."

What has been done without knowledge is not worthy of much esteem.

Even a little bit of well-oriented effort is more productive than a whole lot of disoriented effort.

Even a worm changes forms for no apparent reason.

People or things that may seem insignificant at one particular point in time are not to be ignored or slighted, for there is no telling what changes the future may bring.

It is the accomplished work that is to be made known.

The *I Ching* says, "A change is believed on the day of completion." If an undertaking is announced and then fails, the effect on general morale is more negative; if an undertaking is accomplished and then announced, the effect on general morale is more positive.

Even the knowledgeable have their works go bad through the detrimental effects of people or of fate.

Even if the knowledge and talent are there, it is unwise to presume upon success. There may also be interlopers and adversaries, and there is no telling what natural forces, like disasters or sudden changes in conditions, may interfere with an enterprise.

Fate can be restrained by making peace with it; humanly caused failure can be prevented by skill.

The adverse effects of unexpected changes or natural disasters can be minimized by accepting their possibility, preparing for them and coping with them when they happen. The adverse effects of interlopers and adversaries can be minimized by skillful human relations both inside and outside the group.

In failure, the puerile talk of the obstacles.

When something fails, it is more productive to reflect on what more or what else one could have done than to complain of how hard it was.

One who seeks to accomplish something must be ruthless; the calf seeking milk assails the mother's udder.

Weakness of will is a handicap in an unrelenting world.

Failure at work comes from lack of effort; success at work does not belong to those who count on luck.

Steady development of skills is more effective and more secure than just getting by from task to task.

The idle one cannot support dependents.

The responsibilities and pleasures of family life, and the development of character their experiences promote, are a lot to lose by laziness.

One who does not see work to be done is blind.

Sufi master Ali said, "Do not ask about what does not exist, for there is work for you in what does exist."

Tasks should be considered in light of direct evidence, what is un-known and inference.

Take into account what can actually be known, what cannot actually be known and what can be figured out.

Prosperity abandons one who acts without consideration. One should only begin a task with knowledge of one's own capacity.

It is common sense to think before acting. This includes considering what kind of information and planning are necessary to make a con-structive start. The first thing to assess in structuring an undertaking is the extent of one's own capabilities, so that planning can be realis-tic and cooperation can be effective.

One who eats the leftovers after having satisfied his people is one who consumes ambrosia.

The *I Ching* says, "Good people distribute blessings to reach those below them, while avoiding presumption of virtue."

Avenues of profit increase through all accomplishments.

Vocations, avocations and hobbies all enrich life in some way. At times an avocation or a hobby may be as profitable as a profession or a vocation. Taking an interest in life and being versatile in one's activ-ities creates an atmosphere of greater enjoyment, a ground of greater potential and also a reservoir of greater resilience in changing times.

The coward does not think of what is to be done.

Fear of failure is not the same thing as knowing when something is impractical. Fear of failure paralyzes initiative; knowing what makes something practical or impractical concentrates and releases energy.

Let one who seeks work do the job cognizant of the employer's ways. One who knows the ways of the cow gets to enjoy the milk.

The Master of Demon Valley said, "When there is collusion but not solidarity, there is overt alliance but covert alienation."

The self-possessed should not reveal secrets to the base.

A Japanese proverb says, "The mouth is the door of calamity."

One who is soft by nature is slighted even by dependents; the harsh authoritarian is feared by all.

The essence of Taoist practical philosophy is balancing flexibility and firmness. Flexibility without firmness deteriorates into pliability and weakness; firmness without flexibility hardens into rigidity and oppressiveness.

One should apply discipline as is appropriate.

Reward without merit and punishment without fault undermine the morale of an organization.

The world does not think much of one with little strength, even if he is learned.

The world values concrete effect over abstract theory. Someone who has a lot of ideas but never accomplishes anything rarely gains popular respect.

Overburdening depresses a person.

Depression causes people to see things pessimistically, which in turn deepens depression. This undermines initiative, making ordinary tasks themselves seem overburdening, thus propelling the cycle of depression further.

He who announces the fault of another in company betrays his own fault. Self-destructive indeed is the anger of those who are not self-possessed.

Those who show themselves too ignorant, angry or spiteful to understand the value of compassion and tact in effective criticism will not likely be treated with compassion or tact themselves.

Nothing is unattainable to those who are truthful.

Confucius said, "Someone who is perfectly sincere can affect things thereby."

Success at work does not come through recklessness.

Taking risks and taking chances are not the same thing; boldness and recklessness are different states of mind. Gain gotten by chance can also be lost by chance; considering that it may be necessary to take risks sometimes, this must be backed up by basic constancy and deliberate planning.

One who is afflicted by calamity or suffering pain forgets it when it is no longer impinging. There is no continuity when time is wasted.

Realizing that the misery of a trying situation will eventually go away, one can avoid letting distress and downheartedness set the tone of life, and be the more ready to go on without wasting time with depression and regret.

Ruination through risk is better than ruination without risk.

When you are ruined through risk, you know you took your chances; when you are ruined without risk, you know you were sleeping on your feet. There is less regret in knowing you took your chances than in knowing you were asleep on your feet.

Taking the goods of others in pledge is purely self-interest.

If there were no self-interest, a loan would be a gift.

Giving is righteous.

There are many different rationales, forms and patterns of giving followed around the world, but there is also something common underlying their diversity. Thus it could be said of every society that "giving," in some form, "is righteous." The structure of the giving recognized as righteous in a particular culture tends to show where the society's heart is.

One who is wealthy but perverse is not noble, but malicious.

People without conscience might draw great wealth from the produce and labor of a community or society but remain callous to the needs and desires of the people. They might outwardly be considered community leaders in political affairs by virtue of their holdings, and yet be considered bandits by the people and lack the popular support needed to be effective in action.

What does not increase virtue or wealth is desire; opposition to them is courting misfortune.

Acting on whims undermines character and dissipates capacity. When integrity disintegrates and resources dwindle, misfortune cannot be far off.

People who are exceedingly honest by nature are hard to find. One with integrity despises supremacy gained dishonorably.

Confucius said, "To me, wealth and status wrongly gained are like ephemeral clouds."

A single fault eclipses a multitude of virtues.

A scholar once asked a Zen master why people harp on a relatively minor flaw in an otherwise exemplary person. The Zen master said that it is precisely because the person is otherwise exemplary that a relatively minor flaw is particularly noticed.

Don't be aggressive toward a great adversary.

Citing an ancient maxim, the *Tao Te Ching* says, "Let us not be aggressors, but defend."

Conduct should never be excessive or remiss.

A Zen proverb says, "Going too far is as bad as not going far enough."

A lion does not graze on grass, even if tormented by hunger.

A Zen proverb says, "An elephant does not walk a rabbit path."

Trust is to be preserved, even at the cost of life.

Confucius said that a state could dispense with arms before food, and could dispense with food before trust. Questioned about dispensing with food before trust, Confucius explained, "There has always been death, but without trust it is impossible to stand."

A listener who betrays is abandoned, even by his wife and children.

If people betray confidences, others will stop having confidence in them.

Ear should be lent to what is meaningful and profitable, even coming from a child.

The question to ask is whether something is useful, not where it came from. One of the greatest Zen masters said he would learn from anyone who was more enlightened, even a seven-year-old child; and he would give advice to anyone who was less enlightened, even a hundred-year-old elder.

The unbelievable should not be voiced, even if it is true.

The Sufi master Ali said, "People oppose what they don't know anything about." Voicing something beyond the pale of current beliefs invariably incurs opposition and incites disturbance. This environmental condition is one reason for constructive use of discretion and tact.

Many good qualities are not to be disregarded on account of a little flaw. Flaws are commonly found even among the learned; there is no jewel that does not break.

Because a minor flaw in an otherwise exemplary individual can distract the attention of ordinary thinkers, a good leader does not dwell morbidly on a weakness but restores duly constructive attention to the person's strengths.

Courtesy that is excessive should never be trusted.

If courtesy seems forced rather than heartfelt, one wonders the reasons why.

In an adversary, even a friendly deed is hostile. Even as it bows down, the beam of the pump uses up the water in the well.

A "glad hand" of friendliness may be extended in order to take something. It may be necessary to know and understand others well to perceive their intentions.

One should not neglect the opinion of the good. By association with those imbued with virtuous qualities, even those lacking in such qualities come to have them. Water in milk becomes like milk; in alloy with gold, silver becomes golden.

The great Zen master Kuei-shan wrote, "Association with the good is like walking through mist and dew; although your garments are not drenched, in time they become imbued with moisture." Confucius said, "Good people form associations for education and action."

The unenlightened seek to hurt benefactors. Evildoers have no fear of criticism.

Biting the hand that feeds is a sign of ignorance; having no conscience is a sign of sociopathy.

The energetic subdue even the hostile; prowess is the wealth of kings. The indolent one has neither here nor hereafter; opportunity is lost through lack of exertion.

Energy and ability can build nations; complacency and indifference can ruin generations.

Useful resources should be recognized as a fisherman does water.

An expert fisherman knows what fish live where. An expert leader knows what possibilities people and things may attain.

The suspicious are not to be trusted; poison is always poison.

People who cannot trust cannot be trusted. At the very least, they will be suspicious of your motives in trusting them, and thus have no compunction about betraying your trust.

In the acquisition of wealth there should be no association with enemies. After having attained wealth, one should not trust an enemy.

If you get ahead by compromising with people who are basically antagonistic to you, then you will compromise your liberty, security and integrity in the process of acquiring wealth. If you allow self-seekers to ingratiate themselves with you after you have already achieved success, it will be harder for you to use your wealth wisely.

A steady relationship is also based on wealth; a friend should be protected, even the son of an adversary.

Without resources, how could one protect a friend in need?

Until you see an adversary's weakness, action or combat are to be avoided; one should strike an enemy's weak spot. One should not reveal one's own weakness; adversaries aim at weak spots.

The Art of War says, "A skillful attack is one against which an enemy does not know where to defend, while a skillful defense is one against which an enemy does not know where to attack."

An enemy is not to be trusted, even when you have him captive.

The Art of War says, "Be subtle, subtle even to the point of formlessness; be mysterious, mysterious even to the point of soundlessness: thus you can control the enemy's fate."

Bad business on the part of one's own people should be stopped: for disgrace in their own people brings pain to the high-minded; damage to a single limb brings a person down. Good conduct overcomes the enemy.

Within a large and complex operation, deviation from accepted norms may go uncorrected in isolated cases, counting on the overall integrity of the whole. This could lead to internal demoralization and external friction, possibly causing major losses by minor negligence. For an organization to be viable in a competitive society, it needs to maintain acceptable and efficient standards of conducting its business.

The base are fond of dishonesty; a good idea shouldn't be given to a base person—they are not to be trusted. A bad person causes injury, even if treated well; a forest fire burns even the sandalwood trees.

It is one thing when the base are known for their baseness, another when malevolence is deeply hidden. Chinese manuals of leadership and strategy give numerous ways of testing people's character, yet there is still a Zen saying: "The difficulty of knowing people is what ails sages." Learning who is worthy of confidence is a crucial task of leadership and a skill of individual self-government.

A person should never be disrespected. One should not torment a person who can be forgiven.

Good leaders and good neighbors do not overlook the good in others, and they respect the need for human dignity. Even when people have made mistakes or gone wrong, it is better and more useful to seek redeeming qualities than to dwell on their errors.

Fools wish to voice aloud the secret intimated by their superiors.

Those who breach the security of their own organizations endanger their own positions and lose the trust of others as well.

Devotion is manifested by its results. The result of direction is dominion. The fool finds it hard to give even what is due.

The quality and degree of attention, care and concentration devoted to a task or an enterprise will be reflected in its fruition. When effort is directed correctly and effectively, then mastery can be attained. One who expects to reap rewards without expending due effort is not thinking realistically.

One who lacks firmness perishes, even after attaining great dominion. For one who lacks firmness, there is neither the here and now nor the hereafter.

When one can be easily swayed under the influence of external pressures or seductions, or if one can be destabilized by subjective wishes or fears, it is impossible to be resolute. Without firmness of will and resoluteness of action, one cannot succeed in either worldly endeavors or spiritual strivings.

Do not associate with bad people; in the hands of a drunkard, even milk is despised.

Association with the wrong people fosters bad habits by learning through contact and also ruins one's reputation in the community. When one's behavior and character have become warped, and one is no longer trusted by decent people, failure and loss follow naturally.

What determines utility in crises at work is intelligence.

Prudence and forethought may not be enough to prevent the arising of unexpected difficulties. What counts in such circumstances is not regret and recrimination, but intelligent application to resolution of the problem.

Health comes from moderate eating: No food should be eaten while digestion is incomplete, whether it is wholesome or not. Sickness does not approach one who digests food thoroughly.

A traditional Japanese prescription for good health is to eat only to the point where the stomach is 80 percent full. The prophet Muhammad said that a hypocrite eats enough for seven stomachs, while a believer eats only enough for one. Christian doctrine also refers to gluttony as one of the seven cardinal sins. Perhaps a similar caveat could be applied to all forms of consumption. Overconsumption leads to jading of taste, while jading leads to increased overconsumption and further waste. Ultimately wealth is consumed without enjoyment, pleasure or profit.

A growing disease in an aged body should not be overlooked. Eating in a state of indigestion is harmful. Sickness is even worse than an enemy.

A growing disease in an aged body may refer, besides the obvious meaning, to corruption in a long-established organization, system or society. Just as an aged body has less resistance to disease, so a complacent society may be lackadaisical about addressing decadent tendencies.

Eating in a state of indigestion is harmful to health because it increases indigestion, discomfort and general strain on the whole system. Roman aristocrats of imperial days used to eat as much as they could at banquets, then go vomit in the vomitorium and come back to eat their fill again. And again and again, it seems, perhaps until they passed out. Perhaps it is no wonder the Roman empire was overrun in time by hardier people from the north.

The wealth of Rome on which the imperial aristocrats wined and dined themselves silly was based on the wealth produced by their slaves and the peoples they conquered in Europe, the Middle East and Africa. Rome had the power to subdue and subjugate many peoples until the establishment so sickened itself by overconsumption that its imperial might crumbled away under the onslaughts of tribal warriors rising against their enfeebled masters. So for a body as powerful as the Roman empire, "sickness is even worse than an enemy."

Generosity goes with wealth.

Neglect of this principles was undoubtedly one of the symptoms of the illness that felled the Roman empire, and probably of every other empire in history as well. All empires fall in time, or they fall apart, because they were based on gross overconsumption by a relative few at the expense of the majority of people. Confucius said, "Those above secure their homes by kindness to those below."

The clever and the covetous are easy to deceive; intellect is veiled by craving.

This is also one of the basic principles of classical Chinese strategic philosophy. It is important to know how vulnerable others are to deceit in accord with their desires; it is even more important to know the level of one's own vulnerability to deception through wishful thinking.

Cynical people may be those who have had painful experiences through disappointment of hopes and consciously or unconsciously chose cynicism in the form of automatic, defensive rejection of hope itself. Cynics abandon hope without abandoning desire to take whatever immediate satisfactions can be gotten. They make this choice in preference to the more difficult undertaking of deliberate reexamination of the two-way relationship between fundamental hopes and effective realities.

When there is much work to do, great reward should be made an inducement.

When rewards and penalties are used for motivation and restraint, it is axiomatic that they should be reliable, predictable and suited to the importance or gravity of the deed or misdeed, not the status of the person. The Master of the Hidden Storehouse said, "When trust is complete, the world is secure. When trust is lost, the world is dangerous. When the common people labor diligently and yet their money and goods run out, then contentious and antagonistic attitudes arise, and people do not trust each other.

"When people do not trust each other, this is due to unfairness in government practices. When there is unfairness in government practices, this is the fault of officials. When officials are at fault, penalties and rewards are unequal. When penalties and rewards are unequal, this means the leadership is not conscientious.

"When the leadership is conscientious, then penalties and rewards are uniform. When penalties and rewards are uniform, then officials obey the law. When officials obey the law, then order reigns. When order reigns, the common folk find their places and interact trustingly."

If people can trust that their services and achievements will be rewarded for their merit, then they can be motivated to do their best. If people suspect that sycophants and cronies will garner the lion's share of credit and profit, rarely will people not become cynical.

Work that is to be done by oneself alone is to be examined.

Some things require collective effort, some things must be done alone. The first thing to examine is whether a particular task can be delegated, or calls for cooperation with others, or should be done by oneself alone. If it is something that one needs to take care of oneself, then there is no counting on information or feedback from others, so one has to be sure to take personal account of all factors relevant to the job, including the necessary knowledge, practical planning and continuous monitoring of progress all along the course of the task. Thus a task one is to do alone should be thoroughly examined from the start.

In fools, daring should be restrained.

The daring of the prudent is close to confidence, based on a foundation of knowledge and experience. The daring of the foolish is close
to madness, based on a foundation of heedlessness and recklessness.
There are times when daring may be necessary, in order to make progress or to break through an impasse of some kind. The daring of fools,
however, seldom works out for the best. Even when it does seem to
work out, that is not by virtue of the daring of fools, but by virtue of
the luck of fools.

*There's no arguing with fools; to fools, one must speak like a fool.
Iron has to be cut by iron.*

To try making sense by reasoning with a fool is itself foolish. Rationalize by means of the fool's brand of folly, however, and the fool may
hear what you have to say.

Those who lack intelligence have no companion.

The Sufi master Ali said, "The richest of riches is intelligence, and
the greatest poverty is stupidity. The loneliest isolation is conceit,
and the most noble value is goodness of character."

The world is maintained by justice.

Socrates said, "It is by justice that the universals of the world exist,
and its particulars cannot exist without it."
   The Taoist Huainan Masters said, "Humanity and justice are the
warp and woof of society; this never changes."

Justice and injustice follow even the departed.

The effects of justice and injustice continue even after the event; the
good and evil people do throughout their lives outlive them in the
end. Buddha said, "One who does evil suffers regret in this world and
after death, regretful in both. One suffers regret knowing one has
done wrong, and suffers more when gone to a state of misery. One
who does good rejoices in this world and after death, joyful in both.
One rejoices knowing one has done good, and rejoices even more
when gone to a state of felicity."

Compassion is the birthground of justice; the roots of justice are truth and charity.

Compassion is the birthground of justice because understanding or commonality of feeling is what gives rise to consideration for others; and consideration for others, and by extension for society and humanity at large, is a basic ingredient of human motivation for doing justice. Truth and charity are roots of justice in that truth and charity are the avenues by which genuine needs are recognized and fulfilled; and recognition and fulfillment of real human needs are elemental functions of justice.

One overcomes the world with justice; even death protects one who stands on justice.

When the Chinese philosopher Wen-tzu asked the Taoist sage Lao-tzu about justice, Lao-tzu said, "If you are in a superior position, you help the weak; if you are in a subordinate position, you maintain control over yourself. Don't indulge in your whims when you are successful, and don't get excitable when you are in straits. Follow reason uniformly, without bending it subjectively. This is called justice."

Where evil occurs as false justice, there great contempt for true justice results.

When people see that the current operation of conventional organs and practices of justice in their society is actually resulting in manifest injustice, they may long for real justice, unless they have seen or heard of so many travesties of justice that they despair of real justice.

Then again, when people in positions of power use their authority to sanction personal whims to the detriment of the larger body of a society, their contempt for true justice is greatest of all.

Contempt for true justice can thus arise among both the victimized and the victimizers. This can result in violent confrontation, which under these conditions may be just as likely to be initiated from one side as the other and is probably even more likely to be initiated by both sides, each in its own way, both sides having lost faith in true justice, each in its own way.

Those whose destruction is imminent are recognized by temperament, determination and conduct.

People who are temperamental, willful and devious tend to lose the trust of others and wind up surrounded only by those who aim to exploit their temper, obsessiveness and craft.

Warped intelligence indicates self-destruction.

Typical modes of destructive misuse of intelligence include rationalization of unreasonable behavior, perpetrating and justifying dishonest behavior, and intentionally deceiving, attacking or confusing other people. Unfortunately, these phenomena are ordinarily more easily seen in retrospect than in prospect; perhaps the principle is emphasized so strongly in hopes that enough retrospective recognition might foster future perspective and foresight.

To vicious gossips, there is no secret. Don't even listen to others' secrets.

Plato said, "One who pays attention to a statement is a confederate of the speaker." He also said, "Evil people look for people's faults, ignoring their good qualities, just as flies look for rotten parts of a body, ignoring the wholesome." Aristotle said, "A malicious person is an enemy to himself, so how can he be a friend to another?"

It is not right for a director to be an agent.

One who is in charge yet is dominated by the influence of others is not really in charge.

Do not be overbearing to your own people; even a mother is bound to be abandoned if she is bad.

If one presumes upon a relationship and becomes imperious and abusive, alienation will follow. This can happen even in close blood relationships; mistreating people in personal, social or professional relationships results in rejection more readily yet.

Even one's own hand should be cut off if it is poisoned; while a benefactor is kin, even if a stranger.

Jesus said that if your hand offends you, then you should cut it off, for it is better to lose a hand than for the whole body to go to hell. Pythagoras said that a neighbor nearby is more helpful than a brother far away; Ali said that kinship is more in need of friendship than friendship is of kinship.

There is no trusting thieves.

Zen lore warns against treating a thief like a son. There is a specific admonition against "giving a ladder to a thief," or unwittingly giving assistance to the dishonest. A proverb says, "Bring in a wolf, and it'll crap in the house."

Even when there are no problems, it won't do to be negligent. Even a small defect can prevent success.

A Chinese maxim says, "When safe, don't forget about danger." A Zen proverb says, "The spoils of victory are ruined by celebration." Too much enjoyment of the feeling of success and security can undermine attentiveness to subtle changes in external conditions, leading to neglect of adaptive inner changes, ultimately producing gaps in which vulnerabilities and problems tend to arise.

One should acquire wealth like an immortal; the wealthy one is respected by all; the world does not think much of one without wealth, even a great chieftain. Poverty, after all, is a living death for a person.

This is practical observation of what happens in the world; it is social economics, not ideological philosophy. Sufi master Ali noted, "The rich man is at home even when abroad; the pauper is a stranger in his hometown."

An ugly man with wealth is handsome; even if he is ungenerous, seekers do not forsake the wealthy man; the low born, if rich, is superior to the high born.

This is also observation, not philosophy; and these observations are at least as true today, in practical terms, as they were when they were written. Chandragupta Maurya, who became emperor of the greatest Indian empire of all time, is supposed to have been a lowly cowherd and soldier before he met the pundit Kauthilya, who taught him the art of wealth and the conduct of kings.

An ignoble man has no fear of dishonor; intelligent people have no fear for their livelihood. There is no fear of objects for those with controlled senses; there is no fear of death for those who have accomplished their purpose.

Ignoble people have no fear of dishonor, so no one can trust them. Intelligent people have no fear for their livelihood, so no one need worry about them. Those with controlled senses have no fear of objects, so no one can do anything to influence them. Those who have accomplished their purpose have no fear of death, so no one can do anything to intimidate them.

A good man considers himself rich when everyone is rich.

A good man considers himself rich when everyone is rich because he feels his own riches oblige him to give to the needy. When everyone is rich, wealth does not drain away, but can be accumulated and redeployed for development of other forms of enrichment.

No interest should be taken in the possessions of others; interest in others' property is the root of ruination. An object belonging to another should not be taken, even a stalk of straw; taking away others' things is the cause of loss of one's own things—no noose is higher than thieving.

When there is no taking interest in others' possessions, feelings of envy or rivalry cannot arise. In most societies, needy people generally consider it better to beg than to steal; and most thieves, it seems, are generally not needy people, but greedy people. What happens to them in the end depends on whether they were more greedy than needy or more needy than greedy.

Even gruel sustains life, if available in time; medicine is of no use to the dead. At the same time, you yourself are the opportunity for sovereignty.

It may be better to make do with less than to hold out for more if time is of the essence. If minimum needs are not fulfilled in time, there is no use in hoping for something better. Therefore it is important to recognize necessities and possibilities. Most of all, it is essential to take responsibility for one's own needs and capacities, to recognize in one's own being the opportunity for competence, self-mastery and fulfillment.

The sciences of the base-minded are harnessed to evil deeds. Drinking milk increases poison in a snake; it doesn't turn to ambrosia.

From this point of view, the notion that science and religion are inherently incompatible, or the notion that science and the humanities are separate domains, would seem to be rooted in pessimistic assumptions about morality and ability that are already too limited for practical, constructive use.

The popular image of the evil "mad scientist" who tries to control the world or destroy the world is considered fictional, no doubt, because there are many scientists who are not mad. Yet relatively sane scientists and thinkers may find no practical choice but to work in the employ of organizations that are actually trying to control the world in one way or another, and are indeed succeeding in destroying the world in several dimensions, without anyone ordinarily thinking that is actually madness. To the mind habituated to such a situation, it is ordinarily not considered pathological; it is regarded as nothing more or less than the way things are.

Most people are not confronted with scientific statistics day in and day out, but if they were made to become constantly conscious of the enormity of environmental pollution and destruction on the face of the earth, and of the vastness of the amount of productivity and wealth that has been and is being funneled into destructive power, power so immense that it would be sufficient to annihilate every human being in existence several times over, then people would probably either consider that madness or they would soon go mad themselves under the duress of this realization.

There is no wealth like grain, there is no enemy like hunger.

Hunger undermines both physical and mental health. There is no telling what people may do when they get too hungry too often. They easily get sick, and they might go crazy.

Grain and wealth can be expressed by the same word in Sanskrit, for grain is a basic form of wealth. Grain is perhaps the most prolific and economical source of human food energy, far more efficient than harvesting energy from meat. The Hindu custom of eating grain as the staple of the diet and not eating the meat of cattle is not superstition, but hygiene and economics.

One who keeps up impropriety goes hungry; there's nothing the hungry will not eat.

People who continue to misbehave toward others wind up being abandoned and shunned. Then they will be in the position of "beggars can't be choosers."

The senses subject you to old age.

The *Tao Te Ching* says, "Colors blind people's eyes; sounds deafen their ears; flavors spoil people's palates; the chase and the hunt craze people's minds."

Livelihood should be earned from a compassionate employer; one who works for someone who's greedy fans a firefly in hopes of fire. One should choose an employer who's judicious.

Employers screen potential employees; workers should also screen potential employers. If workers see they have no prospects of enrichment or advancement by dint of personal effort because the ownership takes the profits in bonuses and dividends, then the workers will lack motivation to do anything more than get by. If workers see that a firm is unstable because of a quirky mangement or directorate, then they cannot be deeply committed to the enterprise. The *Tao Te Ching* says, "Those who embody nobility to act for the sake of the world seem to be able to draw the world to them, while those who embody love to act for the sake of the world seem to be worthy of the trust of the world."

Longevity, reputation and virtue wane by approaching those who should not be approached.

Associating with the wrong people can lead to unhealthy habits, disrespect and bad morals.

There is no enemy like ego.

Nothing helps you deceive yourself like your ego; nothing helps others manipulate you like your ego. If you think you are invulnerable to deception and manipulation, that too is a suggestion of your ego.

Don't complain of an enemy in company; it is pleasant to hear of an enemy's distress.

When you complain, you are expressing your own distress; thus you please your enemy by showing how distressed you are.

Intelligence is not found in the ne'er-do-well; the advice of a pauper is not taken, even if it is good. A pauper is disrespected, even by his own wife; bees do not approach a mango tree if it has no flowers.

It is expected that one with intelligence would not be a habitual failure. It is not expected that someone who shows a lack of resourcefulness could have any good advice to give. One who lacks resourcefulness and proves to be a habitual failure is not disrespected because of social prejudice, but because of habitual failure and lack of resourcefulness. One who cannot contribute anything to others, even on the level of the nuclear family, will normally be considered a liability anywhere.

Knowledge is wealth for the poor; knowledge cannot be taken by thieves.

The Sufi master Ali said, "Knowledge is better than wealth. Knowledge protects you, while you protect wealth. Wealth is diminished by spending, while knowledge grows by use."

One who acts for the benefit of others is a good person.

This may seem to be a truism, but then again it is possible for some forms of pious behavior to become so ritualized as to lose constructive relevance to society at large. Conceptions of good may also differ, and even conflict, so the practical thinker evaluates the actual effect of action, whatever the rationale.

Learning means tranquility of the senses. The prod of learning turns one away from ignorant behavior.

Learning that results in clear understanding leads to the serenity of certitude with freedom from doubt, and the ability to recognize and consider the range of potential meanings and consequences of actions.

The knowledge of the base-minded is not worth acquiring. Barbaric speech should not be learned. Good manners should be acquired, even those of foreigners.

If the knowledge of base-minded people were uplifting, then they wouldn't be base-minded. If barbaric speech could win people over, it wouldn't be considered barbaric. If considerate behavior were nothing but culture-specific ritual, then people of different backgrounds could never get along with each other.

Don't envy character; a good quality should be learned, even from an enemy: ambrosia can be obtained from poison.

It is self-defeating to envy another's character, for envy itself degrades one's own character. Confucius said he could find a teacher even in a group of three people: when he saw something good, he would emulate it himself; and when he saw something bad, he would correct it in himself.

One should practice the conduct of the upright and never overstep bounds.

The Sufi master Ali said, "You will find the ignorant either remiss or excessive."

A jewel of a man has no price; there is no jewel like a jewel of a woman; a jewel is really hard to find.

In Sanskrit convention, a jewel is used to represent the finest example of something. The best men cannot be bought, the best women are beyond compare. If jewels could readily be found all over the place, they would not be called jewels.

Ill repute is the fear of fears.

Social beings depend on each other and on the groups with which they are associated. That is why ostracization is a classical method of punishment in human societies. The fear of ill repute is ultimately the fear of ostracization, which is frightening because it deprives the individual of social, economic and psychological security. According to the Buddhist *Flower Ornament Scripture,* fear of ill repute is banished only when fear of death itself is transcended.

There is no attainment of learning for the lazy.

In the basic Mahayana Buddhist system of education, diligence is the fourth requirement for enlightenment, after charity, morality and patience, because the many practices involved in waking the whole mind cannot be successfully performed without diligence.

Once when Confucius saw a student sleeping in the daytime, he remarked, "Rotten wood cannot be carved, a manure wall cannot be plastered. What admonition is there for me to give?"

One who wants flowers does not water a withered tree; an undertaking without resources is no different from plowing the sand.

Don't spend time, money and effort on a project that you should realize cannot in the nature of things yield sufficient return to make it worthwhile. While it may seem that no one would ever undertake such a project to begin with, nevertheless it does happen, whether because of wishful thinking, or because of the momentum of certain habits, or because of misperception of realities.

Practical philosophers of classical times would sometimes cite simple common sense as a way of jarring their listeners into asking themselves whether they really had any common sense and whether something else, perhaps such as superstition, custom or other automatic behavior, might not take over their thinking from time to time.

The success of a task is indicated by the operative causes; indications of operative causes are better than astrology. There is no astrology for someone in a hurry.

Buddhist practical philosophy also emphasizes the understanding of causality, including the understanding that causality cannot be understood in reality by a fixed system of interpretation. People often blunder when they want fortune cookie explanations of events and advice for the future because it seems easier that way. The idea of being given guaranteed formulas can be more attractive than the idea of taking the time and effort to observe causal conditions, gathering potentially useful information and knowledge, and sharpening perceptions.

Where there is familiarity, faults are not concealed.

No doubt this is the reason why "familiarity breeds contempt." It also means that cultivating familiarity is a tool of spies and other secret agents, who seek to discover the faults of others as a way of life.

One who is himself impure is suspicious of others.

A Chinese saying has it, "Doubt in the mind, ghosts in the dark." Common sense often tells people that those who are most strident in condemning others may simply be those who feel the most need to justify themselves.

It is hard to overcome innate disposition.

An Irish proverb says, "Heredity will come through the claws, and the hound will pursue the hare." But difficulty is not impossibility. Another Irish maxim says, "A man is better than his birth."

Let the penalty fit the offense, let the response fit the remark. Let adornment accord with circumstances, let conduct accord with the community. Let the undertaking suit the task, let the gift befit the receiver.

According to the Taoist Huainan Masters, "A wise ruler employs people the way a skilled craftsman works with wood. There is an appropriate use for everything, great and small, long and short; there is an application for both the ruler and the compass, for the square and the round."

The Huainan Masters also said, "People have their specific talents;

things have their specific forms. Therefore petty-minded policies will inevitably cause loss of the overall integrity of society."

Excessive courtesy is suspect.

The Taoist classic *Tao Te Ching* says, "Higher courtesy is done, but no one responds to it; so there is forceful repetition." It also says, "Courtesy comes after loss of the sense of duty; manners mean loyalty and trust are thin, and disarray is beginning."

A fool does not see fault in himself; he only sees fault in others.

Buddhism, Taoism and Confucianism teach people to look for faults in themselves when they see them in others. This exercise is used to improve disposition and character in oneself, and to develop empathy and compassion for others.

With courtesy comes deceit. Courtesy is offering the desirable and the preferable. Excessive politeness from longtime acquaintances is suspect.

When you are more courteous to people than their own behavior deserves, they may deceive themselves into thinking you respect them more than you actually do. When you are more polite to people than your relationship requires, they may wonder what you are thinking.

A single milk-making cow is better than a thousand dogs.

Where quality or utility are required, quantity is no substitute for either.

A pigeon today is better than a peacock tomorrow.

One thing may seem more desirable, but something else may be more possible. Perceiving this distinction helps eliminate confusion in decision making.

Too much togetherness causes trouble.

This may be because familiarity breeds contempt or because people are vulnerable to manipulation when their personal weaknesses are known to others.

The one free of anger overcomes all.

In Buddhist practical philosophy, anger is considered one of the most basic poisons of the human mind.

When angry at a wrongdoer, it is the anger at which one should be angry.

Anger injures the body and mind, and it is not a necessary part of recognizing and repudiating wrong. Anger at wrongdoing causes self-injury and, if taken to extremes, may lead the angry themselves into wrongdoing.

Don't argue with the wise or the foolish, or with friends, teachers or loved ones.

It is foolish to argue with the wise, even more foolish to argue with fools. It is painful to argue with friends, presumptuous to argue with teachers and graceless to argue with loved ones.

There is no supremacy without fiendish determination.

This aphorism is not necessarily a recommendation for fiendish determination or a recommendation to struggle for supremacy. What it may suggest is to be sure to assess ambitions rationally, not just entertain them wishfully or pursue them blindly. For maximum economy of effort, it helps to think about aims in terms of costs as well as rewards. It may seem attractive to get ahead of others; it may seem less attractive to have to be watching one's back at all times.

It is no trouble for the wealthy to do good deeds; a journey is no trouble for those who have a vehicle.

Perhaps this may mean that it is simply rational, nothing wonderful, when wealthy people fund charitable enterprises.

One should be employed where one is skillful.

The Taoist Huainan Masters said, "When there is no discrimination, and each individual finds a suitable way of life, then the world is equalized; no one dominates another. Sages find work for all of them, so no abilities are wasted."

The mother is the most important of all teachers. The mother is to be supported in all conditions of age.

The mother's education begins while the child is in the womb, imprinting her offspring's body with the effects of her moods, thoughts and actions. After birth, when infants are distressed by life outside the womb, the mother must identify the particular need and attend to it; without this form of teaching conveying to them a sense of order in the world, infants can lose hope and become autistic at a prearticulate stage. The first three years of life, in which the primary caregiver is normally the mother, are believed to create such a deep impression on an individual as to exert a lifelong influence. There is literally no calculating the debt that is owed to mothers.

Erudition is clothed in manners of speaking.

The Taoist Master of Demon Valley said, "When you have examined people's mentalities, intentions and thoughts, and have gotten to know what they like and dislike, then you can speak of what is important to them, using intoxicating and arresting expressions to hook into the inclinations and thereby hold them and attract them."

The ornament of women is modesty, the ornament of intellectuals is learning, the ornament of everyone is justice. The ornament of ornaments is knowledge combined with humility.

The Sufi master Ali said that there is no faith like modesty and patience, no legacy like culture, no worship like discharge of obligations, no nobility like knowledge and no prestige like humility.

When the children are virtuous, the home is paradise. Children should be given complete education.

A complete education would include learning in the bases of virtue. Virtue has the meaning of morality and also the meaning of efficacy. By understanding the logical principles and effects of moral standards in action, it may be possible to attain successful effectiveness at ethical ways of living and working, resulting in an enhanced sense of security and well-being.

One whose destruction is imminent does not listen to good advice.

One whose destruction is imminent may have already made a habit of not listening to good advice. When things are cracking up or crumbling down, anxiety and hurry will not make a habitually heedless person more sober and attentive. Ali said there is no support surer than consultation, and also that, "One who cautions you is as one who brings you good news."

As long as we have bodies, there will never be no pleasure or pain.

The *Tao Te Ching* says, "The reason we have troubles is that we have bodies; if we had no bodies, what troubles would we have?"

Pleasure and pain follow one who makes them, as children do their mother.

The Buddha said, "If one speaks or acts with a corrupt mind, misery will follow, as the wheel of a cart follows the foot of the ox. . . . If one speaks or acts with a pure mind, happiness will follow, like the shadow that never departs."

Even the smallest favor is deemed enormous by the good person.

Taking favors for granted means loss of appreciation, and eventually loss of favor. Counting blessings, in contrast, no matter how small, is a way to develop a positive attitude and a constructive approach toward the experience of life.

No favor is due the dishonest.

Helping people who hurt others is tantamount to helping to hurt others.

Fearful of having to requite a favor, the ignoble one turns hostile.

Those who want to get but don't want to give will usually find for themselves an excuse that they prefer over recognition of their own self-centered moral sloth. Using hostility to provoke hostility is one manner of creating an excuse for oneself that can be attempted with no moral or intellectual resources at all, fabricating as it does a sense of self-righteousness with the greatest of ease, involving no constructive effort.

The noble one does not neglect to requite even the smallest of favors.

One of the disciples of Confucius used to say, "Neither causing harm nor being importunate—how can this not be good?" Confucius rejoined, "How can this way be enough to be considered good?"

Divinity should never be disrespected.

In Hindu pantheism, everything is the face of God. In Hindu transcendentalism, God is the ultimate source and goal of every soul. In Islamic Arabic, the word for disbelief or rejection of the Divinity also means ingratitude. Everything in nature, including opportunity and choice, everything in the livelihood of humanity, is said to be a "sign of God." From this point of view, an ungrateful attitude toward life, be it presumption or be it bitterness, is considered evident infidelity to the source and meaning of life itself.

There is no light like the eye, for the eye is the guide of beings.

Jesus Christ said the eye is the light of the body. The mind is called an eye, for people are led by what their minds perceive. According to Buddhists, there are five eyes. There is the eye of mortal sense, the eye of extrasensory perception, the eye of wisdom, the eye of objective reality and the enlightened eye comprehending all of these.

Don't piss in the water.

Environmentalism in ancient times is documented in classical Chinese literature of about the same era as this Sanskrit text. It could be argued, naturally, that this aphorism is a metaphor for similar principles in emotional, social and professional life.

As the body, so the consciousness. As the intelligence, so the prowess.

Things that afflict the body stress consciousness with repulsion. Things that please the body stress consciousness with attraction. No life is exempt from either of these things in some form or another. The ability to employ the energy of this stress constructively depends on understanding its mechanism and knowing good measure.

Don't throw fire into fire.

When there is friction in a situation, venting anger will only make it worse.

One should follow what is right at all times. What is wholesome and true leads to felicity.

Confucius said, "If your words are truthful and your actions are in earnest, they will be effective even in foreign countries. If your words are not truthful and your actions are not in earnest, do you think they would be effective even in your homeland?" Buddha said, "Energetic, alert, pure in deed, careful in action, self-controlled, living in accord with truth, the vigilant one will rise in repute." The *Tao Te Ching* says, "Build up virtue, and you master all."

There is no austerity greater than truth. Truth leads to felicity; the world is sustained by truth. There is no fall worse than falsehood.

Truth is austerity in that it means abstention from wishful thinking and self-serving bias. Buddha said, "The abstinence of the ignorant is worth less than a sixteenth part of those who have integrated all truths." He also said, "One who is deluded and ignorant does not become a sage by silence; but the sage is the wise one who, holding the scale, takes to what is best." There is rigor in truth; but also well-being and peace of mind.

Don't get involved in villainy; a villain has no friends.

Sufi master Ali, who was also the caliph, once said when a trouble-maker was brought before him, "There is no welcome for a face seen only on bad occasions."

Worldly subsistence troubles the pauper.

This appears to be an obvious truism. The point seems to be that if one does not take care of worldly subsistence in time, one will be too distracted and preoccupied to accomplish anything else. No doubt it was for this reason that in the traditional Aryan social system there were four stages of life: in the first stage, the main focus was education; in the second stage, the main focus was the establishment of livelihood; in the third stage, the main focus was marriage, family and enjoyment of life; in the fourth stage, the main focus was transcendence of the world and attainment of spiritual liberation.

There appears to be plenty of evidence that personal and social stagnation are caused by demanding the enjoyments of the third stage of life without having developed responsibility and capability in the first and second. Religious frustration can also be caused by trying to work on the fourth stage without having adequate experience of the first three stages of life.

The superhero is the heroic giver.

The heroic image of giving, which was recommended to warrior chieftains, was shared by classical cultures all over the world. In old Irish culture, which was cognate with Indian Hindu culture, generosity was expected of leadership, and a man was not judged by what he had so much as by what he gave.

Culture is an ornament for all; even one who is not well born can be superior to the well born by virtue of training.

This aphorism is one piece of evidence that the so-called caste system of the Aryans was originally not so rigid as to exclude social mobility. While there were regional and temporal variations, it was evidently not until long after Kauthilya's time that the Indian caste system became generally sclerotic. A parallel class system in Ireland, whose language is related to Sanskrit and whose classical culture came from the same source as Hindu culture, shows a similar pattern of early flexibility later rigidified, yet always modified, as in this aphorism of Kauthilya, by the traditional maxim that "a man is better than his birth," meaning that people of all stations in life could improve their condition in life by education and training.

Life span is enhanced through good conduct, and so is reputation.

Good conduct enhances the life span through the benefit of moderation as well as reduction of friction, anxiety and other forms of stress that result from disharmony. A good reputation also contributes to this well-being by minimizing interpersonal resistance in the social and professional environment.

Don't say something useless, even if it is nice.

The Master of Demon Valley said, "The mouth is the door of the mind, the mind is the host of the spirit. Will, intention, joy, desire, thought, worry, knowledge and planning all go in and out through the door." One of the first secrets of success, according to this ancient leadership manual, is to learn to open and close that door at the appropriate times.

Don't go along with an isolated individual, one who is opposed by many people.

The result of going along with an isolated individual who is opposed by many people is subjection to isolation and opposition. Even if misery loves company, such an alliance seems to be of no real worth to either party in the long run. The first question to ask might be why the individual is isolated and opposed to begin with.

Don't cast your lot with bad people; don't join up with the successful if they are base minded.

Even if dishonest people seem to be successful, that is not good enough reason to team up with them. Not only will association with bad people cause others to turn against you, making your place in the world inherently precarious, there is also nothing to stop what you thought was your team from leaving you holding the bag when trouble comes. Base-minded people who are successful at a particular time may, after all, have gotten where they are by deception and backstabbing all along. Connection with people of that nature ultimately leaves you without adequate security or reliable support for lasting success in the world, even if you think for a time that you are getting advantages from working with them.

Debts, enemies and illnesses should be eliminated completely.

Indebtedness, enmity and sickness all have ways of compounding if they are left unattended.

To act in accord with well-being is an elixir of life for a person.

This aphorism may seem like a truism, but it raises the questions of what well-being really is and what is actually conducive to well-being. Too much concern for gain can result in loss; excessive striving for benefit can cause harm. Trying too hard to get ahead or improve one's situation may result in anxiety and stress that damage health and shorten the life span.

Petitioners should not be treated with contempt.

You may or may not be able to fulfill a request, but there is no reason to look down on the person or the need. You may find yourself in the position of a petitioner yourself someday.

Having incited an evil act, the mean man derides the one who did it.

This is a useful illustration of meanness, whose main ingredients include weakness and cowardice. The word "mean" is commonly used in colloquial English in the sense of vicious or nasty, in literary English in the sense of base or ignoble. This Sanskrit aphorism illustrates the functional connection between baseness and viciousness in the corrupt personality.

An ingrate cannot avoid hell.

Ingrates go to hell when their habitual failure to appreciate goodness accumulates into a critical mass, producing a sensation of bitterness and discontent that never goes away but fluctuates between chronic and intense manifestations.

Growth and decline depend on the tongue; the tongue is a storehouse of both poison and elixir. One who speaks pleasantly has no enemy. Even if not true, hard words remain a long time. Nothing offensive to a ruler should be voiced; they are pleased by musical speech that is delightful to hear.

On the art of persuasion, the Master of Demon Valley says, "When speaking with those who are in a positive mood, go by the exalted and the lofty; when speaking with those who are in a negative mood, go by the humble and the small. Seek the small by lowliness, seek the great by loftiness. Follow this procedure, and what you say can be expressed anywhere, will penetrate anywhere and can suit any situation. It will thereby be possible to persuade individuals, to persuade families, to persuade the world."

One who is motivated by personal duty has integrity.

Confucius said, "Ideal people understand things in terms of duty; lesser people understand things in terms of profit."

A beggar has no dignity.

Muhammad the Prophet said, "If any of you takes a rope and gets up early and goes into the mountains and cuts firewood and sells it, and eats from this and gives charity from this, that is better for you than to ask of others."

Even an enemy should not be caused to lose his livelihood.

When people are deprived of a means of livelihood, that not only hurts them and their families, but also drains others on whom they become dependent. Even in conflict with enemies, to treat them in this way would be counterproductive because it would inevitably create an inherent source of instability, undermining general peace and well-being.

Don't anger an elephant while wielding only a castor-bean plant. Even the biggest cotton tree is no tying post for an elephant. No matter how tall, a softwood tree cannot make clubs. No matter how bright, a firefly is not fire.

According to the classic Chinese *Art of War* by Sun Tzu, "If you know others and know yourself, you will not be imperiled in a hundred battles."

Size is not a basis of virtue.

Virtue means efficacy. A small-scale operation may be more efficient than a large one.

As is the seed, so is the fruit. Awareness is in accord with learning. As is the family, so is the behavior. A cultivated nimb tree does not become a fragrant mango tree.

A nimb tree (*Azadirachta indica*) has bitter fruit by nature. What we get out of an undertaking depends on what we put into it. How we think and view the world depends on how we have been socialized and trained. How we normally behave depends on the examples we learned to consider normal in our formative years. Cultivation can have some effect, but it cannot change basic character.

Don't abandon happiness that has come to you. One comes upon sorrow by oneself.

The Sufi master Ali said, "Take of the world what comes to you, and turn away from what turns away from you." He added, "If you cannot do this, at least be decent in seeking."

There should be no night rambling; and one should not sleep only half the night.

The *I Ching* says, "Ideal people go inside and rest when the sun goes down."

One should look into reality with the help of those with knowledge.

Whithout the help of those with knowledge, there is the danger of being impeded by subjective bias.

One should not enter the house of another without reason.

Recognition of the right to privacy and quiet enjoyment of home seems to be fundamental to individual freedom, civil liberty and domestic tranquility.

People do wrong even though they are aware of it.

Education, public opinion and common sense may not be sufficient to eliminate wrongdoing and crime.

Public conduct is headed by education; where there is no education, one should follow the ways of the learned. There is no education more important than conduct.

When moral education is clearly at variance with the conduct of leaders of society, the body public subjected to contradictory impacts may become cynical, disillusioned and disaffected, losing respect for both leadership and education. The Taoist Huainan Masters said, "When people are influenced by their rulers, they follow what the rulers do, not what they say." Confucius said, "If you are personally upright, things get done without any orders being given. If you are not personally upright, no one will obey, even if you do give orders."

With spies for eyes, a ruler sees even the distant.

The Huainan Masters said, "A ruler who does not descend from the upper part of the temple yet knows beyond the four seas is one who recognizes things by means of things and knows people by means of people. There is no limit to what accumulated power can lift. Whatever is done by the knowledge of many succeeds."

The Huainan Masters also said, "If you ride on the knowledge of the multitude, it is easy to gain dominion; if you use only your own mind, you cannot even preserve yourself."

The Huainan Masters also said, "Leaders see with the eyes of the whole nation, hear with the ears of the whole nation, think with the knowledge of the whole nation and move with the strength of the whole nation. For this reason, the directives of the leaders reach all the way to the lower echelons, while the feelings of the masses come to the notice of the leaders."

Society goes along with what has already happened.

Repetition of the familiar and development of habits are characteristic actions of the brain, both individual and collective. This is often useful to a certain point, like a kind of automatic pilot; but it may interfere with creative thought and action needed to adapt to changes.

One should not speak ill of anyone on whom one is dependent.

It is common sense not to bite the hand that feeds you. It also makes sense to consider the variety and extent of the whole range of inter-dependent relationships, near and far, involved in the operation of the world of everyday life: the sources of supplies and services; the sources of social roots; the sources of education, gainful employment and recreation on which people depend for their livelihood and live-liness.

The essence of discipline is control of the faculties.

There are different forms of discipline, according to the inner and outer conditions of society, but the essence of discipline itself is to master one's own faculties. The concept of discipline seems to have picked up some baggage over the ages, apparently due to the visibility of its exaggerations into monolithic authoritarianism and suppres-sion of the individual. The original concept of discipline illustrated in this aphorism is quintessentially individualistic, in that control of one's own faculties enables one to be independent of control by manipulation of either or both the internal and external environ-ment.

A paradisical state is not permanent; it lasts only as long as the result of virtues: and there is no misery worse than fall from a para-disical state.

According to Buddhist teaching, virtue without wisdom has three phases of negative consequences. The first phase is when good deeds are done in hopes of reward, distracting people from clarifying the essence of mind. The second phase is when pleasurable states that develop as results of good deeds become objects of attachment and possessiveness. The third phase is when the pleasurable states are worn out, while habituation to them remains; this gap between actu-ality and conditioned expectation produces extra misery.

Liberation is the cure of sorrows.

Buddha said, "Be free of the past, be free of the future, be free of the meantime; be transcendant. When your mind is completely liberated, you no longer suffer birth and old age."

The enmity of the noble is better than the allegiance of the ignoble.

From the enmity of the noble one may learn to recognize one's own mistakes and faults; by the allegiance of the ignoble one may learn to disguise one's own mistakes and faults.

Hard words destroy the family.

Plato said, "It behooves those who take the young to task to leave them room for excuse, lest they drive them to be hardened by too much rebuke."

There is no greater pleasure than contact with one's children.

People today might say this depends on the quality of one's relationship with one's children, but then again, it doesn't take that much to surpass the pleasure of abandonment.

In an argument, keep justice in mind.

Don't get carried away by emotion or confused by verbal maneuvering; just pursue what is right and true.

When at leisure, one should think of what is to be done.

This is the way to keep on top and ahead of things. If leisure is all used up in rest and diversion, and none is given to leisurely reflection and creative thinking, this can produce exaggerated cycles of lethargy and tension, thus reducing the recuperative value of leisure as well as the effectiveness of renewal in its aftermath.

One whose destruction is imminent thinks of bad plans.

It is often hard to think straight when hard pressed. That is no doubt why it is better to think ahead when there is free time, as the previous aphorism recommends. Strategies formulated on the spot in moments of crisis and states of high anxiety are too often distorted by emotion, or based on too narrowly focused attention, to be effective in practice.

For one who needs milk, what is the use of an elephant?

A common feature of bad planning is reliance on quantitative abundance in place of qualitative exactitude.

There is no power of subjection equal to a gift.

Using debt or gratitude to influence or manipulate people is an insidious practice known in the Japanese vernacular as "making someone wear gratitude." An early Muslim said, "In the lifetime of the Prophet, a gift was a gift. Today, it is a bribe."

One should not long for that which is at the disposition of another. Only an immature person enjoys ill-gotten gains; bitter fruit is eaten only by crows.

Coveting what is rightfully at the disposal of others creates psychological complications; taking what is rightfully at the disposal of others, whether by stealth, by deception or by force, creates social complications.

An ocean does not quench thirst.

A successful individual may be surrounded by many people in good times, but they may all prove useless when a real need arises.

Even grains of sand stick by their own kind: the wholesome do not enjoy the company of the unwholesome; a swan does not frequent a burning-ground.

People may put on appearances to make a certain impression on others, but their habitual associations will ultimately reveal their true character.

The world goes on for the sake of wealth: the world is bound by wishful expectation, but prosperity does not abide with those given to wishful expectation. There is no firmness in those given to wishful expectation.

When Confucius remarked that he had never seen a person who was firm, one of his students mentioned someone as an example. Confucius retorted, "He is covetous—how can he be firm?"

Death is better than meanness.

Mean people also have to die. The quality of mean-spirited living, however, whether considered in terms of cause or in terms of effect, might make it seem that death would be better.

Desire drives away shame.

Mencius said that people should have a sense of shame in order to reach the point where they have nothing to be ashamed of. This element of personal cultivation naturally affects professional life as well. Confucius said, "Can an ignoble man serve the government? No. He worries about getting something, and once he has got, he worries about losing it. As long as he worries about losing, there's no telling what he might do."

One should not praise oneself.

Ali said, "The loneliest isolation is conceit."

One should not sleep by day.

Buddha said, "People who are negligent are as if dead."

One who is blinded by prosperity does not even see what is at hand, or listen to a good word.

The *Tao Te Ching* says, "To keep on filling is not as good as stopping. . . . Though gold and jewels fill their houses, no one can keep them. When the rich upper classes are haughty, their legacy indicts them."

A guest is to be treated properly.

Hospitality is a basic thread of the fabric of many traditional societies. In old Irish culture, the westernmost relative of Hindu culture, hospitality was considered so fundamental that free public hospitality houses were official institutions.

An enemy appears to be a friend; a mirage appears to be water.

According to the Chinese warrior-philosopher Sun Tzu, subterfuge and deception are normal practices in strategic arts.

Pseudoscience seduces the ignorant.

Kauthilya also said, "Indications of operative causes are better than astrology." Brahmins of India and druids of Ireland, heirs of a common tradition of high antiquity, both included natural sciences among their domains of study. The idea of scientific objectivity is not something new, and not specifically Western, just as pseudoscience is not confined to premodern societies. Numerous sages and prophets in various ancient cultures opposed superstition, often at considerable cost to themselves. Confucius, it is said, "did not talk about strange things, powers, chaos or the spiritual." Abraham, Moses, Buddha and Muhammad also discouraged popular superstitions of their times.

The company of the good is paradise. The noble one thinks of others as self.

Buddha said, "The sight of the noble is good, association with them is always happy. One who never sees fools will be happy forever."

Buddha also said, "Follow one who is wise, insightful, learned, enduring, dutiful, noble, a genuine human being, authentically intelligent."

One's place is where one can live happily.

The Huainan Masters said, "Let individuals suit their natures, be secure in their abodes, live as best they can and exercise their capabilities." The *Tao Te Ching* speaks of a state in which people can "relish their food, like their clothes, are comfortable in their ways and enjoy their work."

There is no salvation for one who destroys trust.

Confucius considered trust the most basic ingredient of society. He said that it is more important even than food and armament because nothing constructive can be done without trust.

The honorable man considers the suffering of dependents as his own.

When a successful man thought himself more important than those below him in rank, Muhammad the Prophet said to him, "Are you made triumphant and provided sustenance except by the powerless among you?"

The Prophet also said, "You see the believers in their mutual kindness, love and sympathy, as if they were a single body. When one of its members is ailing, the rest of the body joins it in sleeplessness and fever."

The ignoble man hides what is in his heart and speaks of something else.

When asked how to work for rulers, Confucius replied, "Don't deceive them, even if you have to offend them."

An irrational man is equivalent to a demon.

With someone who allows no possibility of reasonable interaction or rational discourse, such that there is no way to predict the effect and outcome of one's own behavior, one will have a devil of a time dealing gracefully. It may very well be that this is precisely the reason why some people will actually choose irrationality under certain circumstances. When people seem unreasonable, therefore, it may be useful to see whether they are truly irrational or strategically so. It would probably be useful to check one's own rationality as well.

One should not travel unaccompanied.

Company on the road can improve morale and multiply resources for dealing with the unforeseen. Complete strangerhood may abnormally loosen or radically undermine normal restraints on behavior.

The reasonable have no enemies.

Confucius said, "If you are exacting with yourself while forgiving to others, then you will put enmity at a distance."

One should not reveal one's own weakness.

In terms of strategic science, to reveal one's own weakness is to make oneself vulnerable. The energy then spent on remedial defense is not available for constructive action.

It is the patient one who sees everything through.

Confucius said, "Those whose strength is insufficient give up along the way."

Money should be saved for hard times.

Among the fundamental management principles adopted by the Japanese industrial magnate Matsushita Konosuke, one of the most successful businessmen of the twentieth century, was to maintain a thick cash cushion, a specific level of reserve established to keep the enterprise operating effectively through difficult periods.

Do tomorrow's task today; do the afternoon's in the morning.

The *Tao Te Ching* says, "Do it before it exists; govern it before there's disorder."

Morality conforms to convention.

The ethical evaluation of an action depends on the agreements informing the system of values. When different systems of values are compelled to interact, they may compete, or conflict, or find common ground, or come to new ways of understanding.

All-knowledge means knowledge of the world. Even if one has formal learning, without knowledge of the world one is the equivalent of an ignoramus.

There is no point in pursuing knowledge that is irrelevant and useless. Without knowledge of the world, the possible relevance and utility of formal learning cannot be established.

Application of learning is vision of reality. Knowledge of reality also illuminates work.

To put learning into practice requires an effective understanding of the actual context in which it is to be applied. Knowledge of objective conditions also makes it clear what is useful and what is possible in a given time and place.

There should be no bias in litigation.

In ancient Europe, judges were druids, considered the most just of people. Druids were European equivalents of Brahmins in India, both having descended from a common tradition in remote antiquity. The old Irish legal specialists known as brehons, themselves druids and descendants of druids, were famed for their ability to render decisions so fairly that both winners and losers were satisfied. Accurate and comprehensive knowledge of facts and precedents are emphasized in druidical law, and bias and wrangling are counted among four archetypical elements of folly.

The Huainan Masters said, "Just as a balance is fair insofar as it weighs things impartially, and a plumb line is correct insofar as it determines straight lines impartially, so a ruler who applies the law without personal likes and dislikes can thereby command."

Custom weighs even more than law.

Custom is an original source of law. The Huainan Masters said, "Law derives from justice; justice derives from what suits the community. What suits the community is what accords with the hearts of the people. This is the essence of government. . . . Law does not come down from the heavens, nor does it spring up from the earth; it develops among people."

The soul is witness to a transaction. The soul, indeed, is witness to everything.

Becoming inwardly conscious of the witnessing soul is an exercise in awareness of motives and actions, for the purpose of enhancement of conscience.

One should not be a false witness; false witnesses fall into hell.

If conscience is false, there is no way of harmonizing motives and actions with truth and reality, and therefore no way of avoiding perpetual friction, aggravation and overall stress to the whole system.

The elements are witnesses of concealed evils; one reveals one's own evil.

This may be the fundamental principle behind the story of *The Portrait of Dorian Grey.* Hidden vice may leave social face intact as long as it remains concealed, but eventually a toll is taken on the body and the personality. Buddha said, "Don't underestimate evil, thinking it won't affect you. As dripping water can fill a pitcher drop by drop, a fool is filled with evil even if he accumulates it little by little."

Pious, just, delighting in the welfare of the religious, able to protect the people, he who has mastered his faculties is a king. Let him preserve his own domain, keeping it under control, devoted to truth and justice; having overcome hostile armies, let him protect the land with justice.

The Taoist Huainan Masters said, "The ancient establishment of rulers was not for the service of their desires. . . . Rulership was set up because the strong oppressed the weak, majorities did violence to minorities, the cunning fooled the simple, the daring attacked the timid, people kept knowledge to themselves and did not teach, people accumulated wealth and did not share it. So the instinction of rulership was set up to equalize and unify them."

One in whose domain the sacred syllable om *is chanted by sages is a king, a yogin, who is not afflicted by disorders.*

Integrity of the cultural fabric of a nation promotes stability and resilience. A combination of political and cultural integrity is difficult to shake. Great leaders of vast heterogeneous empires—Charlemagne,

Harun al-Rashid, Tamerlane and others throughout history—have understood the value of intellectual, religious, and other cultural elements in the establishment and maintenance of national polities and international alliances.

One who is protector of the helpless, refuge for refugees, guide to the lost, haven for the fearful, supporter of the disenfranchised, friend, kinsman, patron, resort, benefactor, boon, teacher, father, mother and brother to the world, that one is a leader.

In olden times, people with inclinations toward leadership could begin by behaving in these ways to the extent of their capacities. As this gradually won other people's affections and loyalties, their capacities for further outreach and uplift would increase in proportion.

Punishment of the bad, reward of the good, increase of the treasury by proper method, impartiality to supplicants, preservation of sovereignty: five are the stated duties of leaders.

It may be useful to note areas where punishment of the bad remains a feature of leadership, but not reward of the good. There is also the question of fair distribution of punishments and rewards, based on deeds and not social status.

Fair taxation is a basic issue every government has to consider from time to time. What does the public get for what it gives, what does the government give for what it gets?

If the subjective desires of a select few are met while the objective needs of many people, even whole communities, are virtually disregarded, then real social stability is impossible, even if a semblance of stability can be temporarily obtained by rigidification.

Preservation of sovereignty ostensibly means readiness to repel invasion, but armed invasion is not the only threat to sovereignty. There are various ways of exerting influence inside another country, open and covert, including influence through institutions devoted to commerce, industry, finance, education and so on. Getting a country so deeply into debt that the amount of revenue that must be devoted to debt service staggers the economy may be another kind of threat to sovereignty, especially when a large percentage of the debt is held by other governments. There may also be certain types of people within any given country or organization whose cooperation could be purchased by outsiders; they are actively sought, and if not found may be deliberately cultivated. Leaders have to be careful about all of these things in order to preserve true sovereignty for their nations.

Indifferent to the drinking goblet, delighting in virtue, sharing enjoyment with others, willing to learn science and willing to fight in war: these are five characteristics of a leader.

Alcoholic drink was disapproved by Hindus and Buddhists because of the way it diminishes the power of self-mastery, thus eroding the basis of morality.

Self-mastery is considered essential to leadership in Kauthilya's philosophy, and this self-mastery is supposed to be expressed in the moral quality of leadership.

The relationship of the leadership to the social body is a primary example of its moral expression. The Huainan Masters said, "When subjects do not get what they want from their rulers, the rulers cannot get what they seek from their subjects."

Willingness to learn is another mode of pragmatic moral expression. In this context, the term *science* includes natural and human sciences. The willingness of leadership to learn keeps the paths of social progress open.

Willingness to fight to defend the nation also reflects the moral sense of the leadership. Although this may seem to be taken for granted, history shows that some leaders will sell out to more powerful adversaries or abandon their nations in favor of comfortable exile when hard times come.

One thing is to be learned from the lion, one from the crane, four from the cock; five things are to be learned from the crow, six from the dog and three from the donkey. When a man wants to do a task, great or small, let him do it with all dispatch: this is called the one thing learned from the lion.

The Taoist philosopher Lao-tzu speaks of doing the great while it is still small, even of doing things before they exist. The sooner something needing attention is taken care of, the less room for further complications to develop and the more energy available for constructive action.

Controlling his senses, the wise man is like a crane; let him accomplish all tasks by knowing the potency of the place and time.

Knowing the potency of the place and time means seeing what is actually possible, and when. Control of the senses enables one to have the clarity of mind to attain and utilize this perception. Thus avoiding random action, one can channel energy with optimum efficiency.

Rising early, fighting, sharing with kin and enjoyment of the fruits of one's own efforts: these four should be learned from the cock.

Rising at daybreak is a basic way of attuning the individual body to the solar season. This allows a maximum use of daytime energy throughout the year.

Fighting means being able to defend oneself and one's family, neighbors, community and so on. This was one way that people on the path of chivalry came to be leaders of nations.

Sharing with kin affirms the original sense of relatedness from which social contracts arose.

Enjoyment of the fruits of one's own labors confirms meaning in work. Muhammad the Prophet said that there is no better food than that earned by one's own labor; and he also related that David, the Hebrew king, never ate any food but what he earned by the work of his own hands.

Privacy in sex, boldness, timely withdrawal, vigilance and wariness: these five should be learned from the crow.

On one level these five are particularly apt for warriors, but they also apply to other people as well, according to the different contexts of their lives.

Privacy in sex is not only simple decency, but also an essential aspect of real intimacy.

Boldness is ability to take initiative and act with alacrity and decisiveness.

Timely withdrawal is ability not to go too far or rely too much on boldness alone.

Vigilance is necessary to watch the timing of events and actions, the changing conditions and the ongoing consequences.

Wariness is that part of watchfulness devoted to preventing trouble before it happens, thus saving energy for other constructive or creative activities.

Desiring much yet content with little, sleeping deeply yet quick to awake, loyal and brave: these are the six virtues of canines.

Desiring much stimulates progress, while contentment with little eliminates aggression. Sleeping deeply promotes rest and restoration; being quick to awake promotes clarity of mind. Loyalty implies a sense of duty; Confucius said that to see one's duty and not do it implies a lack of bravery.

Even when exhausted he will bear a burden, not minding heat and cold, always going along content: these three things should be learned from the donkey.

Sometimes there is frustration, but that need not keep one from working. Sometimes there may be a lot of pressure, and sometimes there may be slumps, but that need not dominate the mind. One may wish for anything, but not everything is possible; knowing what is enough protects the soul from wear and tear.

The sagacious one who practices these twenty verses set forth here will overcome all adversaries and remain invincible.

It is not only the individual qualities described, but the whole range of their combinations that gives rise to the potency here attributed to them.

Replanting the uprooted, gathering the flowering, strengthening the weak, lowering the overgrown, dividing up the superabundant, loosening the compacted, removing sharp thorns, protecting spontaneous growth: one who is like a gardener, skilled in undertakings, remains long in sovereignty.

These seem to be perennial tasks of government, in whatever form: resettlement of the disenfranchised, fair taxation of profits, assistance of the needy, regulation of growth, prevention of monopolies, elimination of congestion, isolation of criminals and education of the young.

Designs conceived by the hostile are as if divinely thwarted; the leader who stands on the straight path is naturally blessed.

The Huainan Masters said, "Anything can be overcome except the Way."

A virtuous quality in a leader, and in a minister, is one by which state finances are improved.

The Huainan Masters said, "What is to be done for prosperity today, and what is to be done for justice tomorrow—this is easily said. What is to be done for justice today, and what is to be done for prosperity tomorrow—this is hardly known."

One who spends irrationally, one who is argumentative, one who is sickly and one who consumes everything, quickly perishes.

Irrational spending leads to financial ruin. Contentiousness leads to hostility. Sickliness leads to isolation. Overconsumption leads to lack.

Better to have no country than a country with a bad ruler. Better to have no friend than a bad friend. Better to have no student than a bad student. Better to have no wife than a bad wife. How can there be happiness in a badly ruled country? How can there be solace in the friendship of a bad friend? How can there be enjoyment in a home with a bad wife? How can there be honor in teaching a bad student? There is no trusting a bad friend, no enjoying a bad wife; there is no tranquility in a bad kingdom, no life in a bad place.

Social order, friendship, family and education all influence the quality of life.

Clothed in armor, fierce, proceeding indirectly, hooded, yet susceptible to direction, rulers are like snakes.

The armor of a ruler is organization; the ferocity of a ruler is ambition; the indirectness of a ruler is tactical diplomacy; the hood of a ruler is delegation of authority; a ruler's acceptance of direction is consultation.

The root of law and order is the leaders, and the root of sacred lore is the learned. Where the learned are respected, there law and order is everlasting.

The learned are respected where cultural values are honored and their integrity is maintained. Because cultural values inform customary law and social order, common respect for these values is the primary force that maintains law and order.

One who gives up his own kind and takes to another goes to his own dissolution, as does a leader by following an alien rule.

Confucius said, "Those whose paths are not the same do not consult each other."

Sovereignty and success, status and purity, erudition, longevity, and health—this is the fruit of justice.

The concept of justice had broader meaning in ancient philosophies than it does in common usage today. Socrates said, "It is by justice that the universals of the world exist, and its particulars cannot exist without it." Here in Kauthilya's aphorism, justice appears to imply fairness in professional conduct, fairness in social relations, fairness in respect for truth, and fairness in employment and treatment of the body. The aphorism does not suggest, however, that the beneficial results of justice are themselves the aims of fairness; it only says these are effects of justice. Confucius said, "Cultivated people understand things in terms of justice; small people understand things in terms of profit."

He protects the country, always devoted to true justice; having overcome enemy armies, let him provide security as is right for a lord.

The leadership of an entity such as a nation or a corporation can effectively lead only if it can keep the entity together by maintaining the internal integrity of its operation while protecting it from external threats.

A leader who gets angry at a minister for no reason will be maddened by venom, as if bitten by a cobra. A leader should not frown or get angry without reason; when they are not at fault, the leader should protect ministers with justice.

Arbitrary behavior arousing resentment can have serious consequences within an executive group whose effectiveness at the head of an enterprise requires sincere cooperation. The reverberations of random disruptions can drive people to distraction.

What is strange about a learned man versed in sacred lore becoming a sage? What is strange about a just man adroit in political science becoming a leader?

It may be assumed, particularly today, that attainment of positions of leadership comes about only through personal ambition and desire for power. That would seem to rule out the possibility of truly impartial justice. It might happen, however, that honesty, intelligence and knowledge could achieve leadership naturally, without selfish ambition or drive, as naturally as the learned might become wise. The contrived and the natural way would produce two different kinds of candidate; we are asked to question ourselves *why* we would expect one kind more than another.

It is a wonder when a beautiful young girl becomes a chaste woman; it is a wonder when a man tormented by poverty does nothing wrong at all.

Sociological approaches to the problem of crime date back more than two thousand years in China as well as in India. The Taoist Huainan Masters said, "No one has ever heard of anyone who avoided breaking the law and risking punishment when both hungry and cold."

The helpless, the poor, the young, the old, the distressed, the unjustly slighted—a leader is the refuge of them all.

The followings of prophets and revolutionary leaders all over the world have swelled with people whose needs have been forgotten or disregarded by the existing order.

The leader is the strength of the powerless, crying is the strength of infants; silence is the strength of imbeciles, falsehood is the strength of thieves.

For masses of the individually powerless, unification and organization make it possible to attain great power.

For Taoists the ability of infants to cry all day without getting hoarse is an example of the potency of naturalness.

For fools there is wisdom in not voicing folly.

For thieves there is nothing more important than deceiving the eye, ear, thought and attention of those around them.

The leader's wife, your teacher's wife, your friend's wife, your wife's mother and your own mother—these five are thought of as mothers.

That is, these people are respected as if they were one's own mother.

A prostitute will desert a man gone broke, people will abandon a defeated leader; birds will abandon a tree whose fruit is gone, and guests will abandon a house after eating.

This seems to be a reminder that if you find that you suddenly acquire a lot of "friends" when you have become successful, you may or may not care to determine whether they like you for who you are or for what you have.

The leader should amass wealth justly on the one hand, while on the other should use that to foster the finest freemen.

When revenue is invested in the development of human resources, the resulting increase in productivity will also increase revenue. The developmental cycle can then be repeated on a progressively larger scale.

Even incompetent ascetics accumulate material goods; so why not protectors of the earth, on whose resources the people depend?

Wealth is not the goal of leadership itself, but it is a means of executing the obligations and responsibilities of leadership.

Momentary success is hard to gain; once gained, it can fulfill human needs. If it is not put to good use here, when will this opportunity ever occur again?

Wealth is valued for what can be attained and accomplished by the means it affords. One who only hoards wealth and does not put it to good use cannot obtain the full benefit of wealth.

It is true that pleasures delight the mind, it is true that enjoyments are powerful; but life is inconstant, unsteady as the stagger of a drunken woman. Having attained momentary affluence, set your mind on permanent truth; for success vanishes in a moment, along with oneself.

The impulse to consume one's success can be balanced by recollecting the transitoriness and frailty of conditional things, including the world and the human body. This realization lends balance and sobriety to the experience of success.

In alliance, in conflict, in almsgiving, in gaining fame, in self-gratification, even in attaining liberation, wealth is the leader's ally. One who has resources has friends, one who has resources has associates; one who has resources is a man of the world, one who has resources is learned.

Assistance, tribute, hospitality, defense, charity, publicity, recreation and education all require resources.

Where does it come from to begin with? And when it disperses, where does it go? The way of wealth is inscrutable.

An accumulation of circumstances, events and actions, none of them anything in itself, can reach a critical threshold, past which a certain pattern takes shape and repeats itself. The accumulation of a fortune by one person inevitably depends on the actions of countless people, the majority of whom may be unknown to each other and unaware of their part in the making of a fortune somewhere. When a fortune is consumed, by the same token, it dissolves into the environment, eventually passing into the hands of people who know nothing of its origin.

The works of the stupid man who has lost his wealth all come to an end, like a stream drying up in the summer heat. Friends abandon one who has lost his riches; so do children, friends and society. They resort to him again when he is wealthy; so wealth is a man's friend in the world. Where there is water, swans resort; when it dries up, they leave. They resort there again when there's water there. A man should not be a friend like a swan.

Most classical philosophies on the art of living, if not all of them, recommend mindfulness of the danger of ruin when in the flush of success, to avoid complacency and laziness. The other side of this is responding to adversity with self-improvement, to avoid bitterness and despair. Even if you accept, as a warning and a precaution, that others may abandon you when you are in difficulty, nevertheless you should not yourself be one to abandon others when they are in need.

Picking each blossom individually, without cutting the roots, be like a gardener in his garden, not like a charcoal maker.

How to utilize resources without using them up is one of the main problems of modern civilization.

Milk is enjoyed after milking, not after slaughtering; a country is to be enjoyed by rulers through methods like milking. The milk of the cow is not obtained after drying her up; likewise, tribute is not obtained from a country by beleaguering it unfairly.

Exploitation of office and excessive taxation are ultimately counterproductive, undermining the bases of wealth in both private and public sectors.

As a bee collects honey from flowers, so should a ruler take in revenue, amassing a store. A country is said to be like honey; and the honeybees are not to be killed: a ruler should draw the yield of the earth and also protect it, as one would look after a calf. An anthill,

*a honeycomb, a waxing moon, royal riches and charity increase bit
by bit.*

Wealth that is obtained gradually, without unfairness or exploitation,
can accumulate in relative security. The greater the accumulation,
the greater the capacity for altruistic action. When both means and
ends are considered acceptable and there is no resentment or opposition toward either the accumulation or the employment of the
wealth, then the cycle of growth, distribution and expansion may
continue unobstructed, within the limits of environmental conditions, until a natural equilibrium is reached.

*Flies seek open sores, rulers seek wealth; the low seek a fight, the
righteous seek peace.*

Flies seek open sores to feed on. Rulers seek wealth to support the
aims of the nation. The low seek to fight as a way to prevail. The
righteous seek peace as a way to prosper.

*Read, son; what good is laziness? One who does not read becomes
a porter, while a scholar is honored royally. Read, son, every day!
Read, son, always; keep it forever in your heart. A king is honored
in his own land, knowledge is honored everywhere. Scholarship and
rulership are never equal: a king is honored in his own land, the
sage is honored everywhere.*

Profound respect for learning was characteristic of the great classical
cultures of China and India, but this was not peculiar to the East. In
classical Ireland, one of the oldest Western cultures, scholars of the
highest rank were equal in status and privilege to kings. For centuries
after the fall of the Roman empire, many of the teachers of the
schools of Western Europe were either Irish or from the Irish tradition.

Scholars were not only more socially mobile than most people,
they also had more opportunities for travel. Scholars in ancient
China, Ireland, India, Japan and elsewhere would travel extensively
as part of their professional training. Courts eager for knowledge of
the outside world, meanwhile, seeking knowledge of useful things or
techniques, of possible allies, of potential enemies, would normally
extend hospitality to learned and skilled people from all over.

Without learning, an individual's horizons would be severely limited in the ancient world. This is still the case in the modern world.

A ruler born blind is better than one without learning; the blind one sees by means of a scout, while the one void of learning sees not at all.

In the *Instructions of Cormac,* a classical Irish manual of leadership, kings are advised to encourage the sciences and to learn arts, languages and skills in various kinds of work. Kauthilya also said, "Song, dance, painting, instrumental music, mathematics, practical arts, political economics and the science of archery: the ruler should actively preserve these."

One arrow shot by an archer may kill or not; but the design of a sage can destroy a country, including its ruler.

Classical learning included strategic science, which is of most critical importance for rulers in particular. The Taoist Master of Demon Valley said of this science, "Petty people imitating others will use this in a perverse and sinister way, even getting to the point where they can destroy families and usurp countries." Unless it is known and understood, there is no way to develop effective defense against it.

A ruler who has suffered misfortune should not be anguished; he should also cut down the ego's success, and neither be depressed nor elated.

Buddhist thinkers also deemed it wise to consider adversity a good opportunity for development of detachment, critical self-examination and compassion for others.

Those who are self-possessed do not become depressive, even in distress; does not the moon reemerge after it has been eclipsed?

The caliph and Sufi master Ali said, "Patience comes down according to misfortune; so if anyone strikes his hand on his thigh in his misfortune, his work comes to naught."

A ruler is to be insightful, mild, free from foibles, inaccessible, sacrificing, equanimous in hardship and ease.

A leader needs insight to see how to motivate people and restrain them, according to conditions. A leader needs mildness for sympathy and tact, to protect people's feelings and preserve goodwill. A leader needs inacessibility for professional integrity, to avoid being swayed by private interests of factions, cliques and self-seekers. A leader needs to be sacrificing in consistently placing the interests of the nation or the group above personal preferences. A leader needs to be equanimous in hardship and ease in order to avoid infecting the social, professional or national body with a sense of fearfulness or a sense of complacency.

One should always restrain fickle opinion and restrain false talk in freemen, priests and the servant class.

A Zen proverb says, "When one person tells a falsehood, myriad people pass it on as truth." The influences of fickle opinion and false gossip can cause incalculable loss of potential by crippling and distorting common sense and blurring perceptions of reality.

Justice is preserved by power, knowledge is preserved by application; a ruler is protected by gentility, the home is protected by a good wife.

If people are powerless themselves and are not protected by the powers that be, who will give them justice when they are wronged by deceit or by force?

If knowledge is not applied in some concrete way—be it art, ethics, education, manners and customs, technology, law, literature—then it disappears from human consciousness.

If the leadership is harsh and oppressive, it will always have enemies.

If the wife has no interest in home life, a household will break up.

Night rambling is poison; the favor of a king is poison. A wife whose heart is with another is poison; undetected illness is poison.

Night rambling drains energy, by its own nature and by the nature of its various complications.

The favor of a king brings envy, jealousy and the danger of loss of favor.

A wife whose heart is with another is not like a wife.

An undetected illness goes without treatment.

One should sit with good people and always associate with the good. Let both debate and friendship be with the good; do nothing whatever with the corrupt. One should abide with the learned, the cultured, those who know what is right, those who speak the truth—stay with them even in prison, rather than rule with mischief makers! One eye is discernment, the other is association with the good; whoever lacks these two eyes surely soon falls into a pit of delusion. Who is an enemy, who is a friend? Who is indifferent, who is impartial? Who is venerable, who is estimable? The simpleton who fails to recognize these is lost everywhere.

Confucius said, "Three kinds of friends are beneficial, and three are harmful. When friends are honest, sincere or knowledgeable, they are beneficial. When friends are pretentious, fawning or opportunistic, they are harmful."

The great Zen master Zhangtang said, "The difficulty of knowing people is what ails sages." The famous strategist Zhuge Liang wrote, "Nothing is harder to see than people's natures. Though good and bad are different, their conditions and appearances are not always uniform. There are some people who are nice enough but steal. Some people are outwardly respectful while inwardly making fools of everyone. Some people are brave on the outside yet cowardly on the inside. Some people do their best but are not loyal. Hard though it be to know people, there are ways."

The Sufi master Ali advised, "Do not befriend a fool, for he hurts you when he wants to help you. And do not befriend a stingy man, for he will distance himself from you when he is most needed. And do not befriend a profligate, as he will sell you for a trifle. And do not befriend a liar, for he is like a mirage, making the distant seem near to you and the near seem distant."

Untrained employees, an ill-bred ruler, false friends and an immodest wife: these four are painful sorrows, spikes to the head.

Failure to train employees thoroughly may cost more than it saves in the long run. Position and power may be more easily corrupted without personal cultivation on the part of those who hold them. False friends abuse trust, undermining faith in humanity. An immodest wife compromises the stability of the home by creating questions about its integrity.

A ruler should give up indulgence in diversions; those who are devoted to pleasure are manipulated by existing enemies. Gambling, hunting, women, drink, touring and slumber—a king perishes quickly through addiction to these.

According to classical Chinese strategic science, anything that has form can be attacked and overcome. An indulgence, habit or addiction, as a rigidly fixed form, presents a stationary target for poachers, as well as a constant preoccupation of energy.

A man who will rationalize violation of well-informed convention, of civilized norms, also perishes quickly, in this world and the next.

As times change and a society ages and struggles to adapt, people begin to ask themselves what constitutes well-informed convention and civilized normalcy. Taoist philosophers tried to solve this problem by focusing on the sources of conventions and norms, and the reasons why conventions and norms became conventional and normal. That way, they envisioned, stability would not have to be won at the cost of adaptability. The Huainan Masters said, "Whatever is inappropriate in the policies of former regimes is to be abandoned, while whatever is good in the affairs of latter days is to be adopted. There has never been any fixed constant in manners and culture, so sages formulate manners and culture without being ruled by manners and culture." Thus emphasis lies on keeping well informed, in order that norms and conventions can be well formulated.

A king who is pretentious and proud of his retinue and possessions is soon overcome by enemies, at court and at war.

The *Tao Te Ching* says, "Those who assert themselves are not illustrious; those who glorify themselves have no merit; those who are proud of themselves do not last."

Society as a whole is controlled by authority, for the innocent man is rare. It is through fear of punishment that society as a whole partakes of enjoyment.

The Taoist Huainan Masters said, "Now that society's virtues are declining and mores are growing weaker, to want to govern a decadent populace with simple laws is like trying to ride a wild horse without a bit and bridle." They also said, "What restrains and punishes is law. When people have been punished and yet are not resentful, this is called the Way."

An ignorant person is pitiful, infertility is pitiful, people without food are pitiful, a country in anarchy is pitiful.

The Huainan Masters said, "When people have more than enough, they defer; when they have less than enough, they contend. When people are deferential, then courtesy and justice arise. When people contend, violence and disorder occur."

Fortunate are those who do not see the breakup of the country, the destruction of the family, the estrangement of a wife, the ruin of a son.

These things occur with greater frequency, affecting even greater numbers of people, as the fabric of a society decays.

Wealth again, a friend again, a wife again, land again—all this can be regained, but not the body, ever again!

The *Tao Te Ching* says, "Which means more to you, your body or your goods?"

One should not stay where five things are not found: worldly means of livelihood, security, modesty, courtesy and morality.

To stay where there is no way to make a living will lead to dependency or crime. Where there is no security, there can be no freedom from anxiety and no peace of mind. Where there is no modesty, courtesy or morality, there is nothing to mitigate interpersonal contention, friction and conflict.

One should abide in a place where there is abundant respect and abandon where there is lack of respect. One should shun even the company of angels if there is no respect.

When people are not respected, their potential for good is not nourished and enlivened. When people do not respect others, they interact without deference and consideration, thus creating chronic irritation.

A bad country, a bad custom, a bad wife, a bad river, a bad friend and bad food—these are always shunned by the wise.

A result of chronic irritation is unease and illness. One of the ways to aim for a healthy life overall is to consider the mental and physical impact of the events, habits, people and things in the environment.

One who stands by in sickness, in calamity, in famine, in danger from enemies, at the door of the ruler and at the burial ground, that is a friend!

Ali said, "A friend is not a true friend unless he protects his brother in three situations: in his misfortune, in his absence and at his death."

Someone who thwarts you behind your back yet speaks kindly to your face should be avoided, for such a friend is a pitcher of poison with milk on top.

When people enjoy being flattered, they may not think of it as a test or as a cover for backstabbing. One of the classic Chinese Thirty-Six Strategies is "Hide a sword in a smile."

Association with good people is a basis of success, above all; a grain that has grown to the size of the husk does not grow anymore.

A Zen classic says, "It was our parents who gave birth to us, our companions who raised us." The caliber of people with whom one habitually associates is the "size of the husk" within which character and potential grow and develop.

Good qualities should be mentioned, even if they are an enemy's; faults should be mentioned, even if they are a guru's. A statement should be accepted if it is reasonable, not out of respect for a guru.

One of the fundamental principles of Buddhist doctrine is "rely on truth, not on personality." Confucius also said, "A cultured individual does not promote people just because of what they say, nor ignore what is said just because of who is saying it."

A man who wants to trust an enemy is considered to have gone to sleep up in a tree and fallen down. One should not trust a defeated enemy who has come to be friendly; a crow sees a burnt-out cave as full of owls, even when the fire is out. One should not trust a false friend, nor trust a friend, for that matter; someday a friend in anger may reveal all secrets. One should not trust the unfaithful, nor trust the faithful too much; for when insecurity arises from trust, it cuts right through the roots.

The Sufi master Ali said, "Do not trust the disaffected."

The remnant of an illness, the remnant of a fire, the remnant of an enemy and the remnant of a debt: these can act up again and again, so one should see to it that no remnant remains. An enemy should not be ignored by the wise, even an enemy with little power; for even a little fire, when it grows, will reduce a forest to ashes. Never ignore an enemy just because you know he is trifling; in time his maliciousness acts out, like a spark of fire in straw.

Stopping destructive forces while they are still minimal in power is an example of the Taoist technique of "doing the great while it is still small." In a collection of sayings called "Stopping Gaps," the Taoist Master of Demon Valley said, "When things are perilous, sages know it, and preserve themselves in solitude. They explain things according to developments, and thoroughly master strategy, whereby they discern the subtle. Starting from the slightest beginnings, they work against tremendous odds. What they provide to the outside world, strategies for nipping problems in the bud, all depend on stopping gaps."

One should not be too straightforward. Go see the woodland: the straight trees are cut down, while the crooked ones are left standing there.

The *Tao Te Ching* says, "Be tactful, and you remain whole; bend, and you remain straight."

Success is on the tip of the tongue; friend and kindred are on the tip of the tongue. Even imprisonment is on the tip of the tongue; certain death is on the tip of the tongue. O tongue, you are fond of pungent things; why not speak sweetly? Speak sweetly, auspicious one; this world is fond of sweetness. Everyone is pleased by a gift of pleasant words, so that is what should be said; what poverty is there in speaking?

Ali said, "Speak, and be known, for a man is hidden under his tongue." He also said, "Many a spoken word is more piercing than an attack." Buddha said, "Do not say anything harsh; what you have said will be said back to you. Angry talk is painful; retaliation will get you." The Qur'an says, "Speak nicely to people."

By negotiation, by giving, by division, by invasion and by power: by all means is an enemy to be destroyed by rulers of men at all times.

The *Tao Te Ching* says, "When you make peace between enemies in such a way that resentment is sure to remain, how can that be called skillful?"

An enemy may be fought by means of another enemy who is obliged for a favor, just as a thorn stuck in the foot may be removed by a thorn held in the hand.

In the Thirty-Six Strategies, setting one's own adversaries against each other is called "borrowing a sword to kill another."

The soft are killed by gentle means, by gentle means the tough are killed. Nothing is impossible by gentle means, so gentleness is fiercer.

This is also an essential principle of Taoist life philosophy and martial arts. The *Tao Te Ching* says, "What is softest in the world drives what is hardest in the world." It also says, "A great nation flows downward into intercourse with the world."

A great gathering of people can deflect an enemy; a rain-bearing cloud can be withstood by grass. A large number of people, even if individually powerless, are irresistible when united; a rope is made of mere straws twisted together, but with it even an elephant may be tied.

Many means of uniting people are commonly used to tap the power of masses, including convention and custom, organization and order, ideology and education. The Huainan Masters said, "When a group of people unifies, a hundred people have surplus strength. To rely on the power of one individual, therefore, is sure to result in insecurity."

When total destruction occurs and there is danger to lives, one should earnestly protect lives and goods, even by bowing to an enemy. At certain times, there is alliance with an enemy, at certain times, there is division with a friend; the sage awaits the right time, depending on opportunity, to do what is to be done. One should carry a foe on one's back as long as the time is adverse; then when the time comes, one should destroy the foe, like smashing a pot with a stone.

Strategy may employ ideology, and may serve ideology, but a strategy does not necessarily reflect an ideology. Certain Asian martial arts are essentially based on the principle and practice of not resisting the strength of adversaries but utilizing it to your own advantage, avoiding destruction and conserving energy in the process. The ability to survive destruction, regain equilibrium, and ultimately prevail by adapting to changing conditions depends upon the capacity to perceive and predict situations and possibilities accurately, and to act in such a way as to effectively make the best of each time and condition.

Do not let another know your own shortcoming, but know the other's shortcoming; hide like a turtle withdrawing its limbs, but observe the other's condition.

Letting others know your shortcomings makes you vulnerable to them. Knowing others' shortcomings helps you make yourself invulnerable to them. Kauthilya also said, "One should conceal one's own vulnerabilities, and consider others' vulnerabilities." When asked how he overcame his opponents, Ali said, "I never met any man who did not help me against himself."

The deed conceived in the mind should not be revealed in words. The secret should be preserved in code and applied in action.

Security is one of the cornerstones of planning. Meddlers do not even have to be ill intentioned to spoil plans by their interference.

Only one seeking to accomplish something enters into alliance; when one's aim is fulfilled, there is no alliance. Therefore, all works should be done in such a way as to leave something more to do.

The *Tao Te Ching* says, "To govern the human and serve the divine, nothing compares to frugality. Only frugality brings early recovery; early recovery means buildup of power." If political or professional alliances are pursued in such a way as to exhaust themselves, instability and even enmity can result. The same thing can happen in social and romantic alliances.

Alliance should never be made for the sake of supremacy or power; when it's gone, there's no respect, and when it's there, it consumes resources.

Alliances made for supremacy or power may flower at their peak if they do in fact succeed, then sour when their heyday has passed. If you make alliances with others for your own supremacy or power, you may find that others have made alliance with you for *their* supremacy or power.

The covetous may be won over by material goods, the arrogant by respectful behavior, the inexperienced by enticement, and the sage by docility and truthfulness. The superior should be met with respect, the powerful with diversion, the inferior with generosity, the equal with energy.

One of the capacities of leadership is to recognize different human characters and understand their psychologies. This capacity makes it possible to alter behavior according to type in order to deal effectively with a wide variety of individuals, groups and situations.

One should abandon a law that is void of compassion.

Ali said that an expert jurisprudent "does not cause people to despair of God's mercy."

One should abandon a teacher who is lacking in knowledge.

Ali said, "God does not oblige the ignorant to learn until having obliged the learned to teach."

One should abandon a wife with an angry face.

Pythagoras said, "Sitting on a roof's edge is better than living with a turbulent woman."

One should abandon unfriendly relatives.

Ali said, "Kinship is more in need of friendship than friendship is in need of kinship."

Be attentive to the affairs of others, be quick to accomplish your own affairs; be helpful in the affairs of friends, be energetic in affairs of state.

Confucius said, "Be respectful at home, serious at work, faithful in human relations."

Separation from a loved one, disgrace of one's people, unsettled debt, service of a bad ruler and a friend who turns away from you because you are poor: these five things burn the body without fire.

Pining, ostracization, encumbrance, servility and abandonment can lead to nervous breakdown.

Abandon a temperamental boss; abandon a stingy one even more readily than a temperamental one. Even more than a stingy one, abandon one without discernment. And even more readily abandon one who is ungrateful for services rendered.

Work is such an important part of life, materially and mentally, that working for the wrong employer can be among the most stressful and dispiriting things one can do.

Birds abandon a tree whose fruits are gone, swans abandon a pond that has dried up. A woman abandons a man of no means, counselors abandon a fallen leader. Bees abandon a flower that's lost its freshness, deer abandon a forest that's been burned. Everyone has an agenda; who is appreciative, who is whose beloved?

Understanding the true nature of human relations, whether they are based on personal affections, psychological affinities or opportunistic associations, is critical to effective management of social and professional life.

Without associates, no undertakings arrive at success; therefore, association is the way for a ruler to go in all endeavors.

The Huainan Masters said, "If you ride on the knowledge of the multitude, it is easy to gain dominion; if you only use your own mind, you cannot even preserve yourself." They also said, "Leaders see with the eyes of the whole nation, hear with the ears of the whole nation, think with the knowledge of the whole nation and move with the strength of the whole nation."

Trees on a riverbank, a lover in other houses and rulers without advisers—these quickly go to ruin, without a doubt. Like trees on riverbanks and loose women, if a ruler has no advisers, his sovereignty passes away. Like trees on a riverbank and a woman with no support, a leader with no counselors does not live long.

Ali said, "There is no backup like consultation."

Whatever an employee does, good or bad, increases the merit or demerit of the director.

In Japan, it is considered proper for superiors to take responsibility for the errors of their underlings. There is thus great interest in seeing to it that employees are well screened, well trained and well deployed. Confucius said, "Cultivated people are easy to work for but hard to please. If you try to please them in the wrong way, they are not pleased. When they employ people, they consider their capacities. Petty people are hard to work for but easy to please. Even if you please them by something that is wrong, they are still pleased. When they employ people, they expect everything."

A leader perishes through bad advice, an ascetic through attachment, a son through indulgence, an intellectual through lack of study, a family through bad children, morality through association with mischief makers, women through intoxication, agriculture through neglect, affection by absence, friendship by coldness, affluence by lack of restraint, and wealth by relinquishment or heedlessness. A bad woman ruins households, a bad son ruins the family. A bad counselor ruins rulers, a country is ruined by thieves. Knowledge is ruined by nonapplication, women are ruined by constant amusement, a field is ruined by bad seed, rulers are ruined by the faults of those in their service.

The *I Ching* says, "Cultivated people consider problems and prevent them."

A physician addicted to drink, an untalented performer, an uneducated intellectual, a cowardly warrior, an unpleasant boss, an ignorant recluse, a ruler surrounded by bad advisers, a troubled country, a wife who is proud of her youthfulness and enamored of others: the enlightened let go of these right away. A cruel wife, a foolish son, a messenger unthinking in his words, unfriendly relatives and peers: for one who abandons these is great happiness.

Confucius said, "See what people do, observe the how and why, and examine their basic premises."

Employees should be known to be of many kinds, superior, inferior and middling; they should be assigned to correspondingly appropriate tasks. A ruler should assign workers to appropriate tasks after having first examined them to see whether they are superior, middling or inferior.

The Master of Demon Valley said, "If you observe how everyone and everything can be beneficial in some way and harmful in some way, then you can produce excellence in undertakings." The Huainan Masters said, "There are physical and mental limits to what a person can do. This is why someone with one body occupies one position, and someone with one skill works at one craft. When their strength is up to a task, people do not consider it onerous; when their ability suits a craft, people do not consider it difficult."

Employees who are not lazy, who are contented, who have good dreams when asleep and who are wide awake when awake, who are equanimous in good times and bad, employees who are firm and stable, are hard to find in the world. Just as gold is tested by four means—by rubbing, cutting, heating and beating—so is a person tested by four things—by family, conduct, character and work. Employees may be known as they execute a mission, kinfolk when calamity comes, a friend in times of trouble and a wife when wealth is gone.

Testing people is a critical concern of traditional philosophies of social organization and leadership. The Huainan Masters present a number of practical ways to bring to light the human qualities cited by Kauthilya as parameters of assessment. The test, naturally, differs according to conditions: "There are ways to evaluate people. If they are in positions of high status, observe what they promote. If they are wealthy, observe what they give. If they are poor, observe what they refuse to accept. If they are low in status, observe what they refuse to do. If they are covetous, observe what they will not take. See if they can turn difficulties around, and you can know if they are courageous. Move them with joy and happiness, and you can observe their self-control. Entrust them with goods and money, and you can assess their decency. Shake them with fear, and you can know their discipline."

Between a bad man and a snake, the snake is better; a snake only bites at times, but a bad man with every step.

This applies to both personal and professional life. The classical Zen master Kuei-shan said, "Familiarity with the evil increases wrong knowledge and views, creating evil day and night." Plato said, "Do not befriend evil people, for the most they can give you is safety from them." The Huainan Masters said, "If the wrong people are entrusted with responsibilities, the very nation is imperiled; superiors and subordinates oppose each other, the officials are resentful, and the common people are disorderly. So a single inappropriate appointment means a lifetime of trouble."

When the world comes to an end, the oceans overflow their shores; oceans go for a break in the shoreline, but good people never exceed their bounds.

Ali said, "Contentment is kingdom enough; goodness of character is prosperity enough."

In sages are all good qualities, while in a fool are bad ones alone; so a single insightful individual is better than a thousand fools.

Buddha said, "A fool who is conscious of his folly is thereby wise; the fool who thinks himself wise is the one to be called a fool."

One with good qualities should be employed, one lacking good qualities should be avoided. In the sage are all virtues, in the fool only faults.

Ali said, "Do not befriend a fool, for he hurts you when he wants to help you."

Those who are profound, attentive, soft-spoken, self-controlled, truthful, capable, aware of what is to be and knowledgeable of the reality of motivations mostly become employees of successful, intelligent pragmatists.

The profound are able to work steadily for long-term goals. The attentive are able to learn readily and seize opportunities. The soft-spoken are able to get along well with others. The self-controlled are capable of great discipline and sacrifice. The truthful are reliable and trustworthy. The capable are productive and effective. Those who are aware of what is to be are capable of efficient planning. Those who know the reality of motivations can tell with whom to collaborate and whom to avoid.

There are three merits for leaders in employing the wise: a good reputation, living in paradise and great enrichment. There are three disadvantages for a leader in employing fools: a bad reputation, impoverishment and also going to hell. Therefore, a leader should always employ the virtuous and avoid the virtueless, so that justice, pleasure and prosperity may grow. A ruler should reject employees who are hypocritical, deceitful, destructive, irresolute and unen-thusiastic, incompetent, and cowardly. One who is cruel, dissolute, avaricious, irresolute, tactless, unruly and extravagant should not be appointed to a position of authority. One who lacks patience and devotion, who is rivalrous and greedy, and who is incompetent and fearful should be rejected by a leader.

The Taoist Master of the Hidden Storehouse said, "Of all the tasks of government, none is as great as finding people for public service. To prepare people for public service, nothing is as good as mastery of political science; and the best political science of all is bringing peace to people.

"As far as the ability to bring peace to people is concerned, gener-ally speaking you will scarcely find 4 or 5 percent of those who have it if you test them by writing. If you test them verbally, you may find 10 or 20 percent. If you test them by psychology, behavior and atti-tude, you will find a full 80 to 90 percent. This all refers, of course, to a felicitous age with a wise rulership having the clear perception and discriminating choice to make it possible."

A fool should be shunned, for he is actually a two-footed animal: he wounds with the arrow of his words, like an unseen thorn. In company with a multitude of fools, whose behavior is animalistic, all virtues are covered over, like the sun by clouds.

Buddha said, "If you do not find a prudent companion, a wise associ-ate leading a good life, then journey alone, like a king abandoning a domain he has conquered, like an elephant roaming the forest. It is better to walk alone; there is no companionship with a fool. Walk alone, like an elephant in the forest, with few desires, doing no evil."

An embedded thorn, a loose tooth and a bad administrator are best rooted out.

The Master of the Hidden Storehouse said, "Once you become an administrator, your mind should be impartial, your demeanor should be harmonious and your speech should be correct. Impartiality should not be overbearing, harmonization should not be random and correctness should not be offensive."

A ruler should get rid of a servant who is lazy, talkative, rigid, cruel, habit ridden, deceitful, discontent and disloyal.

The Master of the Hidden Storehouse said, "What was pure diligence in perfecting government for service of the nation in ancient times has now become pure diligence in cultivating reputation in service of the self." He also said, "Leaders do not worry about not trusting anyone; they only fear trusting those who cannot handle business."

The Huainan Masters said, "When the directives of the leadership are ignored because of factionalism, and the law is broken out of treachery, and intellectuals busy themselves fabricating clever deceits, and mettlesome men occupy themselves fighting, and administrators monopolize authority, and petty bureaucrats hold power, and cliques curry favor to manipulate leadership, then the ancients would say the nation has perished even though it may seem to exist."

One of good family, morals and qualities, keeper of all laws, astute, and responsible should be appointed chief justice.

Confucius said, "Cultivated people understand things in terms of justice. Petty people understand things in terms of profit." Ali said, "An expert jurisprudent is one who does not cause people to despair of God's mercy, does not cause them to lose hope of refreshment from God and does not cause them to feel exempt from the design of God."

A ruler should not be like a subject in actuality, but people should be like a true ruler. Just behavior and its opposite in the entire populace start with the ruler.

The Huainan Masters said, "No one has ever heard of a country being chaotic when individuals are orderly, and no one has heard of a country being orderly when individuals are unruly. If a rule is not straight, it cannot be used to make a square; if a compass is not correct, it cannot be used to make a circle. The individual is the rule and compass of affairs; and no one has ever heard of being able to rectify others while being crooked oneself."

When mother gives poison, father sells son and government takes everything, who will be my savior? Where the ruler is himself a

thief, and so is the minister and the priest, what shall I do then?
Where protection comes from, so also does danger come from there.

Danger comes from the same sources as protection because of reliance on sources of protection and trust in them. If a source of protection is corrupted or compromised, the severity of the effect is in proportion to the degree of the reliance and trust that had been reposed in it.

Where the ruler is just, the people are righteous; where the ruler is bad, the people are bad. Where the ruler is indifferent, the people are indifferent. The people follow the ruler; as is the ruler, so are the people. The king is responsible for evil done by the people; the priest is responsible for the ruler's evil. The husband is responsible for the wife's evil; and the teacher is responsible for the student's evil. People are destroyed by a ruler like a lion, by a minister like a tiger, by an official like a vulture.

The Huainan Masters said, "In ancient times, under sage leadership, the laws were liberal and penalties easygoing. The prisons were empty, everyone had the same mores and no one was treacherous. Government in later times was not like this. Those above were rapacious beyond measure, while those below were covetous and inconsiderate. The common people were poor and miserable, and they fought with one another. They worked hard but did not achieve anything. Clever deceivers appeared, and there came to be many thieves and robbers."

They also said, "When rulers are very crafty, their subjects are very devious. When rulers have many obsessions and interests, their subjects do a lot of posturing. When rulers are uneasy, their subjects are unsettled. When rulers are very demanding, their subjects are contentious. If you don't straighten this out at the root but concern yourself with the branches, this is like stirring up dust as you try to clean a room, like carrying a bunch of kindling as you try to put out a fire."

The Creator had not given fragrance to gold, nor fruit to sugar cane, nor flowers to sandalwood; a scholar is not given riches, nor a ruler long life. None is wiser than this.

Scholars are supposed to be devoted to knowledge, not to material goods. Rulers are supposed to be devoted to justice, not to an easy life.

Who does not become conceited on acquiring riches? What materialist has had an end to his troubles? Whose heart has not been broken by women? Who indeed is dear to kings? Who is not within range of time? What beggar has attained dignity? Who has gone safely on the way in bad company?

Confucius said, "For those who do not think ahead, there is trouble near at hand."

In the happiness of the people is the happiness of the ruler; and in the welfare of the people is the ruler's welfare. The ruler's concern is not his own pleasure and benefit, but the pleasure and benefit of the people.

The Huainan Masters said, "If leaders can truly love and truly benefit the people, then everyone can follow. But even a child rebels against a parent who is unloving and abusive."

The people help the just one who is beset by serious trouble.

Ali said, "The first compensation of the insightful and patient one for his understanding and tolerance is that the people side with him against the ignoramus."

This science is all a matter of mastering the senses; one who behaves otherwise, without controlling the senses, will soon perish, even though king of the four quarters.

The *Tao Te Ching* says, "Those who overcome others are powerful; those who overcome themselves are strong."

Most rulers who are dominated by anger have been killed by the anger of the people, it is heard; those who are dominated by lust are destroyed by enemies and diseases caused by destructive habits.

Rulers dominated by anger are hated for temperamental harshness and cruelty. Those who are dominated by lust consume disproportionate time, energy and resources, ultimately draining them of both political and personal power.

Like an elephant blind drunk driven by an inebriate, which tramples everything it comes upon, so does a ruler who is blinded by ignorance and directed by an unseeing minister.

A large body of people has a lot of power, or a lot of potential, inherent in its mass. Properly channeled, this power can do a great deal of good; misguided, it can do a lot of harm. In his *Book of Family Traditions on the Art of War*, the seventeenth-century sword master Yagyu Munenori, teacher of the Japanese shogun or leader of the military government, wrote, "When those close to the ruler have been after their own interest all along, not acting in consideration of the ruler and thus serving in such a way that the people resent the ruler, when the time comes it is those close to the ruler who will be the first to set upon him. This is the doing of those close to the ruler, not the personal fault of the ruler. It is desirable that the potential for such situations be clearly perceived and that those distant from the rulership not be excluded from its benefits."

A ruler guided by learning is devoted to the guidance of the people; he enjoys the earth unopposed, devoted to the welfare of all beings.

Once when Confucius traveled to a certain state, he remarked to one of his pupils, "How the population has grown!" The pupil asked, "Since they have a large population, what is there to add?" Confucius said, "Enrich them." The pupil then asked, "Once they are rich, what else is there to add?" Confucius said, "Educate them."

The one who breaks his word, and whose behavior is contrary to that of the people, becomes untrustworthy to his own kin as well as to others. Therefore, one should assimilate, in conduct, dress, language and customs.

The Taoist classic *Chuang-tzu* says, "Be careful, be prudent, be correct yourself. As far as appearances are concerned, nothing compares to conformity. As far as attitude is concerned, nothing compares to harmony. Nevertheless, there are problems with both of these. When you conform, you don't want to be absorbed, and when you harmonize you don't want to stand out." Confucius said, "Cultivated people harmonize without imitating. Immature people imitate without harmonizing." The *Chuang-tzu* also says, "If by appearing to conform you become absorbed, you will be upset, destroyed, ruined, downtrodden. If you stand out for your interest in cooperation, that will turn into a reputation that will be harmful to you."

One who is loved by the people accomplishes a task even with little assistance, because of having cooperation.

Someone who is loved by people receives cooperation without asking for it. Someone who pretends to love people in order to get assistance may not fare so well.

A self-possessed ruler brings success to an unaccomplished people. A ruler who is not self-possessed destroys a prosperous and devoted people.

A self-possessed ruler has the patience and industry to foster development. A ruler who is not self-possessed lacks the discipline and foresight to maintain a state of general well-being. A ruler who is self-possessed leads the people. A ruler who is not self-possessed exploits the people.

An evil-natured ruler, who governs others even though lacking in self-possession, will either be assassinated by the people or be subjugated by enemies.

A ruler who exploits and mistreats the people may be destroyed by their wrath directly, or abandoned to competitors.

The self-possessed one with a loyal populace, even of a small area, enjoys the earth, wins and does not lose.

The *Tao Te Ching* describes a realm of self-possessed contentment in these terms: "A small state with few people may have the people keep arms, but not use them. It inspires them to regard death gravely and not go on distant campaigns. Even if they have vehicles, they don't drive them anywhere. Even if they have weapons, they have no use for them. It lets the people go back to simple techniques, relish their food, like their clothes, be comfortable in their ways and enjoy their work. Neighboring states may be so close that they can hear each other's dogs and roosters barking and crowing, yet they have made things such that the people have never gone back and forth."

Whatever the personal conduct of the ruler, so does the conduct of the populace become.

Confucius said of this phenomenon, "The quality of the leader is like wind, the quality of the people is like grass; when the wind blows, the grass bends."

One who acts at whim, blind for lack of learning, is either obstinate or pliant.

According to Taoist psychology, an ideal mentality or personality combines firmness with flexibility. Firmness without flexibility to balance it results in rigidity, aggressiveness and obstinacy. Flexibility without firmness to balance it results in weakness, indecision and pliability.

Ignorance and lack of discipline are causes of vice in a person; indeed, the uncultivated and unruly see no ill in vice. The whole of learning is this: mastery over the senses.

Ali said, "Captives of desire, desist, for one who is attached to the world is not sacred by anything but the screech of misfortune. People, assume your own responsibility for disciplining and refining your selves, deflecting them from their habits."

One who rules by four things—justice, conventional norms, order and example—will conquer the four corners of the earth.

The Huainan Masters said, "Law derives from justice; justice derives from what suits the community. What suits the community accords with the hearts of the people. This is the essence of government. . . . When leaders establish law, they personally act as models and exemplars. It is for this reason that their directives are carried out throughout the land. Confucius said, 'When people are personally upright, others go along with them even though they are not commanded to do so; when people are not upright themselves, others will not follow them even if ordered to do so.' Thus when leaders are themselves subject to regulations, then their directives are carried out by the people."

Justice is thwarted by injustice, a ruler is destroyed by indifference.

The Huainan Masters said, "When sages carry out justice, their concern comes from within—what personal profit is in it for them?"

One should tolerate minor errors and be satisfied even with a small income.

Tolerating minor errors increases the capacity to keep focused on overall aims. Satisfaction with a small income increases the desirability of work with inherent meaning and reward. By choosing work that is inherently rewarding and focusing on long-term goals, one may attain success and prosperity without anxious ambition.

The action of a leader is based on direct experience, indirect evidence and inference.

Even direct experience must be examined for authenticity of consciousness, memory and understanding in order to rule out misperception, faulty recollection and illusion; indirect evidence must also be examined for probity of sources; and inference must be examined for soundness of reason.

A ruler who is hard to get to see is induced by those around him to do the opposite of what should or should not be done.

Yagyu Munenori wrote, "Surrounding rulers are treacherous people who pretend to be righteous when in the presence of superiors yet have a glare in their eyes when they look at subordinates. Unless they are bribed, they present the good as bad, so the innocent suffer and the guilty gloat. To see the potential for this happening is even more urgent than to notice a concealed scheme."

All urgent tasks should be attended to and not overlooked; something that has gone too far becomes difficult or even impossible to take care of.

The *Tao Te Ching* says, "Plan for difficulty when it is still easy, do the great while it is still small. The most difficult things in the world must be done while they are easy; the greatest things in the world must be done while they are small."

Sovereignty can be accomplished only with assistance; a single wheel does not move. One should have advisers, therefore, and listen to their opinion. One who does not have the power of magical formulas should attend people of wisdom or associate with those advanced in knowledge; thus does one obtain superior access. Indra's circle of counselors consists of a thousand sages; this is his eye. Therefore he is said to have a thousand eyes even though he has only two.

The Huainan Masters said, "The abilities of one man are not sufficient even to govern a single household. But follow the measures of true reason, based on the nature of the universe, and the whole world is equal." They also said, "If you ride on the knowledge of the multitude, it is easy to gain dominion; if you only use your own mind, you cannot even preserve yourself." Ali said, "Consultation is a source of guidance, and one who thinks his own view is enough runs a risk."

Which shall it be, one who likes you or one whom you like? Go to one who likes you; that is the best way of alliance.

Someone who likes you is a better choice of allies than someone whom you like because his loyalty to you will not be inspired by your liking him the way it will be inspired by his liking you.

One with increased power, however, is not to be trusted; for prosperity is a changer of minds. Indeed, hardship produces firmness of friendship.

Changes in circumstance may provoke reevaluation of alliances. Considering this may happen, it is important to observe the influence of conditions on the mentalities and attitudes of associates and friends.

Assistance is a sign of a friend.

Assistance has many forms. Muhammad the Prophet said, "Help your brother, whether he be an oppressor or one of the oppressed." People asked, "We help him if he is oppressed, but how can we help him if he is an oppressor?" The Prophet said, "By stopping him."

Familiars take over everything and act is if they were in charge. Classmates, even if trustworthy, are disrespectful because of having been playmates.

Delegating authority arbitrarily to familiars by assumption, by association, by mistake, by accident or by default may lead to damages even beyond those caused by consequent bungling and incompetence, through systemic deterioration caused by general loss of faith and confidence in the prevailing order.

Those who are alike in ways that have to be kept private secrets, having the same habits and vices, avoid causing offense out of fear that their vulnerabilities are known.

Such people can therefore not be relied upon for objective views, forthright opinions or criticism, even if constructive.

Spies should be killed, using the bait of trust, trapping them when they swallow it. One should not let enemies pretending friendship thrive at one's expense. A clash between equals results in destruction of both, like unfired pots smashing each other.

Spies can be nullified by disinformation if they can be induced to believe it. Enemies posing as friends can be identified in a time of trouble. Invincible warriors are those who know how to win at minimum cost and know how to choose when to fight.

An army returning to engagement without hope of life gives rise to irrepressible force; so do not harass a broken army.

Sun Tzu said in *The Art of War*, "Do not stop an army on its way home. A surrounded army must be given a way out. Do not press a desperate enemy. These are rules of military operations." Mei Yaochen explained, "Under these circumstances, an opponent will fight to the death. An exhausted animal will still fight, as a matter of natural law."

By day, the crow kills the owl; at night, the owl kills the crow. On dry land, a dog tears a crocodile to pieces; in the deep, a crocodile tears a dog to pieces.

A particular capacity is not of fixed value in itself; its value depends upon the conditions under which it is employed. In a diverse environment, a variety of abilities can find domains of successful expression.

In a fight between a dog and a pig, the ultimate victory belongs to the butcher.

It is for this reason that many a fight has been fomented by many a meat merchant. The message to people involved in a fight is to examine their situation and see whether they might not be in the position of the pigs and dogs, with third parties standing by waiting to butcher their remains. This might save them energy and keep them whole.

In indolence is certain loss of what has been gained and what is to come; results are obtained by action, and so success is gained.

Consuming without producing uses up results of past efforts and provides nothing for future needs.

Wealth, justice, pleasure: these are three kinds of aim. It is best to gain them in order.

When immature youths come to expect adult pleasures before they are able to assume adult responsibilities, they may grow up into immature and irresponsible adults.

Since it is the root of justice, and pleasure is its friend, the attainment of wealth linked to justice and pleasure is the attainment of all aims.

Wealth may be used to support the securing of justice and pleasure for oneself as well as others, but attainment of wealth without justice or enjoyment does not improve the quality of life. With no constructive aim, pursuit of wealth is reduced to blind ambition or obsession, doomed in that sense to failure even in success.

A king with few reserves devours both urban and rural populations.

Habitual deficit spending by authorities reduces the proportion of tax revenues available for public works and thus erodes the population's enjoyment of its own productivity.

Men of no means do not attain their aims, even by hundreds of efforts. Objectives depend on material resources, like elephants herded by elephants. A kingdom with depleted resources, even if gained, only becomes a liability.

Ali said, "Form partnerships with those who have abundant income, for they are fitter for wealth and better suited to its reduction."

Revenue should be collected from a kingdom like fruit from a garden, when ripe; doing so in a way that would cause resentment should be avoided, as it brings danger of self-destruction.

The Huainan Masters said, "Unprincipled rulers take from the people without measuring the people's strengths; they make demands on their subjects without assessing how much their subjects have."

Just as fish swimming in water cannot be detected drinking the water, appointees in charge of works cannot be detected misappropriating funds.

The Huainan Masters said, "When society is orderly, the common people are upright and cannot be seduced by profit. When society is disorderly, the elite are villainous and cannot be stopped by the law."

Even the course of birds flying in the sky can be discerned, but not the course taken by appointees who conceal their true condition.

The Huainan Masters said, "If the ruler is truly upright, then honest people are entrusted with affairs, and the treacherous go into hiding. If the ruler is not upright, then evil people achieve their aims, and the trustworthy go into concealment."

Even if one is not a thief, one who happens to be seen on the scene of a theft will be arrested on account of dress, armament or accoutrements like the thief, or on account of proximity to the stolen goods.

Circumstantial evidence may not be admissible in court, but it can still be persuasive, or at least cloud minds. Remembering this fact of life is part of prudence.

Employees paid in milk will kill the calves.

Killing the calves results in more milk at first, then less milk later, from fewer cows. This may be taken as a colorful warning about sacrificing long-term development on account of greed for short-term gains.

There is no corrupting one who is not corrupt, like water treated with poison; sometimes a remedy cannot be found for the corrupt.

Buddha said, "One without a wound on the hand may remove poison by hand; the poison will not get in where there is no wound. There is no evil for one who does none."

The steadied intelligence of the resolute, once polluted, will not return until it has come to an end.

Polluted intelligence will not be purified until the defects of pollution become evident. The *I Ching* says, "When you come to an impasse, change; by changing, you get through."

When a lot of money has been stolen, proof of even a small part in it means liability for all of it.

While the individual profit from a crime is reduced by collaboration with others, individual liability for crime is increased by the actions of collaborators. With the cost of failure far greater than the reward of success, the risk outweighs the advantage. Those who cannot be restrained by social conscience or moral principle may thus take a lesson from calculation.

To the extent that a ruler divulges dangerous secrets to people, to that extent, by that act, the independent one becomes subject to control. The works of the unguarded, even if exceptionally successful, will undoubtedly come to naught, like a broken raft on the ocean. One who is given to carelessness, intoxication, talking in his sleep or sensuality, or who has been relegated to obscurity, or treated with disrespect, betrays secrets. Betrayal of secret plans causes insecurity in the ruler and the people dependent on him. Love and hate, joy and sorrow, resolve and fear: the wise conceal their secrets by contradictory expressions and gestures.

The Master of Demon Valley said, "Sages sometimes open up in an evident manner; sometimes they are closed and secretive. They are open to those with whom they sympathize, closed to those with whose truth they differ. As to what will do and what will not, sages examine and clarify people's plans to find out if they are in harmony or at variance.

"Whether they separate or join, there is that which sages maintain; so they first go along with the aims of others: then when they want to open up, they value thoroughness; and when they want to shut down, they value secrecy. Thoroughness and secrecy are best subtle, for then they are on the trail of the Way. Opening up is to assess people's feelings; shutting down is to make sure of their sincerity."

In all cases of a suit concerning marriage or inheritance, professional rivalry, enmity of peers, establishment of standards for religious ceremonies, or association, or other legal disputes, anger is the foundation and cause of injury.

In the classical legal tradition of Ireland, which was related to the Hindu law of India, angry pleading is called one of the "three doors of falsehood," quarreling is one of "three things that make the wise foolish," contention is one of "three signs of folly" and bitterness is one of "three things that show a bad man."

A case in dispute has four elements: the law, the procedure, customary usage and government decree. The last of these can override the former. The law is based on truth, the procedure is based on witness, customary usage is based on the community, government decree is based on the ruler's authority. In a case where a custom-ary norm is violated, according to established order or legal canons, the case should be decided on the basis of justice. Where a rule is contradicted by the logic of justice, let logic be the authority: there a written text is invalid.

Every human organization, it seems, has a body of rules, whether written or otherwise; established ways of monitoring events and maintaining order; conventional habits of thought and behavior; and some form of leadership or authority. If there is so much concern for the formalities of the system that new realities cannot be accommo-dated, then the logic of justice may be sacrificed in its own name.

What is right and meaningful should be taught, not what is wrong and meaningless.

There are many differences in what is considered right and meaning-ful or wrong and meaningless, according to time, place and people. Comparing them to see what is universal and what is particular may yield certain insights into human nature and human conditions.

One severe in punishment will be feared by the people. One mild in punishment will be looked down upon. One who punishes appro-priately will be honored. Well-informed criminal justice concen-trates the attention of the people on legitimate aims and desires. Wrongly inflicted punishment coming from whim, anger or igno-rance, outrages even renunciants living in the forest; how much more so householders! Lack of criminal justice results in the rule of fishes: without the containment of criminal justice, the powerful devours the weak. People of all classes and stages of life are pro-tected by the ruler's system of criminal justice; devoted to their own duty and occupation, they function in their own spheres. As the root of discipline, criminal justice brings security to the people: for youths regarding the dispenser of punishment as occupying the position of the king of death do not commit crimes. Rulers who execute criminal justice eliminate crime among the people and bring security. Criminal justice keeps the world whole, this world and the next world, when applied by the ruler according to the crime, whether to his own son or to an enemy.

Zhuge Liang wrote in *The Way of the General:* "Rewarding the good is to promote achievement; penalizing wrongdoers is to prevent treachery. It is imperative that rewards and punishments be fair and impartial. When they know rewards are to be given, courageous warriors know what they are dying for; when they know penalties are to be applied, villains know what to fear. Therefore rewards should not be given without reason, and penalties should not be applied arbitrarily. If rewards are given for no reason, those who have worked hard in public service will be resentful; if penalties are applied arbitrarily, upright people will be bitter."

When weaknesses are eliminated, there are no guilty people; but when guilty people are removed, weaknesses can still spoil others.

Inhibiting criminal or antisocial behavior is one thing; eliminating the psychological bases of such behavior is another. The Huainan Masters said, "When laws are set up and a system of rewards is established, and yet this cannot change the mores of the people, it is because this does not work without sincerity."

Those who are impartial to all beings and are trustworthy are liked by the people.

Buddha said, "One who is harmless to all living beings is called noble." Muhammad the Prophet said, "There is a reward for your treatment of all living beings."

Fact should be heard from actual eyewitnesses.

Fact must be distinguished from hearsay before accurate judgment and effective action are possible.

Causes of popular discontent: Not giving what is due, inflicting what is not due. Not punishing the guilty, violently punishing the innocent. Imprisoning those who do not deserve it, not arresting those who should be taken into custody. Suppressing righteous customs. Cleaving to injustice and impeding justice. Doing what shouldn't be done, leaving necessary tasks unrewarded. Offending the noble, dishonoring the respectable. Hostility to elders, unfairness, cheating. Not reciprocating favors, not fulfilling promises.

Doing what is not profitable, thwarting what is profitable. Not providing protection from thieves and enriching oneself. Undermining manly efforts and impugning the merit of works. Ridiculing the good while being kind to the corrupt. Unprecedented acts of violence and injustice. Suppression of established wholesome customs, pursuit of iniquity and prevention of justice result in impoverishment, covetousness and antipathy among the people. Ruination of welfare and security through negligence and laziness on the part of the ruler results in impoverishment, covetousness and antipathy among the people. When impoverished people are desirous, they become disaffected; the disaffected go over to an enemy or assassinate the ruler themselves.

Popular discontent compromises general security within and without, undermining internal strength while increasing danger from external pressures. Therefore, issues of justice are not merely abstract moral questions of human nature; they encompass all the concrete, practical matters of everyday life at every level of social organization, from individual and family to nation and state.

Groups are unassailable to others by virtue of cohesion.

The things that foster popular discontent are unwholesome and ruinous in themselves as they are, and yet they are even more so through their damaging effect to the cohesion of the social fabric. Betrayal of trust, for example, in whatever form it occurs, has particular results according to the nature of the trust that has been betrayed; in addition to that, it also fosters general loss of trust, which in its time causes an even more extensive range of destructive effects.

Like worm-eaten wood, an undisciplined royal family breaks as soon as it is put under pressure.

Many royal families have crumbled after a few generations; few have maintained power for centuries. A proverb says that the discipline of a family can be seen in its third generation.

One who knows the workings of the world should cleave to a ruler who has self-control, wealth and subjects, in a way that is pleasing and beneficial. One may cleave to someone without wealth or sub-

jects, but not someone without self-control; for one without self-control will not attain great sovereignty, even if he inherits it, because of his disregard for practical philosophy and his association with useless people.

The Huainan Masters said, "When political leaders ruin their countries and wreck their lands, themselves to die at others' hands, a laughingstock of all the world, it is invariably because of their desires."

A fire may burn part of the body, or all of it; a king can destroy or promote you, family and all.

Employment in the service of the powerful may present the prospect of unparalleled opportunity, but it also carries with it the potential for complete ruination.

One gains security in one's position by not breaking promises or being contentious.

Breaking promises undermines trust; contentiousness undermines goodwill. One who is not trusted or liked by others will not win cooperation or support, and thus cannot be secure in a position of responsibility.

One should not lose the opportunity to express the interest of the ruler, one's own interest, along with the welfare of friends, as well as the interest of others, at the right place and time, as long as it is consistent with what is just and advantageous.

Advocating legitimate interests at appropriate times and places helps to promote social conscience and general fair play. Expressing the interests of others also helps to create a sense of solidarity that enhances the cohesion and morale of the group.

When consulted about works that call for intelligence, immediate and future, one who is expert should say what is suitable, consistent with justice and welfare, without being intimidated by the crowd.

Those who try to say what they think others want them to say, hoping to curry favor, or who are afraid to say something of which others may disapprove, fearing opposition or dismissal, cannot be reliable informants or advisers in situations that call for independent objectivity.

Those who induce one to be rash, unjust and extravagant, they are enemies masquerading as friends.

Socrates was asked, "Who is the worst of people?" He replied, "One who helps you follow caprice."

One should deflect horrors from others and not speak of horrors oneself.

One who neither condones vicious gossip nor engages in it will gain the trust and respect of serious-minded people.

The patient one should endure like the earth even what is destructive to himself.

Earth is widely used as a symbol of patience, tolerance, endurance and humility. In his *Awakening to the Tao*, the neo-Taoist Liu I-ming wrote, "If people can be flexible and yielding, humble, with self-control, entirely free of agitation, cleared of all volatility, not angered by criticism, ignoring insult, docilely accepting all hardships, illnesses and natural disasters, free from anxiety or resentment when faced with danger of adversity, then people can be companions of earth."

Capable people have been banished merely because of displeasure. Even useless people seem dear when they act in accord with knowledge of desires.

Both employers and employees can use the lesson of this observation to examine whether rejection or acceptance is based on technical professional criteria or human psychological factors. An ideal workplace, no doubt, would demand both professional and social skills on the part of both employers and employees, to combine technical competence with interpersonal harmony.

The wise should always see to self-preservation first, for those who are dependent on kings are said to be living in fire. When asked, one should say what is pleasing and beneficial; one should not say what is not beneficial yet pleasing. What is unpleasant but beneficial should be said privately, if the hearer is willing to listen. Better to answer with silence than to speak of anything odious.

The Master of Demon Valley said, "Those who speak without seeing what type of person they are talking to will be opposed, and those who speak without finding out the state of mind of the person they are talking to will be denied."

When accomplishments are destroyed, power is undermined, knowledge is marketed, rejection is quick, direction is overbearing, trust is lacking or there is conflict with the powerful, these are grounds for quitting.

These grounds for quitting all concern things that inhibit creativity, teamwork and productivity. When factors that nullify the worth of effort are found to be intrinsic elements of the structure of a work situation, there may be no remedy but to quit.

Training guides the one with potential, not the one without potential.

The capacity to discover the potentials of individuals and develop them accordingly is a mark of an effective system.

Learning can only guide the good listener who is attentive, who has the discernment to grasp and remember, and the intelligence to infer and exclude.

Confucius said of his teaching method, "If I bring up one corner, and the student cannot come back with the other three, then I do not go on."

Just as virgin lumber immediately absorbs anything with which it is painted, an innocent mind regards whatever it is told as authoritative teaching. Unenlightened teaching is a great evil.

Just as learning requires certain duties, including the exercise of attention, recollection and reason, teaching implies certain responsibilities because of the influence that education has on the psychology and character of individuals and societies.

Discipline and self-mastery are learned from authorities in the individual sciences.

Generalists and dilettantes ordinarily lack the degree of concentration and expertise found in specialists, and may also lack the degree of general self-discipline needed for mastery of an art or a science. This is why royal courts of olden times, both East and West, traditionally included technical experts and sages of various kinds in their composition.

The learning from which are derived justice and wealth is the essence of learning of all learning. This established science, with these established devices, has been articulated for the acquisition and protection of this world and the next. It fosters and protects justice, wealth, and pleasure; this science destroys injustice, poverty and hatred.

These are the main guidelines for the application of the strategies outlined in this classic: they are properly used to foster and protect justice, wealth, and pleasure, and to destroy injustice, poverty and hatred. This needs to be said for the reason that malpractice of such devices can and does lead to the reverse of the intended effects; it is therefore imperative to examine strategies for their potential effects in context, and exercise reason and conscience in their application.

Wisdom arises from learning, discipline from wisdom and self-possession from discipline.

Wisdom that arises from learning has a nonsubjective basis. Discipline that arises from wisdom has a noncoercive basis. Self-possession that arises from discipline has an independent basis.

Religious scriptures deal with right and wrong, economics deals with wealth and poverty, politics deals with good and bad policies. Examining logically, philosophy benefits the world, stabilizing the intellect in both adversity and prosperity. Philosophy is perennially regarded as a lamp for all sciences, a means for all tasks, a refuge for all religions.

Aristotle said, "Logic is a tool for all sciences."

A state must have people. Without people, like a barren cow, what is produced? When there are no people, there is no community, and with no community there can be no state.

The Huainan Masters said, "Those who can become rulers must be able to find winners. Those who can win over opponents must be strong. Those who can be strong are those who are able to use the power of other people. To be able to use the power of other people, it is necessary to win people's hearts. To be able to win people's hearts, it is necessary to have self-mastery. To be capable of self-mastery, it is necessary to be flexible."

One who would undertake what is possible should undertake feasible works; one who would undertake what is good should undertake that which is void of ill; one who would undertake what is auspicious should undertake that which will result in good.

To plan a successful undertaking, it is necessary to consider the feasibility of the project, the potential for problematic side effects and predictability of positive results.

Time comes but once to a man who wants time; it will be hard to get time again when he wants to work.

It is easier to miss a moment of opportunity because of lassitude or lack of inspiration than it is to find a moment of opportunity whenever one happens to feel energetic or inspired.

No one would want physical destruction, even for a huge fortune.

People would not be so inclined to chronic overwork in pursuit of material success if they kept in mind that they were destroying their health for wealth they would not be able to enjoy.

There is success and failure on every path.

Some diplomats and attorneys are more skilled than other diplomats and attorneys. Some teachers and physicians are more skilled than other teachers and physicians. Some plumbers and carpenters are more skilled than other plumbers and carpenters. Some farmers and herders are more skilled than other farmers and herders. Some people may never succeed in anything they try.

Power changes the mind.

Modern psychological experiments designed to study the influence of systematic control over others on the minds of conventionally normal people confirm that power does indeed change the mind; and not, evidently, for the better. In this context, the observation is probably expressed as a warning, to the effect that it is insane to pursue external power without also seeking internal strength to maintain psychological balance and moral integrity.

Like understands like.

Confucius said, "Those whose paths are not the same do not consult one another." The Master of Demon Valley said, "When there is intimacy in spite of distance, that means there is hidden virtue; when there is alienation in spite of nearness, that means there is disparity of aims."

Sons captivated by pleasure do not attack their father.

People who are happy in their own situations do not think of rebelling.

It is courage that repels calamity.

Caution and forethought may not be sufficient to avoid calamity because not all conditions are under anyone's control. Once calamity has befallen, furthermore, cleverness and resourcefulness can hardly be mustered in a crisis without inner fortitude and willpower.

One should go the way that is conducive to welfare.

Profit or position that may seem desirable or advantageous may not translate directly into enhanced welfare if so much attention and energy are consumed by obtaining and securing profit or position that none of their practical benefits can be made available for the general well-being.

There is hardly one among thousands who can be a leader.

Since leadership requires exercise of greater responsibility than the average individual has, it must also require greater than average capacity. The Zen master Huitang wrote, "The way of sages is like sky and earth, nurturing myriad beings, providing everything. The ways of ordinary people are like rivers, seas, mountains, streams, hills and valleys, plants, trees, and insects, each fulfilling only its own measure, not knowing outside of that what is complete in everything."

In vast areas, medicinal plants are found growing both in land and in water.

Talent may be found in a wide variety of circumstances. The broader the frame of reference, the more chance of finding people of ability. Zhuge Liang wrote, "For strong pillars you need straight trees; for wise public servants you need upright people. Straight trees are found in remote forests; upright people come from the humble masses. Therefore when rulers are going to make appointments, they need to look in obscure places."

Both divine and human action make the world go 'round.

Human effort is necessary for successful endeavor, but there are always factors beyond human control, which skillful planning must also take into account.

Effort is what effects the accomplishment of undertakings: peace is what makes possible the safe enjoyment of the results of work.

In an unstable environment, energies may be so diffused by the strain of coping with challenges and changes that it is impossible to realize or to enjoy the fruits of constructive effort. Comprehensive planning therefore takes this into account, not focusing simply on desired goals, but on the total context within which aims are to be pursued and realized.

Human minds are fickle: like horses, people change while engaged in tasks.

Because people are changeable, it is not necessarily effective to delegate authority for a project without also providing for feedback and monitoring.

The wise can wound the heroic, even though the latter are more powerful, as a hunter does an elephant. An arrow shot by an archer may or may not kill one of those targeted; but a plan launched by a wise man can kill even babies in the womb.

Individual powers and skills are each limited in application and effectiveness; the potential force that can be unleashed by strategic organization of all accessible powers and skills, however, is incalculably more than the sum of its parts.

One should always associate with those advanced in discipline in order to develop discipline, for that is the root of discipline.

Keeping the company of people who are more accomplished or more developed is a fundamental educational strategy, based on the principle of learning by osmosis as well as formal instruction and informal conversation.

A gambler will keep on gambling, even at night by lamplight, even when his mother has died; and if questioned when in trouble, he becomes angry. So the self-possessed one, who is attentive to elders and has conquered the senses, should give up destructive anger and lust, from which ruin begins.

Being too much under the sway of desires and feelings, without balance and sobriety, results in general heedlessness and irresponsibility, which in turn open the way to many a misstep in life.

A potential cause of distress to the citizenry should be remedied at once by the alert.

The Master of Demon Valley said, "A gap is an opening; an opening is a space between barriers; a space between barriers makes for tremendous vulnerability. At the first sign of a gap, it should be shored up, or repelled, or stopped, or hidden, or overwhelmed. These are called principles of stopping gaps."

For the sake of a kingdom, even a father will attack sons, and sons a father; how about ministers?

Ali said, "One who has authority is like someone riding on a lion; he is envied for his position, but he knows his situation better."

Even a trivial problem becomes trouble for one who is beleaguered.

When already on the verge of being overwhelmed, most anything could become the proverbial straw that breaks the camel's back. Then again, since great pressure is known to affect one's sense of proportion, remembering this aphorism might help to reestablish a sense of perspective when relatively minor problems occur in the midst of a larger crisis.

Like a forest fire, energy born of difficulty motivates.

It is more constructive and less disheartening to use trouble for motivation than to succumb to bewilderment or a sense of defeat.

No one should be disrespected; everyone's opinion should be heard. A sage should make use of a meaningful statement, even if from a child.

The *Tao Te Ching* says, "Observe yourself by yourself, observe the home by the home, observe the locality by the locality, observe the nation by the nation, observe the world by the world." The Huainan Masters said, "Leaders see with the eyes of the whole nation, hear with the ears of the whole nation, think with the knowledge of the whole nation and move with the strength of the whole nation."

Proper duty is conducive to paradise and eternity; when it is violated, society will be destroyed by confusion. One who does one's own proper duty is happy in the hereafter and in this life as well.

The Huainan Masters said, "No one has ever heard of a nation being chaotic when individuals are orderly, and no one has heard of a nation being orderly when individuals are unruly." They also said, "When society is orderly, the common people are upright and cannot be seduced by profit."

One should enjoy pleasure without compromising duty or wealth; then one will not be without happiness. Indeed, the three are inseparably connected to one another. Excessive indulgence in any one of them, be it duty, wealth or pleasure, hurts that one and the other two as well.

The Huainan Masters said, "The behavior of sage kings did not hurt the feelings of the people, so even while the kings enjoyed themselves the world was at peace."

There is no one without desire.

The *Tao Te Ching* says that sages desire to be without desire; but that is still on account of desire, and is itself a desire.

Wealth escapes the infantile one who keeps consulting the stars. Wealth is the "star" for wealth; what can the stars do?

Wealth may be reliably produced by judicious investment of resources in productive enterprise under suitable conditions; taking a gamble on fortune or luck reflects greed and laziness in the form of wishful thinking.

One with theoretical knowledge but no practical skill will be disappointed in action. The fitness of a person is determined by practical capability.

Ali said, "Knowledge is linked to action; so one who knows acts, as knowledge calls for action and will depart if it is not answered."

A steady worker does not stop working until the job is done.

The *I Ching* says, "Cultivated people persist to the end."

Fire dwells in timber.

With the potential for construction comes the potential for destruction.

What comes of itself should not be disregarded.

Ali said, "Take of the world what comes to you."

The self-possessed one should protect himself.

Confucius said, "They are wise who do not anticipate deception and do not consider dishonesty, yet are aware of them from the start."

One who is wise and self-disciplined should guard himself from his own people as well as others.

People need not be ill intentioned to cause trouble; anyone can make mistakes. Too much reliance on others puts one at the mercy of their shortcomings. Confucius said, "At first, the way I dealt with people was to listen to what they said and trust that they would act on it. Now I listen to what they say and then observe whether they do act on it. This was what was within my power to change."

Calmness and effort are the source of profit and security.

The *I Ching* describes the ideal condition of the individual as "serene and free from agitation, yet sensitive and effective; sensitive and effective, yet serene and free from agitation." Calmness makes it possible to perceive realities clearly; effort makes it possible to act on realities effectively.

Capacity, situation and opportunity foster one another.

Zhuge Liang wrote, "When opportunities occur through events, but you are unable to respond, you are not smart. When opportunities become active through a trend, and yet you cannot formulate plans, you are not wise. When opportunities emerge through conditions, but you cannot act on them, you are not bold."

The leader of a group should be properly benevolent to the group, well liked, patient, with loyal people and act according to the collective will.

According to the instructions for kings attributed to the great Irish high king Cormac, among the qualities of leadership are generosity, affability, patience, fairness and modesty. Kings are also enjoined to hold frequent assemblies, a principal method of expressing the collective will in an ancient form of democracy.

One's own body should be preserved, not material goods; why care for impermanent material goods?

The Sufi master Ali said, "The man who gets the worst bargain and is the most unsuccessful in his endeavors is the one who wears out his body in seeking his wealth but is not assisted by destiny toward his aim, who leaves the world with his sorrow and pain and arrives at the hereafter bearing his responsibility."

References and Further Reading

Citations from parallel literature quoted in the commentaries are taken from the following sources.

Buddhism/Zen

Dhammapada: The Sayings of Buddha. Translated from the Pali, with commentary, by Thomas Cleary. New York: Bantam Books, 1995.
Zen Lessons: The Art of Leadership. Translated from the Chinese by Thomas Cleary. Boston: Shambhala Publications, 1989.

Confucianism/I Ching

The Essential Confucius. Translated from the Chinese and presented by Thomas Cleary. San Francisco: Harper San Francisco, 1992.
The Tao of Organization: The I Ching for Group Dynamics, by Cheng Yi. Translated from the Chinese by Thomas Cleary. Boston: Shambhala Publications, 1988.

Greek Philosophers

Living the Good Life. Translated from the Arabic by Thomas Cleary. Boston: Shambhala Publications, 1997.

Strategy/Military Science

The Art of War, by Sun Tzu. Translated from the Chinese by Thomas Cleary. In: *Classics of Strategy and Counsel*, vol. I. Boston: Shambhala Publications, 2000.
The Book of Five Rings. Translated from the Japanese by Thomas

Cleary. In: *Classics of Strategy and Counsel,* vol. II. Boston: Shambhala Publications, 2000. Includes *Family Traditions on the Art of War* by Yagyu Munenori.

Mastering the Art of War. Translated from the Chinese and edited by Thomas Cleary. In: *Classics of Strategy and Counsel,* vol. I. Boston: Shambhala Publications, 2000. Includes *The Way of the General* by Zhuge Liang.

Sufism/Islam

The Essential Koran. Translated from the Arabic by Thomas Cleary. San Francisco: Harper San Francisco, 1993.

Living and Dying with Grace: Counsels of Hadrat Ali. Translated from the Arabic by Thomas Cleary. Boston: Shambhala Publications, 1995.

The Wisdom of the Prophet: Sayings of Muhammad. Translated from the Arabic by Thomas Cleary. Boston: Shambhala Publications, 1994.

Taoism

Awakening to the Tao, by Liu I-ming. Translated from the Chinese by Thomas Cleary. Boston: Shambhala Publications, 1988.

The Book of Leadership and Strategy: Lessons of the Chinese Masters. Translated from the Chinese by Thomas Cleary. Boston: Shambhala Publications, 1992. Contains sayings of the Huainan Masters.

The Essential Tao. Translated from the Chinese and presented by Thomas Cleary. San Francisco: Harper San Francisco, 1991. Contains the *Tao Te Ching/Leo-tzu* and the *Chuang-tzu.*

Thunder in the Sky: Secrets on the Acquisition and Exercise of Power. Translated from the Chinese, with commentary, by Thomas Cleary. In: *Classics of Strategy and Counsel,* vol. II. Boston: Shambhala Publications, 2000. Contains the books of the Master of Demon Valley and the Master of the Hidden Storehouse.

Wen-tzu: Understanding the Mysteries; Further Teachings of Lao-tzu. Translated from the Chinese by Thomas Cleary. Boston: Shambhala Publications, 1992.

LIVING A GOOD LIFE

Advice on Virtue, Love, and Action
from the Ancient Greek Masters

INTRODUCTION

Grecian culture and thought are universally acknowledged to be among the main roots of Western civilization, and the inspiration of the European Renaissance. Grecian cultures and philosophies were originally of considerable variety and were also commingled with other cultures and ways of thought, including the already ancient as well as the contemporarily current. Elements of Minoan, Egyptian, Chaldean, Indian, Persian, and Hebrew cultures were absorbed by inquisitive Greek peoples over the centuries, producing dynamic new syntheses.

The Greek empire declined in time, superseded in the West by the Romans, but the high culture of the Graeco-Roman synthesis remained essentially Greek in many important ways. When the center of Roman culture was destroyed by Teutonic tribes, therefore, both Latin and Greek literature and culture faded in the Western part of the former empire. The antagonism of the Roman Church to the Greek accelerated the disappearance of Greek scholarship from Western Europe.

It was not until the twelfth century, seven hundred years after the sack of Rome, that the rendering of Greek classics into Latin got underway on a broad scale for wider use in Western Europe. They were not translated only from the original Greek at that time, however, but also from classical Arabic versions. By the twelfth century, under the impact of Saracen culture in Spain and Italy, Arabic had largely superseded Latin as the dominant learned language of continental Western Europe. The process of transferring Graeco-Arabic learning into the domain of Latin Christendom in preparation for the Renaissance was just beginning.

The Arabic versions of Greek classics had been made several hundred years earlier. This translation work reached its peak in the eighth and ninth centuries under the patronage of the Abbasid

Caliphate. This massive endeavor was part of a major new Islamic cultural synthesis embodying the sayings of the Prophet Muhammad, "Seeking knowledge is encumbent upon every Muslim," and "Seek the word of wisdom, wherever it may be found."

The Abbasids were descendants of the Quraish, an aristocratic clan of hereditary shrine keepers of Mecca in olden times. The Quraish were well known for collecting information and artifacts of the religions and beliefs of the peoples of other lands with whom they engaged in trade. Muhammad the Prophet, who is said to have welcomed wise men from the East, was himself a member of the Quraish clan. Up until the zenith of its empire, the Abbasid Caliphate drew its top ministers from the Barmakis, a family of hereditary Buddhist priests and shrine keepers in what is now Afghanistan.

By the twelfth century, when Arabic versions of Greek classics were translated into Latin under Saracen influence, many studies and commentaries on Greek classics had been composed by Persians writing in Arabic. Jewish scholars and philosophers also used the Arabic language, not only for studies of Greek thinking, but even for Hebrew grammar and Biblical interpretation. Arabic schools in Saracen Spain attracted Christians, Jews, and Muslims. Interested in science, religion, mysticism, and philosophy, people of all three faiths worked side by side, revitalizing civilization in Western Europe.

After the rendition of Greek classics into Arabic, the challenge of Greek rationalism to Islamic pragmatism was answered, both theologically and mystically, by certain Sufis who demonstrated the compatibility of reason and religion. Astronomy, mathematics, medicine, and other natural sciences were consequently developed to a high degree by Sufis and other Islamic workers. Influences of this new cultural synthesis extended through most of Western Europe, in time affecting education and literature as far away as England.

Abstract theology and natural science thus made great strides under the impact of Graeco-Arabic learning, stimulating the revival and enrichment of the Western consciousness. Among the diverse communities of ordinary people within Saracenic culture, meanwhile, aphoristic literature from the Greek sources gained particularly great popularity. Rendered in simple, clear Arabic, concerned only with practical content and meaning rather than literary embellishment and philosophical speculation, collections of wise sayings attributed to Greek ancients became the most widespread vehicle of popular Graeco-Arabic culture.

This book is a collection of translations from these popular Arabic versions of Greek wisdom lore. It is presented in five parts. The first part consists of sayings attributed to a variety of ancient philosophers, including Pythagoras, Diogenes, and Hermes, as well as Socrates, Plato, and Aristotle. These are arranged according to topic. The second part consists entirely of sayings attributed to Plato, the third part of sayings attributed to his disciple Aristotle. The fourth part is a collection of Neo-Platonic meditations whose Arabic attribution is simply "The Greek Master."

The fifth part of this book contains parallel selections from other wisdom literature of the world, including Taoist, Confucian, Buddhist, and Islamic. This last section is included to illustrate something of the commonality of human concerns in an extended global context, much as the Graeco-Arabic wisdom literature appealed to the widely recognized heritage of Greek civilization as a means of connecting Jewish, Christian, and Islamic sensibilities in a community of common conscience and consciousness.

PART ONE

Aphorisms of the Masters

MONEY

[1]

One day money was mentioned in the presence of Pythagoras. He remarked, "What do I need with something that is given by fortune and luck, preserved by meanness and stinginess, and annihilated by generosity and liberality?"

[2]

Socrates said, "The intellectual is a doctor of faith, and money is a sickness thereof; so when you see the doctor bringing the sickness on himself, how can he treat anyone else?"

[3]

Plato said, "The wealthy one is not the one who amasses money, but the one who manages it well and knows how to save and to spend."

[4]

When told that a certain person was rich, Diogenes said, "I would not know that until I knew how he manages his money."

[5]

Aristotle said, "Let your interest in seeking wealth be graciousness to friends."

[6]

Plato said, "A miser is as ready to give up his honor and dignity as he is eager to keep his money; a generous man is as intent on keeping his honor and dignity as he is open-handed with his money."

[7]

Told of a man who had a lot of money, Diogenes said, "I wouldn't be happy for him without knowing that he used his money well."

[8]

A king presented Pythagoras with a gift, but the philosopher returned it to him. When the king questioned him about it, Pythagoras said, "It was because of the fact that the giving of what is there and the seeking of what is wanting are from richness or poverty of soul. Thus I did not want you to be generous to my greediness or for you to be enriched at the price of my impoverishment."

[9]

Pythagoras said, "Love of money is the beginning of evil, because the operation of evil is connected to love of money."

CHILDREN

[1]

Pythagoras was told, "Had you married, a child would have been born to you that would have made you happy."

The philosopher retorted, "It is out of my love for children that I have given up seeking to have children."

[2]

Socrates was asked, "Why do you always associate with the young?"

He replied, "I do it as horse trainers do; for they look to train young colts, not old nags."

[3]

Socrates said, "How ugly are the decorations of decorators, though they imitate beautiful form! Yet sons neglect to emulate their worthy fathers!"

[4]

Plato said, "Don't force your children into your ways, for they were created for a time different from your time."

[5]

Socrates was asked, "What use is education to the young?"

He replied, "If they get nothing more from it than that it restrains them from bad habits, that is enough."

[6]

Plato said, "It behooves those who take the young to task to leave them room for excuse, lest they drive them to be hardened by too much rebuke."

POLITICIANS AND PHILOSOPHERS

[1]

The corrupt dictator of Sicily asked Pythagoras to stay with him, but the philosopher said to the dictator, "Your intelligence is lost, at odds with what would profit you; your constitution is agitated, uprooting your foundation. So do not try to get me to stay with you, for it is not a condition of healers to be ill along with the ailing!"

[2]

When Socrates was asked why he didn't visit the king, he said, "Why should I?"

He was told, "He is our master, and we are his servants; so whoever is closer to him is superior to whoever is more remote."

Socrates retorted, "But he is enslaved to what I have mastered, and he is ruled by what I rule."

This anecdote was reported to the king, who summoned Socrates and said to him, "I hear you said I am enslaved to what you have mastered, and ruled by what you rule. What are you referring to?"

Socrates said, "The passions. They are your rulers, while I rule them; they are my servants, while you are their slaves!"

The king exclaimed, "You have spoken truly! Well said, by God! Do you want some money?"

Socrates replied, "By God, I do not have any place to store even a coin, let alone anything else. And what would I do with money?"

He was told, "It will be useful to you in this world."

Socrates said, "And it will hurt my afterlife, distracting me from purity of obedience and making me fearful and scared, making me responsible for guarding it, and complicating my routine."

[3]

When Alexander asked Aristotle to go with him to the lands of Asia, Aristotle said, "I don't want to impose slavery on myself when I am free."

[4]

It was related that Socrates used to sun himself on top of the barrel in which he used to take shelter. The king stopped by and said to him, "Hey Socrates! What hinders you from coming to us?"

Socrates replied, "Preoccupation with what sustains life."

The king said, "If you came to us, we would have met your requirements in that regard," assuming that Socrates meant livelihood, whereas he had meant life everlasting.

Anyway, Socrates said, "Had I found that with you, I would have stayed with you as long as the need for it stayed with me."

So the king said to him, "Ask for what you need."

Socrates responded, "My need is for you to remove your shadow from me, for you have been interfering with my enjoyment of the sunshine."

Then the king called for sumptuous clothing of silk brocade and other materials, and gold and jewels, to be given to Socrates. But Socrates said, "O king, you have promised that which sustains life, but you are offering that which sustains death. Socrates has no need of stones from the earth, or the stalks of plants, or the spittle of caterpillars. What Socrates needs is with him wherever he bends his steps."

[5]

When he left the presence of a king, Pythagoras was asked what the king was doing. The philospher replied, "He is impoverishing the people."

[6]

Plato said, "Intoxication is forbidden to the ruler, because he is the protector of the state, and it is disgraceful that the protector be in need of someone to watch out for him."

[7]

Alexander said to Aristotle, "Advise me, since you are not going along with me."

So Aristotle told him, "Make your deliberateness the bridle of your hurry, make your strategy the emissary of your force, and make your pardon the basis of your power; then I guarantee you the hearts of your subjects, as long as you don't oppress them by violence against them or make them reckless by pampering them."

[8]

It was said that when Alexander conquered a certain city he put its inhabitants to the sword after winning victory over them. So Aristotle wrote to him, "You were mistaken in doing this, because those people were your enemies in war, but when you conquered them they became your servants; and it is vile for a man to mistreat his servants. So in victory it behooves one to lay down the weapons of wrath with the weapons of warfare."

[9]

Alexander told Diogenes that he himself was the greatest king. Diogenes said, "I am Diogenes the Cynic; I fawn on the good and the virtuous, and I bark at and bite those who are different from that."

Alexander asked Diogenes, "Do you fear me?"

Diogenes asked back, "Are you good or bad?"

Alexander said, "Good."

Diogenes said, "I do not fear, but rather love, one who is good."

[10]

Alexander went to a certain place to make war on its people, but the women fought back against him, so he desisted and refrained from fighting them, saying, "If we overcome this army, there is no honor in it for us; and if we are overcome, it will be an enduring shame."

WISDOM

[1]

Asked about wisdom, Pythagoras called it "Knowledge of the realities of things existing in a single state eternally."

[2]

Aristotle's teacher, Plato, asked him, "What is the proof confirming God Most High?"

Aristotle said, "Nothing of God's creation gives more cogent proof of God than anything else."

[3]

Plato said, "The business of a philosopher is to know the essences of things, not their superficials."

[4]

Aristotle said, "Whoever wants to see the form of his naked soul should make wisdom his mirror."

[5]

Pythagoras said, "Wisdom is the medicine of souls."

[6]

Aristotle said, "I used to drink yet increase in thirst, until I knew the Truth, sublime Its splendor; then my thirst was quenched without drinking."

[7]

Plato used to pace when he wanted to teach, in deference to wisdom. And he used to say, "Call upon the self to serve wisdom, not sitting down in disrespect toward it."

He also said, "The specialty of wisdom is the comprehension of what is knowable. And along with comprehension of what is knowable, it is the purification of the soul. And along with its purification of the soul, it makes its possessor like the Primary Cause, in that the purpose of wisdom is to grace human souls and repel depravities from them."

[8]

Pythagoras said, "Fathers are the cause of life, but the wise are the cause of wholesome life."

[9]

Aristotle was the mentor and teacher of Alexander the Great. Alexander's esteem for him reached the point where he was asked whether he had more love for his mentor or his father. Alexander said, "My mentor, because my father was the proximate cause of my being, whereas my mentor, Aristotle, was a cause of bettering my being."

It is also reported that Alexander said, "My father was the cause of my temporal existence, whereas Aristotle was the cause of my eternal life."

[10]

Aristotle said, "Desire for intelligence is better than desire for wealth."

[11]

Plato said, "Among the things that facilitate an individual's search for wisdom is help from luck. And by "luck" I do not mean that whereof the cause is unknown, but rather divine fortune, which illumines the intelligence and guides it to the realities of things."

Then Plato was questioned about the influence of this luck. He replied, "It is not of one sort only, for the following reason. When one senses a light by which one's intelligence is illumined, whether one is awake or asleep, let one observe: One who sees no shape or form to the light, but just a simple radiance, should know that it is the divine light. If one sees it in a projected human form, but not that of a recognizable person, one should know it is the light of the intelligence. If one sees it in the form of a recognizable person, one should know it is the light of the self."

CHANGE

[1]

Pythagoras said, "The world is a series of changes, sometimes in your favor and sometimes against you: so when you are in charge, do good; and when you are overruled, bear it."

[2]

Seeing an old man who wanted to take up philosophy but was embarrassed, Socrates said to him, "Don't be embarrassed to become better at the end of your life than you were to begin with."

[3]

Socrates said, "We ought to be distressed at life and happy to die, because we live to die and we die to live."

THE HUMAN SOUL

[1]

Pythagoras wanted to admonish the people and censure them for their neglect of knowledge, so he climbed up onto a high place and cried, "O community of people!" Then when they had gathered, Pythagoras said, "I didn't call *you*—I only called *people!*"

[2]

Pythagoras said, "It is impossible for anything of the noble, lofty divine sciences to be firmly rooted in a soul while it is filled with squalor, since like appeals only to like."

[3]

Plato said, "The superior soul is beyond joy and does not sorrow. That is because joy only occurs when the good aspects of something are seen, and not the bad; and sorrow is on account of seeing the bad aspects of something and not the good. But the superior soul considers something in terms of what it leads to, what it offers, and what its liabilities are; and since the virtues and defects thereof balance each other as far as the superior soul is concerned, neither condition of joy or sorrow overcomes it."

[4]

Aristotle said, "There are four excellences of the soul, with four equivalent excellences of the body.

"Wisdom in the soul has its physical equivalent in perfection.

"Justice in the soul has its physical equivalent in beauty.

"Courage in the soul has its physical equivalent in strength.

"Modesty in the soul has its physical equivalent in health."

[5]

Pythagoras often used to say that it is fitting for a man to have a good build in youth, to be chaste while growing up, to be upright as a young man, to be perspicacious in maturity, and to be a keeper of norms in old age and at the time of death, so that regret does not overtake him after he dies.

[6]

Aristotle said, "Let your concern be with exercise of the soul. As for exercise of the body, take an interest in it to the degree that necessity calls for it; and flee pleasures, for they drain weak souls, though they have no power over the strong."

[7]

Plato said, "If anyone is melancholy, let him listen to the melodies of the noble soul. For the light of the soul dies out when melancholy enters it, while the light of the soul blazes when it is happy and rejoices. Melancholy appears according to longing, to the extent that the one subject to it admits it; and the susceptibility of the one subject to it corresponds to one's purity and innocence of dishonesty and pollution."

[8]

Aristotle said, "The soul is not within the body; rather, the body is within the soul, because the soul is more extensive than the body, and greater in magnitude."

LAW

[1]

Pythagoras said, "Hold yourselves to three things from the law: abandon anger and importunity, avoid overconsumption, and do not sleep excessively."

[2]

Seeing him in a garment so threadbare that it did not cover him completely, a man exclaimed in amazement, "This is Socrates, lawgiver of the Athenians?"

Socrates retorted, "New clothes are not the sign of true law, nor are worn clothes the sing of false law."

[3]

Socrates said, "One who is benevolent by nature adheres to the law."

[4]

Socrates said, "Just as it is by physicians that the sick are purged and restored, so it is by laws that the unjust are reformed."

SELF-DESTRUCTION

[1]

Pythagoras said, "The water that gags is sweet, the bread that chokes is delicious; and therein lies the destruction of people's devices."

[2]

Plato said, "Lust is a powerful snare for falling into evil."

[3]

Pythagoras was asked, "What is passion?"
   He said, "Folly that has occurred to, or happened upon, an idle heart."

[4]

Plato said, "Don't plant a date palm inside your house."

MODESTY

[1]

Pythagoras said, "If you want your life to be pleasant, be content to be thought of as ignorant."

[2]

Socrates said, "If he who knows not would simply remain silent, disputation would stop."

[3]

Pythagoras said, "Don't brag about what you did today, for you don't know what tomorrow will bring."

[4]

Socrates used to study music in his old age. He was asked, "Aren't you embarrassed to be studying in spite of your old age?"
   Socrates replied, "I would be more embarrassed to be ignorant in spite of my age!"

[5]

Plato said, "If not for the fact that in my saying that I don't know is confirmation that I do know, I would have said I don't know."

[6]

Aristotle said, "If I am ignorant and I know I am ignorant, that is to me preferable to being ignorant and ignorant of my ignorance."

[7]

Seeing a woman all dressed up for a trip to the city, Socrates remarked, "I suspect that your trip is not to see the city, but for the city to see you."

VIRTUE AND ACTION

[1]

Pythagoras said, "It is not enough for virtue to exist in the soul without emerging into action by effort. And effort is in training, by means of study, the irascible part of the self that is not submissive to order, so that the self may acquire education, skill, and aspiration for what is best."

[2]

When Socrates was asked about the virtuous man, he said, "The virtuous man at the highest level is the one who strives for virtues of his own accord. The virtuous man at the secondary level is the one who is motivated toward virtues when he hears of them from another. As for one who neglects both imperatives, he is vile and depraved."

[3]

Pythagoras said, "Ignorance of virtues is equivalent to death."

[4]

Plato said, "The good are those for whom undertaking the benefit of people is easier than undertaking their harm."

[5]

Irritated by an imbecile who had stopped Socrates and was annoying him, one of his friends said to the philosopher, "Permit me to restrain him."

Socrates replied, "One who permits malice is not a man of wisdom."

[6]

Plato said, "How hard it is for the covetous one to become virtuous!"

[7]

Pythagoras said, "Don't even entertain the notion of something that is not right to do."

[8]

Aristotle went to visit Plato and saw that he was angry. Aristotle inquired, "What has angered you, Teacher?"

Plato replied, "Something about you, of which a trustworthy individual has informed me."

Aristotle said, "A trustworthy individual does not slander."

Plato's anger then ceased.

[9]

Socrates said, "The error in giving to the undeserving is the same as withholding from the deserving."

APPEARANCE AND REALITY

[1]

Pythagoras said, "One whose face is comely but whose morals are bad is like a vessel that is of gold but has vinegar in it."

[2]

Seeing a man with a handsome face whose behavior was bad, Diogenes said, "The house is nice, but the resident is a devil."

[3]

Men and women used to gather around Socrates to learn wisdom. One day he saw a young student of his fixing his gaze on the face of a woman named Hipparchia, who had a beautiful appearance and was a philosopher. Now Socrates said to himself, "Maybe this youth is distracted at heart and his glance fell on this woman's face while his soul was preoccupied with thought about something else."

Now this young man was of high rank, so Socrates let the matter rest until he realized that he was gazing at her intentionally. Then Socrates said, "Young man, what is this ugly look that has appeared from you, and this preoccupation that has hindered you from reflection and meditation?"

As if excusing himself, the young man said, "I marvel at the beauty of the effects on her form of the wisdom of nature!"

But Socrates said, "No, my son. Don't make the beauty of the representation of individualities a vehicle for desires, lest you be carried away by them into a sticky morass. And it is for you to notice that gazing at Hipparchia's outward form blots out your vision, whereas gazing at her inner form will sharpen your vision."

[4]

When a picture of Socrates was shown to a man who claimed to be a physiognomist, he said, "This is a man overcome by corrupt desire."

People laughed at him and said, "This is Socrates, the most abstinent of people!"

But Socrates said to them, "Don't be hasty, for the man did not lie. I am by disposition guilty of what he said, but I master my self and subjugate my desire."

[5]

Noticing two men who were virtually inseparable, Pythagoras asked what kinship there was between them. He was told, "They are not related, but they are the best of friends."

Pythagoras remarked, "If that were so, then one wouldn't be rich while the other is poor!"

[6]

It was related that a sophist said to Socrates, "How ugly your figure is!"

Socrates replied, "Your comeliness is not yours for you to be praised on its account, nor is my ugliness mine for me to be blamed on its account. That is merely the work of the Fashioner; so whoever finds fault with the work finds fault with the Creator."

[7]

Aristotle said, "Everyone has a resemblance to an animal or something else. For example, one who takes by speed is like a wolf, one who takes by cunning is like a fox, and one who is simple-minded is like a donkey. One who has a good appearance without inner worth is like an oleander, one who is outwardly praiseworthy but inwardly blameworthy is like a date, and one who has a despised exterior but inward excellence is like an almond. And some combine all that is praiseworthy, like the citron, which combines pleasant appearance with nice fragrance and flavor."

KNOWLEDGE AND IGNORANCE

[1]

Pythagoras said to a pupil of his who attached little importance to knowledge, "Young man, if you will not take pains for knowledge, you will suffer the distress of ignorance."

[2]

Seeing a handsome youth who was uneducated and uncultivated, Diogenes said, "However the house may be, it has no foundation."

[3]

Socrates said, "The polish of souls is geometry; the rust of souls is indulgence in animal lusts."

[4]

Aristotle said, "Leisure spent in idleness has sweet roots but bitter fruits; trouble taken in the pursuit of education has bitter roots but sweet fruits."

[5]

Plato said, "The knowledgable one knows the ignorant, having once also been ignorant; but the ignorant one does not know the knowledgeable, never having been knowledgable."

[6]

Plato said, "Knowledge and fortune are of no benefit to one who gets them by theft, or to one who gets them by fraud, because these two depravities only take root in a deranged soul, in which nothing of its potential thrives or bears fruit."

[7]

Socrates was asked, "Why don't you record your wisdom in books?"
    He replied, "How trusting you are of the skins of dead animals, and how powerful your suspicion of living, eternal essences! You want to learn from a lode of ignorance, and you despair of learning from the source of intelligence!"

[8]

Plato said, "As long as you are able to add another's light to your own light, then do it."

[9]

Aristotle said, "Education graces the wealth of the wealthy, and veils the poverty of the poor."

NEGATIVITY

[1]

Pythagoras was asked, "What enervates a man and consumes him?"

The philosopher replied, "Anger and envy; but anxiety is worse than both!"

[2]

Aristotle was asked, "Why is it that the envious are always sorrowing?"

Aristotle replied, "Because they sorrow not only at any adversity that befalls them, they sorrow equally at any good that is granted to other people."

[3]

Socrates said, "Be wary of anger, for when it breaks out it distracts the angry one from everything, until he becomes like a house afire, which fills with shouting and smoke, to the point where no eye can see there, and no ear can hear."

He also said, "Just as one who is drunk cannot know the ugliness of drunkenness as long as he is drunk, until he sees it in another, similarly one who is angry cannot know the ugliness of anger except by seeing its influence on another."

Socrates also said, "Just as leanness of face, jaundice of the nostrils, and hollowness of the eyes are among the signs of death in sick bodies, similarly the change of the face through anger is a sign of death of the soul."

[4]

Aristotle said, "Cupidity is an individual's seeking what he doesn't have, while stinginess is his begrudging of what he has."

[5]

Plato was asked, "How does it happen that stupidity is more fortunate than intelligence?"

He replied, "Because evil infects intelligence, whereas evil does not infect stupidity, since it is itself evil, and evil does not infect an evil."

[6]

Aristotle said, "Specialties of evil include admonition of enemies and meanness to friends."

[7]

Pythagoras said, "Lack of cultivation is a cause of every evil."

[8]

Aristotle said, "A malicious person is an enemy to himself, so how can he be a friend to another?"

[9]

Plato said, "Evil people look for people's faults, ignoring their good qualities, just as flies look for rotten parts of a body, ignoring the wholesome."

[10]

Aristotle said, "An evil disposition is infectious."

He was asked, "How is that?"

He replied, "Because your companion does bad and does good, and when he does that a lot, you become similar to him."

[11]

Pythagoras said, "Three things make the earth quake: the slave who rules, the ignoramus who is sated, and the man whose wife is despised."

[12]

Plato said, "The unworthiness of a man is known by two things: he talks a lot about what is of no use to him, and he tells of what is not asked of him and not desired of him."

[13]

Aristotle said, "Affection and well-being are united against their enemies, anger and malice, which are harmful to them."

[14]

Socrates was asked, "What is the worst of states?"
    He replied, "Decrepitude and destitution."

[15]

A man said to Aristotle that Plato was stupid. Aristotle said, "If someone else told you this, don't believe him; and if it is you who tell that, I don't believe you."

[16]

Plato said, "One who pays attention to a statement is a confederate of the speaker."

[17]

When a certain person was insolent to him, Aristotle said to him, "Graceful forgiveness is better, in our view, than requital for your offense. We have no recompense for your offense except forbearance, and no remedy for your outrage but patience.

    "We have, in fact, already seen enough of your obvious inferiority to make us wish to be kind to you and forgiving to you. So do not presume to yourself that I would give up my good nature for your bad nature, or that I would pay you back by doing as you have done, or that I would go your way, for to requite evil and evil is to enter into it."

[18]

Plato said, "When the form of evil operates invisibly, it produces anxiety; and when it operates visibly, it produces suffering."

[19]

Pythagoras said, "When there is no firewood, fire goes out; and when no one is quarrelsome, argument ends."

[20]

Diogenes was asked, "Why are you called a cynic?"

He replied, "Because I confront people of evil and falsehood with truth, and I tell them the truth about themselves. And I fawn on the good and growl in the faces of the bad."

REALISM

[1]

Pythagoras said, "If you want yourself, your family, your children, and your loved ones to live in security forever, then you are an ignoramus, wishing for yourself something you cannot have."

[2]

Pythagoras said, "If you want your son or your servant not to make mistakes, you are seeking something unnatural."

[3]

Pythagoras said, "When you call your son, your errand boy, or your servant, bear in mind the degree of obedience or insubordination of the one you are calling, and the fact that he may obey you or disobey you, in order that this too may inform your confidence and let you know about them, so that you do not make them a cause of trouble in your life."

[4]

Pythagoras said, "Just as faces are not alike, hearts are not alike."

PLEASURE

[1]

Socrates said, "The greatest dominion is that man overcomes his passions."

[2]

Asked about pleasure, Pythagoras said, "Not everything that is pleasurable is beneficial, but everything that is beneficial is pleasurable."

[3]

Asked about sleep, Pythagoras said, "Sleep is a light death, and death is a long sleep."

[4]

Socrates said, "Pleasure is a honey snare."

[5]

A jester said to Socrates, "You have forbidden yourself the amenities of the world."

Socrates retorted, "And what are the amenities of the world?"

The jester said, "Fine meats and sweet wines, sumptuous clothing and beautiful women."

Socrates told him, "I give that to those who are content to be like swine and apes, and who are like beasts of prey in that their stomachs are graves of animals, and who prefer the structure of the unstable body to the structure of the eternal spirit."

FAMILY AND FRIENDS

[1]

Pythagoras said, "A man should be good with his family at all times, so they will not be unable to be an adornment to him among his friends."

[2]

Pythagoras said, "Sitting on a roof's edge is better than living with a turbulent woman."

[3]

Pythagoras said, "A neighbor nearby is more helpful than a brother far away."

[4]

Socrates used to take shelter in a barrel with a little dog. Some of his students asked, "What are you doing with this dog?"

Socrates said, "The dog treats me better, since it protects me and doesn't annoy me, whereas you desert me and yet annoy me too!"

MIND AND MATTER

[1]

When a rich man expressed disapproval of Socrates, the philosopher said, "You would not be able to live as I live even if you wanted to, whereas I would be able to live as you do if I wanted to. And if you had known poverty, it would have kept you too occupied with yourself to feel sorry for Socrates!"

[2]

Socrates said, "Do not be bent on the acquisition of wealth at the expense of scattering your thoughts. Disregard death so that you do not die. Kill the passions, and you will be immortal. Adhere to justice, and safety will stay by you."

[3]

Socrates was asked, "Why do you never sorrow?"

He replied, "Because I never acquire anything whose loss would sadden me."

[4]

Aristotle was asked, "What things should an intelligent person acquire?"

He replied, "Those things which will swim with you when your ship sinks."

[5]

Plato said, "Don't let your holdings consist of things that will depart from you."

[6]

A philosopher wrote to Socrates, censuring him for eating little and wearing worn clothing, saying, "You maintain that compassion is incumbent upon all who are imbued with spirit and soul. You yourself are imbued with spirit and soul, yet you oppress them by paucity of nourishment and coarseness of clothing."

Socrates replied, "You have praised me to my face, which is actually disparagement. You have censured me for coarse clothing, but it has happened that a man will fall passionately in love with a homely woman and leave a comely one. And you have reproved me for eating little, but I only eat to live, whereas you live to eat. Peace!"

[7]

Socrates was asked, "Why don't you purchase some land?"

He replied, "Because I am ashamed before the Owner of the whole earth to dispute over a little patch of it, seeing as how the Owner is gracious and good to me!"

He was told, "But the Owner has granted it to you!"

Socrates responded, "Had it been *given* to me, I would not be made responsible for its produce."

He was told, "Then you could be as its manager, with you living in the middle of it."

Socrates retorted, "The pay is up to the Owner, but the manager may be faithless."

[8]

Aristotle had a valuable country estate, which he put in the care of a manager and did not personally superintend. Someone asked him why he did that; he said, "I did not acquire an estate by virtue of my commitment to properties, but by virtue of my commitment to my education; and by that means, I hope to acquire more properties."

[9]

Plato said, "He is not a consummate sage who rejoices at the wealth of the world, or sorrows at anything of its misfortunes."

[10]

When Socrates was imprisoned, and they assumed he was going to be executed, his students said to him, "Teacher, what do you instruct us to do with your body when you have been executed?"

Socrates replied, "The one who will worry about that is whoever needs the space, or whoever is vexed by the stench of my rotting corpse."

FRIENDS AND ENEMIES

[1]

Pythagoras said, "It is better to be struck by a true friend than to be kissed by an enemy."

[2]

Socrates said, "Among the things that show your friend's intelligence and his sincere advice to you as well as to himself is that he shows you your flaws and expels them from you; he exhorts you to what is best, and also accepts such exhortation from you; and he restrains you from evil, and is restrained from it by you."

[3]

Alexander said, "A man's enemies may sometimes be more beneficial to him than his friends, because they show him his faults, so he turns away from them, fearing their malice, thus keeping his good fortune, and he is on his guard against its loss as far as he is able."

[4]

Plato said, "Don't make friends with someone who is evil, for your character will take evil from his character without your being aware of it."

[5]

Socrates was asked, "What is the most beneficial thing a person can acquire?"

He answered, "A friend who gives sincere advice."

[6]

Aristotle said, "Whoever gives money to a friend has given of what he has accumulated, but one who gives a friend affection and sincere advice has given of himself."

[7]

Alexander said, "I have benefited more from my enemies than from my friends, because my enemies blame me for a mistake, calling my attention to it, whereas my friends present a mistake in a favorable light to me, encouraging me in it."

[8]

Socrates was asked, "Who is the most contemptible of people?"

He replied, "One who trusts no one and whom no one trusts."

[9]

Plato said, "It is a most serious matter for one to be mistaken about someone one trusts."

[10]

Alexander was asked, "How did you acquire such a mighty kingdom in spite of your youth?"

He said, "By winning over enemies and making them friends, and by obligating friends through beneficence to them."

[11]

Plato was asked, "How can one take revenge against one's enemy?"

He replied, "By becoming better oneself."

[12]

Plato also said, "When one of your peers envies you for an excellence that is apparent in you, and strives to inconvenience you or fabricates lies against you about things you have not said, do not counter him with the likes of his attack on you, for he will then excuse himself for his offense against you, and you will open a way for him to do what he wants to you. Instead, you should strive to increase that very excellence for which he envies you; for then you will hurt him without giving him a cause against you."

[13]

Plato said, "Your behavior with your friend should be conduct that does not make you need an arbitrator; and with enemies, conduct by which you will succeed in arbitration."

[14]

Plato said, "Do not befriend evil people, for the most they can give you is safety from them.

[15]

Socrates was asked, "Who is the worst of people?" He replied, "One who helps you follow caprice."

[16]

Aristotle said, "One who annoys you with truth shows you good will, while one who pleases you with falsehood debases you."

[17]

Socrates said, "The error in giving to the undeserving is the same as withholding from the deserving."

JUSTICE

[1]

Seeing his wife weeping as he was being taken out to be executed, Socrates said to her, "What makes you weep?"

She replied, "How could I not weep, when you are being killed unjustly?"

Socrates said, "What? Do you prefer that I be killed justly?"

[2]

It was related that two sophists, Batil the Useless and Fatin the Clever, passed by Socrates as he was being taken off to be executed. They, for their part, had gone to someone to arbitrate in a matter of dispute that they were contesting between them. Now they heard an onlooker exclaim, "He who sentenced you to death has done you wrong, Socrates!"

But Socrates said, "This man's words imply that he is gloating over my misfortune, or that he is commiserating with me, or that he has testimony for me, or that he is making a drunken jest."

The man was then questioned about what information he had, and he did in fact have testimony. Socrates declared, "Urgently as I may need to accept his testimony by pronouncement of his integrity and attestation of his honorable record, nevertheless it is not permissible to accept testimony for a judgment from someone upon whose head there lies deception."

As it turned out, the man who had the testimony was in the habit of dying his hair.

Now Fatin the Clever said to his companion, "If the arbitrator between us had been Socrates, who made this judicious distinction with knowledge of his imminent death, we would not have feared that he would err in his view or be unfair in his judgment."

[3]

Socrates said, "It is by justice that the universals of the world exist, and its particulars cannot exist without it."

[4]

It was related that once Socrates was at a reception where the servant was slow with the food. A man said to the host, "You should punish him as severely as you can."

But Socrates said, "No. Forgive him his mistake; for to improve yourself at the cost of spoiling your servant is better than correcting your servant at the cost of corrupting yourself."

SELF-GOVERNMENT

[1]

Socrates said, "It is desirable that thought should rule before an act, during the act, and after the act: before the act, so that it will not be mean and hurtful; during the act, so that it does not cause a nuisance; and after the act, so that it may be followed up and it may be known what it has led to, and its beginning may be assessed by its end."

[2]

Socrates said, "Kill desire, and you enliven nature."

[3]

Socrates said, "Treat anger with silence, and desire with anger; for whoever is angered at himself because of experiencing its disadvantages is diverted from it."

[4]

Socrates said, "Don't be afraid of death, for the bitterness of it lies in the fear of it."

[5]

An ignorant young man asked Plato, "How did you manage to learn so much?"

Plato said, "It is because I have burned more oil than you have drunk wine."

[6]

Someone said, in the presence of Socrates, "Silence is safer, because mistakes happen when one talks a lot."

Socrates remarked, "That doesn't happen to someone who knows what he's talking about. In the case of someone who does not know what he's talking about, though, he'll make mistakes whether he talks a little or a lot."

[7]

Socrates was asked, "Who does one ask for advice in one's affairs?"

He replied, "The man who is human in deed and not merely in form; for he is above the time. One who is under the time does not see the consequence of anything in it, so he is not consulted in coming to a decision about something."

[8]

When Aesop was taken captive, a man who wanted to buy him said, "Shall I buy you?"

Aesop said, "How can you buy me to be your slave after you have taken me as an adviser?"

[9]

Socrates said, "Your days are three. There is the day that has gone by, which you cannot overtake. Then there is the day you are in, of which you ought to avail yourself. As for your tomorrow, all you can do is hope. But do not rely on hope so much that you neglect work.

"Today and tomorrow are in the position of two brothers. One of them stopped over at your house, but you treated him badly and unhospitably, so he left, blaming you. Then his brother came to you after that and said, 'Hey you! I came to you after my brother, who left you yesterday, and whom you mistreated by your actions. Now be good to me, and that will efface your mistreatment of him. Yet nothing could be more natural for you if you inflict evil on me, that you be ruined by the testimony of both of us against you."

[10]

Pythagoras was asked, "What is hardest for a human being?"
  He replied, "Knowing oneself and concealing inner thoughts."

[11]

Solon the philosopher was asked, "What is most difficult for a human being?"
  He said, "To know one's own imperfections and refrain from what one should not speak of."

[12]

Pythagoras said, "There is no taking back something you have already said or done, so be wary before that."

[13]

Plato said, "We ought to turn away from base things. Base things are the world, so we ought to turn away from the world. And to turn away from the world is to be guided by God Most High."

[14]

When a man complained to him about his circumstances, Plato said, "You will find people to be one of two kinds: there is the one who suffers setback on his own account but his luck has advanced him, and there is the one who has progressed on his own account but his time has set him back. So either be content by choice with your circumstances, or you will have to be content by force of circumstances."

[15]

Socrates said, "When your self asks you for provision for tomorrow, say 'Get me a guarantee for today!' "

[16]

Plato said, "It is no wonder when one in whom passions have died out becomes virtuous; the wonder is when one whose passions contend with him is at the same time virtuous."

[17]

Plato was asked, "Why, of all the cities of Greece, did you choose the city of Academy Garden, seeing as how it is a pestilent place?"

He replied, "So that if I do not refrain from passions for fear of harm to the soul, I will refrain from them out of necessity, to avoid the invasion of harm into the body."

[18]

Plato said, "Place intelligence on your right and truth on your left, and you will be safe all your life and remain free."

PRIORITIES

[1]

When Socrates was told that the speech he gave at a certain time was not accepted, he retorted, "I am not worried about whether it is accepted; I am worried about whether I spoke well on that occasion."

[2]

Plato said, "One who raises himself above lowly ambitions becomes known for his good qualities. One who is known for his good qualities is praised, and one who is praised is loved. But humanity loves no one until God has loved that one."

[3]

Socrates saw a young man who had inherited money from his father but had squandered it, to the point where he was reduced to eating olives and bread. Socrates said, "Young man, if you had restricted yourself to food like this, this would not be your food."

The Life of the World

[1]

Socrates said, "Life has two boundaries: one goes as far as work, the other goes as far as the instant of death. The first one maintains it, the second terminates it."

[2]

Socrates said, "The world is desired for three things: power, wealth, and comfort. But one who is abstemious in the world grows strong, one who is content grows rich, and one with little ambition is at ease."

[3]

Anaxasis said, "The grapevine bears three bunches of grapes: first, a bunch of enjoyment; second, a bunch of intoxication; and third, a bunch of folly."

[4]

Aristotle said, "Don't crave the world, for you only stay in it a little while; how long can you possibly live?"

[5]

Plato said, "When the transcendent Creator only wishes for the world what is good for it, our joy and our sorrow are useless."

SPIRITUAL PERCEPTION

[1]

A man said to Plato, "You are the one who says there is a world other than this one, and a human being other than this one."

Plato said, "Yes."

The man said, "Then show me."

Plato said, "You don't have what it takes to see it."

[2]

Pythagoras was asked, "Why did you come to this world?"

The philosopher replied, "It was not my idea, not my preference! But I saw, where I was, a beautiful picture, and I said, 'Let me have this.' But I was told, 'Not until you journey to this country to carry out an intelligence mission for us, give an account of a wonder, and establish a way of access to us. We will furnish you with provisions, and do our best to help you.'

"So I crossed valleys and peaks, dangers and perils, until I reached this place. And here I am, as I was instructed in the beginning.

"But I see I have enemies here of whom I had no knowledge there, and I have made my way alternately socializing with them and fighting them, until I have come to the point where I am unable to do it anymore. So I fear I may be overcome, and denied everything I was promised."

He was asked, "Why didn't you stay where you were?"

Pythagoras said, "Folks, don't blame me! If you had witnessed what I witnessed, you would have demanded it more, even if the terror were greater and the menace were worse. For whoever profit delights, crossing land and sea is easy!"

[3]

Aristotle said, "There is Something above the substance of the firmament; nothing is greater than It, and there is no way to quantify or measure It. It is beyond change in any manner or mode. There is no limit to Its power. Therefore It performs Its acts outside of time, being by nature effective and thus always in action, without Its action affecting It. Nothing comes from It in a state of potential; rather, things come from It in action, while Its potential always pervades the universe."

[4]

Aristotle said, "By the arrangement of things, their connectedness, their concord, and their order, we know that their Maker is one."

[5]

Someone asked Socrates, "What is God the Exalted like?"

Socrates answered, "Hidden, but not concealed; evident, but not visible."

[6]

Hermes said, "It is indeed difficult to know or talk about the reality of the Creator, for it is not possible for a graspable body to describe what is ungraspable, and what is not perfect does not comprehend what is perfect, and it is hard to connect the eternal with what is not eternal, for the eternal abides forever, while what is not eternal passes away. And that which passes away is imagination, shadow; and the relationship between that which passes away and God, who does not die, is as that between the weak and the strong, or the lowly and the noble."

POLITICAL SCIENCE

[1]

Plato said, "When a nation is tolerant of malpractice in judges and doctors, it is then decadent and near to disintegration."

[2]

Plato said, "It behooves a ruler to start by rectifying himself before he starts rectifying his citizenry, lest he be in the situation of one who wants to straighten a crooked shadow before straightening the rod of which it is the shadow."

[3]

Plato said, "A state starts out with a crude model, then applies realities and perfects obedience to God and to those in authority.

"Then when it has gotten rid of its enemies and its people are secure, their defense against their enemies begins to deprive them of the chance to get some of the bounty available to them.

"Then when they become immersed in the abundance and luxury of life they enjoy, they are too preoccupied with recreation to be of any help. This reaches the point where their social order cannot withstand anyone who has designs on them, and the regime comes to an end.

"They are like fruits, which at first are too unripe to eat, then you see them in an intermediate condition, and then they mature; yet along with their delicious sweetness, the fruits are closest to rotting and changing."

[4]

Plato said, "States begin with justice and fear. Then when they reach midway in development, they are governed by ambition and fear. And when their passing is near, they are governed by ambition and favoritism."

[5]

Pythagoras said, "Prefer being defeated but just to being victorious but unjust."

[6]

Plato said, "The decline of a state includes cleaving to secondary things and neglecting basics, abandonment of works, neglect of construction, extension of hostilities, and infringement of agreements."

[7]

Plato said, "The most beloved of people to a ruler is one whose weakness he reckons to be completely in his passions, and his strength to be entirely in his opinion and his conservatism."

[8]

Plato said, "The first exercise of a prime minister is tolerance of the morals of the masses and concealment of ire; and attention to the morals of the ruler in his relations with others. If the ruler is harsh and rude, the minister deals with people otherwise; and if the ruler is mild and easygoing, the minister deals with people more firmly, in order to approach justice in his work."

[9]

Plato said, "A king is not the one who rules over slaves and *hoi polloi*, but the one who governs the free and the advantaged. And the wealthy one is not the one who amasses money, but the one who manages it well and knows how to save and to spend."

[10]

Plato said, "Among the characteristics of a free man is that his patience in the betterment of those below him is greater than his patience in seeking the favor of those above him, and he tolerates more from those who are weaker than he tolerates from those who are stronger."

[11]

Plato said, "Clemency is attributable only to one who has the power to attack."

[12]

Aristotle said, "When the ruler is just, the judge is honest, and the chief of police is a good manager, the reign lasts and its normal way of life is well established and does not fall into oblivion; otherwise, they become vitiated and pass away."

[13]

Plato said, "The time of a tyrannical ruler is shorter than the time of a just one, because the tyrant is a spoiler and the just one is a restorer; and spoiling something is quicker than restoring it."

SPEECH AND SILENCE

[1]

Plato said, "The difference between silence and inability to express oneself is that silence is keeping the tongue from speaking even while knowing what to say, whereas inability to express oneself is keeping the tongue from speaking because of not knowing what to say."

[2]

Plato said, "When you talk to someone who knows more than you do, get right to the point, without unnatural wordiness and without embellishment. But when you talk to someone who knows less than you do, expand your speech so that he may get in the end what he could not at first."

[3]

Plato said, "Expansiveness is one thing that makes you partially blind, so do not be free with it except to someone who is trustworthy in respect to it and is deserving of it."

[4]

A philosopher wrote to Socrates, saying, "I know the reason you eat so little; but why do you speak so little? You are stingy to yourself with food, and stingy to others with words!"

Socrates replied, "What I need to leave alone, and what I need to leave to others, are no business of yours; and to bother with what is none of your business is too much trouble!

"As for the paucity of my words, I see that God the Blessed and Exalted has made for me two ears and one mouth, so I may listen twice as much as I speak. You, on the other hand, talk more than you listen, and one who talks too much is accused of nonsense and fabrication, of babbling and lying."

[5]

Aristotle said, "When you want to know if a man is master of his desires, then observe how much control he has over what he says."

[6]

Asked about rhetoric, Aristotle described it as, "Putting much meaning in few words, and putting a little meaning in many words."

[7]

Asked what is most difficult, Aristotle said, "Silence."

EDUCATION

[1]

Aristotle was asked, "What is the best of animals?"
    He replied, "The human being graced with education."

[2]

Isocrates said, "It behooves a cultured person to take the best part of all aspects of education, just as the bee takes the best part of every flower."

[3]

Aristotle said, "Education is an adornment for the rich, and a way of life for the poor, by which they live the life of the free."

[4]

Aristotle was asked, "What graces a man among his fellows?"
  He replied, "Education graces the wealth of the wealthy and conceals the poverty of the poor."

[5]

Plato said, "When you admonish a wrongdoer, do so gently, that it may not lead to open hostility."

[6]

Socrates was asked, "What is most gratifying in the world?"
  He said, "Culture, education, and seeing what one has not seen before."

[7]

Aristotle said, "Habituate the self to the humanities, for from them and in them are seen the wonders of thought and the subtleties of reflection."

[8]

Aristotle said, "When the intelligence is sound, education adheres to it as nutrients are incorporated into a healthy body, nurturing it and making it grow. When the intelligence is impaired, it withdraws from any education it is taught, just as someone suffering from a stomach ailment cannot hold down the food he eats. And when an ignoramus chooses to learn something, that education transforms within him into folly, just as wholesome food in the stomach of a sick man turns into disease."

PART TWO
Sayings of Plato

TRUTH

Plato said to his companions, "When you attain truth, it blesses you, and when you abandon truth, it curses me. So make truth your own and act on it, and be wary of error; for therein lies God's satisfaction with you, and my affection for you."

He also said, "Truth is removal of the veil."

PRIDE

The best of what is in pride is being too proud to indulge in the vices of the people, and shunning servility to excess.

ATTENTION

Don't slight a small matter from which a serious matter may arise.

ARROGANCE

Don't be arrogant in victory.

COMPASSION

Don't laugh at another's mistake.

Don't rejoice at another's fall.

ANGER

Don't argue with someone who is angry.

Put up with mistakes from people in a reasonable way.

Gluttony

Refrain from making your insides coffins and graves of animals.

Antagonism

Let your dread of your strategy against your enemy be greater than your dread of your enemy's strategy against you.

Noble and Ignoble

The noble one rises with all who know him, while the ignoble one rises by himself.

Humility

Do not look down on anyone because of his humility; rather, honor him more for his humility.

When an intelligent person is commended for a virtue he does not have, it is not proper that he accept that commendation.

Charity

One who hesitates over a charitable deed should not disdain the work involved.

Conscience

You should do what is essential without anyone impelling you to do it, and refrain from uncalled-for action without a prohibition forbidding you from doing it.

Goodness

When the form of good operates visibly, it produces happiness; and when it operates visibly, it produces delight.

Disposition

There are some people whose disposition is suited for something beyond which they cannot go.

Work

One who chooses to be happy is a lover of labor.

Desire and Intellect

When times change for the better, desires serve intellects; and when times change for the worse, intellects serve desires.

Fortune

Fortune never gives anyone anything without taking it away.

Tact and Truthfulness

When you are with an intelligent man, please him even to the annoyance of those around him; but when you are with a man of weak perception, go ahead and annoy him, even to the pleasure of his subordinates.

Forgiveness

Forgiveness corrupts mean people to the same degree that it improves noble people.

Virtues

Most virtues are disagreeable at first but end up sweet.

Chivalry

The purpose of chivalry is for a man to have a sense of shame on his own account. And that is because the reason for a sense of shame before an elder is not his age or the whiteness of his beard; the reason for a sense of shame before him is the illumination of the essence of the intelligence in him. So when that radiant essence is in us, we ought to have a sense of shame before it, and not approach it shamelessly.

PROSPERITY AND AFFLICTION

The insolence of a man in prosperity corresponds to his humility in affliction.

PROGRESS

Do not antagonize a progressive nation, lest you turn back its progress.

STINGINESS

The souls of stingy people are more strongly shackled than the souls of generous people.

PART THREE
Sayings of Aristotle

DEFINITIONS

Definitions are of four kinds: transcendental, descriptive, logical, and physical.

The transcendental deals with categories of things that are not material forms and are not connected to material forms, and with the elucidation of their differences.

As for the descriptive, that is the definition of things whose substances cannot be distinguished except in imagination.

The logical is the sort employed by dialectitians, who define things in relation to their purpose and form.

As for the physical definition, that deals with categories of things in relation to both their matter and form together.

INTELLECT

Aristotle said, "Everything has a skill, and the skill of the intellect is choosing well."

He also said, "Intelligence is a means to a profitable life."

UNREALITY AND UNTRUTH

The unreal is what does not exist at all; the untrue is what is either exaggerated or understated.

HUMANKIND

Humankind is elevated above all animals only by speech and intellect; so if one is mute and uncomprehending, one reverts to animality.

LOGIC

Logic is a tool for all sciences.

PHILOSOPHY

Asked how many things are required for a person to become a philosopher, Aristotle said, "Three things: need, disposition, and interest."

VALUE

There is nothing in the universe without value, for nature does nothing in vain.

GENEROSITY

The generous one is the one who neither withholds generosity nor mixes it with extravagance.

FRUGALITY

When a rich man eats a meager meal of humble food, it is said he only did it to heal himself thereby, but when a poor man eats it, it is said that neediness drove him to it.

COMPULSION AND CHOICE

A human being is under compulsion in the form of having choice.

CONSUMPTION AND ABSORPTION

Increase in strength is due not to the quantity of nutrients with which you supply your body, but to the quantity of what it absorbs.

FOUR EARS

Have four ears: one pair to listen to what is important to you, and one pair for what does not concern you, so that what is of concern and what is not should not be brought together in one.

Intelligence and Decency

Decency is not cheating anyone, and intelligence is not being cheated by anyone.

Culture and Society

To be in combat without arms is easier than to enter a gathering without understanding.

Revelation and Concealment

Asked what should be revealed and what should be concealed, Aristotle said, "You show gratitude for a benefactor, and you conceal the imperfection of anyone you raise to the status of a true friend."

Enrichment

Asked how a man becomes wealthy, Aristotle replied, "In the case of a ruler, through service; in the case of the general run of humanity, through reliability and efficiency."

Patience

Aristotle said, "Whoever does not have intelligent patience has neither the world nor the hereafter."

When Aristotle went to Alexander to express sympathy on account of a misfortune that had befallen him, he said, "I did not come to you to offer condolence for your trouble, but to learn patience, for I know that you know patience in misfortune is a virtue. Your character, furthermore, is purged of all depravity; and how could you be induced to be the way you naturally are, or taught to behave as you normally do?"

Cultural Gifts

Aristotle wrote to Alexander, "God distributed gifts among peoples, giving bravery to the Persians, horsemanship to the Eastern

Tribes, artistry to the Byzantines, and sublety and philosophy to the Indians."

Righteousness

Among the signs of a righteous man are that he is friendly to his friends' friends and hostile to their enemies.

Friendship

Aristotle said, "Trust in and count on a friend who is knowledgeable; and don't be too fearful, like a slave or a weakling. Do not trust in a friend who is ignorant and greedy, and beware of an enemy who is dissolute and ignorant."

He also said, "One who has no friends has no family and no home; and one who has no family and children has no name and no posterity."

Life and Death

One who is perpetually needy, or chronically ill, or seized with fear, or away from his family and children for a long time, or who makes a living by begging from others, should consider his life as death and his death as repose.

Passion and Intelligence

When passion overcomes intelligence, it changes the good qualities that are the beauty of intelligence into bad qualities, turning patience into resentment, knowledge into hypocrisy, intelligence into craftiness, culture into conceit, eloquence into prattle, liberality into wastefulness, frugality into stinginess, and forgiveness into cowardice.

When this happens to someone, it leaves one so that one sees no health but physical health, no knowledge but that by which one becomes presumptuous, no wealth but monetary profit, no confidence but in material acquisition, and no security but in subjugation of people.

All of that is inconsistent with one's aim, distancing one from one's object and bringing one nearer to perdition.

But when intelligence overcomes passion, it changes the bad qualities into good ones, turning stupidity into discernment, vehemence into acumen, cunning into intelligence, prattle into eloquence, inarticulateness into silence, unruliness into cultivation, recklessness into energy, cowardice into caution, prodigality into liberality, and stinginess into frugality.

The Happy Man

The happy man is the intelligent one whose intelligence is his most perfect characteristic and whose knowledge is his most excellent provision, who is only enriched by contentment, who is only made secure by innocence, who is compelled by increase only to gratitude, and who is shielded from adversities only by prayer.

But one who is void of intelligence is not made more powerful by formal authority, and one who has no contentment is not made richer by material wealth.

Three Falsehoods

A ruler who lies does not count as a ruler, a pious ascetic who deceives does not count as a pious ascetic, a friend who leaves you in a lurch does not count as a friend, and one who does a favor for an ingrate does not count as a benefactor.

Despondency

An intelligent person should not be despondent, for two reasons: either he has a way to get rid of the misfortune that has happened to him, and so he works on it on his own, with a heart undistracted by sorrow; or if he does not see any way to deal with what has happened to him or any way to get rid of it, then he directs himself to a means of being patient.

Charity

A charitable person is not one who seeks to do good only to the good and not the bad, but one who embraces both of them with good. Have you not seen the veracious person speaking truth to someone who has lied to him, and the trustworthy person discharging a trust for someone who has let him down, and the just person being just to one who has oppressed him? Thus is the charitable person good to one who has been bad to him, and forgiving to one who has wronged him, and generous to one who has been stingy to him.

TROUBLES

Troubles turn an enemy into a friend, if he is noble; they turn an envious person into a compassionate one, if he is intelligent; they turn a commoner into a prince, if he is patient.

SINCERITY

The sincerest friend, in terms of affection, is one whose affection does not come from desire or fear.

CONDUCTORS TO TRUTH

We should be grateful to the forbears of a people who were our initiators into contact with something of truth; so how about those who became our actual way to truth!

OBLIGATION

Just as you prefer others being in your debt to your being in their debt, so should your doing good for others be preferable to you over their doing good for you.

CAUTION, ASTUTENESS, AND MINDFULNESS

Be cautious, as though you were inexperienced; be astute, as though you were negligent; be mindful, as though you were forgetful.

CONDOLENCES

Aristotle wrote to a noble lady of his family to console her on the loss of a brother of hers: "I dislike to rush you with encouragement to bear up at the beginning of the calamity, because it is hard for one giving consolation to resist the rush of sadness, just as it is hard for a swimmer to face the current. But it is not graceful for one like you, who is a descendant of people remembered for bravery and greatness of resolve, to show immoderation in grieving, particularly in the case of an event such as has touched you.

"For he parted from this world praised and remembered for the magnanimity of his acts and the greatness of his virtues; and then his death was the best of deaths. Anyone who betrayed him or broke a compact with him will be haunted by censure and shame.

"Be aware that the eyes of the people are looking at you, watching how you will be in this situation. Show, therefore, greatness of will and patience in affliction, as befits your noble origins. Peace."

Seeking and Finding

A man said to Aristotle, "I have been in quest of knowledge for forty years."

Aristotle said, "Many a man who has engaged in commerce for forty years does not have goods for the day."

Leadership Qualities

When a man deals with someone who hates him such that he turns into one of his friends, and treats his friend with justice so that he does not go over to his enemies, he is worthy to be called a leader and to take responsibility for the conditions of governing.

Appropriate Feelings

One should become accustomed from youth to be happy about what one should be happy about, and to be sad about what one should be sad about.

Ponderous People

Aristotle was asked, "Why does a ponderous person weigh heavier on the heart than a heavy burden on the back?"

Aristotle replied, "Because the spirit helps the body with the heavy load, but the spirit bears the ponderous person alone."

STRAIGHT AND CROOKED

An intelligent individual harmonizes with another intelligent one, but an ignoramus harmonizes with neither an intelligent person nor another ignoramus. That is like something straight fitting something straight, whereas something crooked fits neither something crooked nor something straight.

SEEK THE ETERNAL

Do not take a liking to what passes away and whose end is near. Seek the wealth that does not perish, and the life that does not change, the kingdom that never ends, and the permanence that does not dwindle away.

SELF-IMPROVEMENT

Improve yourself for your own sake, and people will follow you.

HERE AND HEREAFTER

Make your life in this world a defense for your afterlife; do not make your afterlife a defense for your life in this world.

PART FOUR

Meditations of the Greek Master

[1]

The Primary Agent is still, without any sort of movement at all. Its stillness produces its image, which is the intellect; but not in a thing, for its image is a vessel, noble and powerful, superior in nobility and power to all lower vessels.

In that image are all science and knowledge, because when it emanated from the Primary Agent, it focused on its cause, and beheld it according to its power and thus became intellect and essence.

This essence is the intellect. So it was primary in its relation to what is subordinate to it, and secondary in relation to what is above it.

[2]

Whoever wishes to know how the true One creates a multiplicity of phenomena should set his gaze on the true One alone, leaving aside all things, which come from It; and should return to Its essence and stay there: for he will see, by means of his intellect, the true One, motionless, standing high above all things intelligible and sensible.

And he will see the totality of things as if they were productions emanated from It and inclining to It. In this way, things start to move, meaning that it is necessary for everything in motion to have something toward which to move, and there is nothing in motion but what moves attracted to what it comes from, for it only desires to attain to It and to assimilate to It.

[3]

The Primary Agent is necessarily still, without movement, insofar as there must be something secondary to It. And Its action must be something secondary to It. And Its action must be without deliberation, movement, or desire inclining to the effect.

The primary effect is the intellect, which emanated from the potency and power of the stillness of the Agent. Then the totality of intelligible and sensible phenomena emanated from It by the mediation of the intellect.

[4]

The intellect became all things only because its Creator is not like anything whatsoever. And the primary Creator does not resemble anything whatsoever because all things come from It, and because It has no attributes and no particular form inherent in it.

And that is because the primary Creator is one, its oneness meaning that it is unconditioned. It has no properties of Its own, because all properties emanate from It. Thus all things are in It, while it is not in any thing, except as cause.

[5]

All things are in the intellect, and it is in things. Things happen to be in the intellect because their forms are in it, and have emanated from it into things, since it is the cause of things lower than it.

However, although the intellect is the cause of things below it, nevertheless it is not the whole cause of a thing, being only the cause of the form of the thing, not the cause of its essence.

As for the Primary Agent, It is the overall cause, because It is the unmediated cause of the essence of the thing, and the cause of the essence of the soul and the forms of things, through the mediation of the intellect.

And the soul and all things are formed in the intellect. They are not in the Primary Cause; they are only emanated from It.

[6]

All intelligible phenomena are delimited. The limitation of a thing is the totality of its attributes and its form. That is because when the Primary Cause created the essence of things, It did not leave them dependent on something without definition, but on what delimits and encompasses, defining them by their forms.

For the boundary of a created thing is its form and stability. And stability is characteristic of the intellect, defining it by the totality of its attributes. Stability is the normal state and constancy of the intellect and intelligible phenomena.

[7]

The unadulterated One is like light, while the secondary unit, which is related to something else, is like the sun; and the tertiary phenomenon is like the moon, which gets its light from the sun.

In the intellect is an essential luminosity, which, however, is not simply luminosity, but a substance that is a receptor of light. As for the thing that illumines the intellect and pours light upon it, that is simply light and nothing else but light. But it is an unrestricted light, pure and unadulterated, which pours its power on the intellect, making it an illuminating, enlightening intelligence.

However, the light that is in the intellect is a thing within a thing, whereas the light that illumines the intellect is not in something else. It is light alone, abiding steadily through its essence and illuminating all things. Some things, however, receive more of its light, and some receive less.

[8]

The true One is the creator of things, but It is not remote from them or separate from them. It is with all things, but is with them as if It were not with them. Its togetherness is evident only with those things that have the power to receive It.

[9]

The One is great, greater than all things; not in terms of mass, but in terms of power. Thus when we say It is infinite, we do not mean It is infinite in terms of mass or number, but that nothing encompasses Its power. And that is because it is above all possible imagination, permanently existing by virtue of Its own essence, void of attributes.

[10]

The One is good, not to Its own essence, for Its essence is goodness pure and true; rather, It is good to all things that have the power to receive the good It pours on them.

Furthermore, It has no motion, because It is before motion, before thought, and before knowledge. And there is nothing in It that It wants to know in the way a mortal knows. Rather, It is the knowledge that does not need to know by another knowledge, because It is pure ultimate knowledge, comprehending all knowledge as well as the cause of the sciences.

[11]

The first created intellect itself has no form. In relation to the primary Creator, it does have form, because it reaches a limit, whereupon it is defined and so comes to have attributes and form.

As for the primary Creator, It has no form, because there is no other thing above It that It would aim to reach, and nothing below It can reach It. So It is unlimited in every way, and thus happens to have no description and no form.

[12]

If the primary Creator were a form, the intellect would be a logos. But the intellect is not a logos, and there is no logos in it, for it was devised as a creation without its Creator having any attributes or form such that It could put that complex of attributes in there as a logos.

So the intellect is not a logos, nor is there a logos in it. But it is the fashioner of the logos in things, because it has attributes and characteristics. When it makes a thing, it imprints some of its attributes on the thing; and that imprint is the effective logos in the thing.

[13]

The primary One cannot be multiple in any way; otherwise the multiplicity that is in It would be attached to another, prior One. Rather, It must be one unadulterated Good. And It must be the Creator of a thing that is one, is good, and has the form of goodness, either as an imprint from the primary Creator, or as the imprint of Its imprint.

The imprint of the Creator is the intellect, and the imprint of the intellect is life. And life is also intellect, just as the imprint of fire is also fire.

However, it is not necessary that what is in the imprint is what is in that which makes the imprint, or what is not in it. That is because the primary imprinter is one, whereas its imprint is the intellect, and the intellect is two, because it is created, and the created as after the creator.

The imprint of the intellect is the soul, and in the intellect is what is in the soul, but there is in the soul what is not in the intellect. That is because the soul is more than two. For that reason, the soul comes to have predilections and act independently. Its independent action is its thought.

Each individual form continues to leave an imprint—and the imprints are more numerous than the form—until it comes to an imprint that does not itself leave an imprint on anything. So the first original imprints but is not imprinted, and the last thing is an imprint that does not make an imprint. And whatever is between the imprinter and the imprinted imprints what is below it and is imprinted by what is above it.

However, the first imprint, which is the intellect, operates an intellectual operation characterized by regularity without any deviation whatsoever, because it is an imprint from an absolutely motionless imprinter.

The second imprint, though, which is the soul, operates a psychological operation that is somewhat predisposed, since it is derived from an imprinter that is in motion. So the soul becomes the thinker.

Now the third imprint is the primal celestial noble body, which operates a local operation that is regular within the particular locale. It is only a local operation because it is an imprint from an operation that has a predisposed inclination, even though it is not itself a local operation.

The fourth imprint is the earthly bodies, which operate locally and erratically in place and manner. So they become mutually opposed in positioning and in power.

All the imprints are connected to the initial action, which is the intellect; and the intellect is connected to the Primary Agent, which is the Creator and Preserver of them all, exept that It creates some of them without mediation, and some of them through mediation.

[14]

The Pure Good is the first to pour good upon things and clothe them in good, as the sun clothes physical objects with light, by which they shine.

[15]

The Primary Good is good, pure and simple, not by virtue of connection with something else, because there is nothing else above It. All things are below It, and receive good from It. It is, furthermore, an agent, though Its action is intellect, life, and self, and everything in which there is life and intelligence.

[16]

The further removed a thing is from matter, the greater the good in it. Whatever is close to matter and comes within its domain, the good in it lessens.

[17]

Evil is simply what is outstanding in the last things, which have not received anything from the Primary Good at all. And just as there is nothing else above the Primary Good, so there is nothing else below the evil things.

It should not be supposed that evil is opposite to the Primary Good, because there is no intermediary between them. The Primary Good, therefore, is that which has no opposite. Good either does not exist, or if it does exist, it has no opposite whatsoever. But it is impossible for Good not to exist, because it is the cause of things.

[18]

Asked what he had gotten from his love of knowledge, the Greek Master said, "When I am sorrowful, it is my consolation. When I am having a good time, it is my delight. When I am listless, it is my motivation. When I am energetic, it is my implement. When I am gloomy, it is my light. And when my gloom vanishes, it is my recreation and my pleasure."

[19]

The soul comes from that world to this one, and again from this world to that world.

[20]

Instruction is but reminder; the soul does not remember its state before its descent into the human body; but it does remember its states after its departure from the human body. If it is ignorant and infatuated with the physical nature, it yearns for its former surroundings and grieves intensely. But if it knows the vanity of this world, it rejoices in departure from the body and disdains this world so intensely that it flees to its own world.

Then when it has come to its own world, it remembers something of its former surroundings in this world. It comes to a state where it does not like this world to occur to its mind, because of the vileness and baseness of this world. And it looks upon powers and ideas, which fill it with enthusiasm, joy, and love for contemplation of all forms of knowledge, such that it is as if forgetful of everything of its surroundings in this world.

[21]

In the other world there is no memory, because there is no past and no future there. Rather, all existents and their forms are there at once. Everything the soul did in this world, and everything else with which it was concerned, is as if something present in its essence, by witness and not by memory.

Furthermore, when the soul departs from the physical world, it is united with the intellect, to be purified of the body and the senses, so that the soul and the intellect are as if one thing. Then the forms of all existents are present to it; so there is neither memory nor forgetfulness, but one single knowledge, complete and permanent.

[22]

The soul does not abide endlessly in this world. If this physical world were endless, the soul would remain in it endlessly. However, since the physical world is finite, it is not possible for the soul to abide in it for an endless time, because it makes the journey from the horizon to the center within a finite time.

[23]

In the natures of the things in this world are congruencies and differences, resulting in attraction and repulsion. Real magic is nothing but knowledge of these things within one another.

[24]

When we depart from this earthly world and go to that sublime world and unite with the universal soul, it is not hidden from us who we are, where we came from, where we went, and where we were.

[25]

When a human being is immersed in the desires of the natural body, he does not ascend rapidly. But if one is unattached to these things, and has taken to the intellect, then natural disposition cannot entice one.

[26]

All things are from the Creator, through the generosity thereof; and the first creation therefore is the primordial matter, then the intellect, then the soul, then the nature, then the body.

[27]

The Primal Good is the Creator, Exalted; and everything else is less good than It, to the extent of the intermediaries between them, because whatever is closer to the Exalted Creator has more goodness.

[28]

The Primal Good is that which does not cease to exist. The secondary good is what this Primary Good created, which is the intellect. Then the tertiary good is the soul, with its arrangement winding up in the bodies. So the good in the body is the soul, for without the soul its constituent parts would dissolve and it would not be a body.

[29]

All good comes to things from the Exalted Creator, by emanation and imprinting. So they have no power from primordial matter to preserve the health that is always beneficial to them. Rather, they have to renew it in one condition after another.

PART FIVE

Notes

The following notes from other wisdom traditions are taken from the following sources (all translations mine):

Taoist Huainan Masters: *The Book of Leadership and Strategy: Lessons of the Chinese Masters* (Boston: Shambhala, 1992).
Lao-tzu: *Sex, Health, and Long Life* (Boston: Shambhala, 1994).
Confucius: *The Essential Confucius* (San Francisco: HarperCollins, 1992).
I Ching: *The Essential Confucius* and *The Human Element: A Course in Resourceful Thinking* (Boston: Shambhala, 1994).
Lao-tzu: *Wen-tzu: Understanding the Mysteries* (Boston: Shambhala, 1992).
The Master of Demon Valley and the Master of the Hidden Storehouse: *Thunder in the Sky: Secrets on the Acquisition and Exercise of Power*. In: *Classics of Strategy and Counsel*, vol. II (Boston: Shambhala, 2000).
Taoist master Lui I-ming: *Awakening to the Tao* (Boston: Shambhala, 1988).
Various Zen masters: *Zen Lessons: The Art of Leadership* (Boston: Shambhala, 1989).
Huanchu Daoren: *Back to Beginnings: Reflections on the Tao* (in this volume).
Qur'an: *The Essential Koran* (San Francisco: HarperCollins, 1993).
Muhammad the Prophet: *The Wisdom of the Prophet: Sayings of Muhammad* (Boston: Shambhala, 1994).
Sufi master 'Ali: *Living and Dying with Grace: Counsels of Hadrat 'Ali* (Boston: Shambhala, 1995).

Money

1. Muhammad the Prophet said, "My heirs will not divide up a single coin. Whatever I leave, besides support for my wives and provision for my workers, is charity."

2. Muhammad the Prophet said, "A time is coming to humankind when the individual does not care whether his gains are ethical or ill-gotten."

3. Muhammad the Prophet said, "I dreamed that two men came to me and took me to a holy land, where we went on until we came to a river of blood. In it stood a man. By the river side there was another man, with stones in his hands, facing the man in the river. When the man tried to come out of the river, the other man threw a stone into his mouth and made him go back to where he had been. And he proceeded to throw a stone into the man's mouth each and every time he tried to come out, making him return to the state he had been in. I then asked, 'What is this?' " Then the Prophet explained, "The one I saw in the river was a profiteer."

4. 'Ali said, "The least of your duties to God is that you do not use God's blessings to help you do wrong."

   Muhammad the Prophet said, "If I had a mountain of gold, it would not please me if I still had any of it after three days, except something set aside for debts."

5. Muhammad the Prophet said, "God Most High has said, 'Spend, O child of Adam, and I will spend on you.' "

6. Muhammad the Prophet said, "Every single day the slaves of God pass, two angels come down. One says, 'O God, give every generous one recompense!' The other says, 'O God, give every miser ruination!' "

   'Ali said, "I am the leader of the faithful, while money is the leader of profligates."

7. Muhammad the Prophet said, "No one should envy anyone but two people: someone to whom God has given wealth and who is thus empowered to spend it righteously; and someone to whom God has given wisdom and who judges by it and teaches it."

8. Whenever food was brought to the Prophet Muhammad, he would ask if it was a gift, or alms for charity. If he was told it was alms for charity, the Prophet would tell his companions to eat it, and would not partake of it himself. If he was told it was a gift, he would eat with them.

9. Muhammad the Prophet said, "If someone is given wealth by God but does not pay the welfare tax, on the Day of Resurrection his wealth will be represented to him as a viper encircling him, striking him with two streams of poison. It will seize him by the jaws and say, 'I am your wealth; I am your hoard.' "

Children

1. 'Ali said, "Having a small family is one of two kinds of ease."

2. Lao-tzu said, "People are supple when they are born, and rigid when they die. All beings, even plants and trees, are tender when born and

brittle when they die. So rigidity is the associate of death, flexibility is the associate of life."

4. The Huainan Masters said, "Those who know the source of law and order change to adapt to the times. Those who do not know the source of law and order change with customs. Manners and duties change with customs. Pedants make it their business to follow precedent, preserving the old based on convention, thinking that government is otherwise impossible. This is like trying to put a square peg in a round hole."

Wen-tzu said, "Different ages have different concerns; when times change, customs change. Laws are set up in consideration of the age, works are undertaken according to the time. The laws and measures of ancient rulers were dissimilar, not because they purposely contradicted one another, but because the tasks of their times were different. Therefore they did not take established laws for rules, but took for their rules the reasons why laws were laws, progressively changing along with the development of civilization."

5. 'Ali said, "You are getting enough from your intelligence if it makes plain to you the ways that lead you astray from your integrity."

6. 'Ali said, "Hearts are in fact desirous, preoccupied, and flighty; so approach them by way of their desires and their preoccupations, for the heart goes blind when it is coerced."

Politicians and Philosophers

1. The Huainan Masters said, "The ruler is the mind of the nation. When the mind is orderly, all nodes are calm; when the mind is disturbed, all nodes are deranged."

The Huainan Masters also said, "To indulge the perversities of an individual, thereby increasing troubles throughout the land, is unacceptable to natural reason."

2. The Huainan Masters said, "When political leaders ruin their countries and wreck their lands, themselves to die at others' hands, a laughing-stock of all the world, it is always because of their desires."

3. The Huainan Masters said, "With the art of the Way it is not possible to seek fame through promotion, but it is possible to develop oneself by retirement. It is not possible to gain advantages by it, but it is possible to avoid injuries."

'Ali said, "Is there no free individual who will leave this unswallowed morsel to those who are attached to it? There is no price for your selves but Paradise, so do not sell them for anything else."

4. The Huainan Masters said, "Sages do not need authority to be noble, do not need wealth to be rich, and do not need power to be strong. Peaceful and empty, they are not subject to outside influences."

5. The Huainan Masters said, "Greedy leaders, and harsh rulers oppress

their subjects and bleed their people to satisfy their own interminable desires. Thus the commoners have no way to benefit from the harmony of heaven or walk upon the blessings of earth."

7. The Huainan Masters said, "The military operations of effective leaders are considered philosophically, planned strategically, and supported justly. They are not intended to destroy what exists, but to preserve what is perishing."

'Ali said, "Whoever hurries with the reins of his expectation stumbles because of it."

8. The Huainan Masters said, "Those who used arms in ancient times did not do so to expand their territory or obtain wealth. They did so for the survival and continuity of nations on the brink of destruction and extinction, to settle disorder in the world, and to get rid of what harmed the common people."

The Huainan Masters also said, "Sages' use of arms is like combing hair or thinning sprouts: a few are removed for the benefit of many. There is no harm greater than killing innocent people and supporting unjust rulers. There is no calamity worse than exhausting the world's resources to provide for the desires of an individual."

The Huainan Masters also said, "Those who make war to gain lands cannot fully become kings of those lands, and those who make war in their own interests cannot make their accomplishments stand."

'Ali said, "Pardon is the tax on victory."

'Ali also said, "When you have overpowered an enemy, show him forgiveness out of gratitude for the ability to overpower him."

9. The Huainan Masters said, "Enlightened people are able to criticize rulers when they see a fault, because they are mindless of reprisal. They are able to defer to the wise when they see them, because they are mindless of social status."

Wisdom

1. Confucius said to a pupil, "Do you think I have come to know many things by studying them?" The pupil answered, "Yes, isn't it so?" Confucius said, "No. I penetrate them by their underlying unity."

Lao-tzu said, "There is something undifferentiated prior to the origin of sky and earth; inaccessible, utterly silent, independent and unchanging; it can be considered the matrix of the universe."

2. 'Ali said, "I wonder at the one who doubts God even though he sees God's creation."

'Ali also said, "I know God the Glorified by the nullification of resolutions, the unraveling of arrangements, and the invalidation of intentions."

3. Confucius said, "Be an exemplary man of learning, not a trivial pedant."

4. 'Ali said, "Meditation is a clear mirror."

7. The Huainan Masters said, "Sages emulate Heaven and go along with its conditions."

9. A Buddhist proverb says, "My parents gave birth to me, but my companions raised me."

10. 'Ali said, "Knowledge is better than wealth. Knowledge protects you, while you protect wealth. Wealth is diminished by spending, while knowledge grows by use."

11. 'Ali said, "Know with certain knowledge that God does not grant any mortal—no matter how great his strategy, no matter how intense his seeking, and no matter how powerful his machinations—more than what is determined in the Recollection of Wisdom."

Change

1. 'Ali said, "Destiny is two days; one for you and one against you. So when it is for you, do not be proud or reckless; and when it is against you, then be patient."

The Huainan Masters said, "Sages cannot cause calamity not to come, but they trust themselves not to beckon it. They cannot ensure that fortune will come, but they trust themselves not to repel it. When calamity occurs, it is not that they have sought that whereby it arises; so even in extremity they are not troubled. When fortune occurs, it is not that they have sought that whereby it comes about; so even in success they are not proud."

'Ali said, "Through changes in circumstances the essence of individuals is known."

3. 'Ali said, "I wonder at the proud one, who was a drop of sperm yesterday and will be a rotting corpse tomorrow."

'Ali also said, "So many entertain hopes of what they do not attain, build houses they do not live in, and amass that which they are going to leave behind them."

The Human Soul

1. Zen Master Bankei said, "Hating people or being jealous of them is the condition of hell; anger and rage is the condition of demonia; covetous thoughts full of greed and stinginess are the condition of ghouls. Regretting afterward and longing for what's ahead is folly, the condition of animals. . . . While born in the honorable human state, taking the quality of clarity which discerns good and bad, right and wrong, and turning it into something worthless, is a miserable, pitiful thing."

Confucius said, "You are worthy of the name *human* if you can practice five things in this world: respectfulness, magnanimity, truthfulness, acuity, and generosity."

2. The Taoist adept Liu I-ming wrote, "The reason why people's minds are not clear and their natures are not stable is that they are full of craving and emotion. Add to this eons of mental habit, acquired influences deluding the mind, their outgrowths clogging up the opening of awareness—this is like water being murky, like a mirror being dusty. The original true mind and true essence are totally lost. The feelings and senses are unruly, subject to all kinds of influences, taking in all sorts of things, defiling the mind."

3. The Huainan Masters said, "When the mind neither sorrows nor delights, that is supreme attainment of virtue."

   A Buddhist proverb says, "When you recognize the essence of mind in the midst of the flow, there is no joy, and so sorrow."

4. 'Ali said, "Physical health comes from having little envy."

5 and 6. Confucius said, "Cultivated people have three disciplines. When they are young and their physical energy is not yet stabilized, they are disciplined in matters of sexuality. When they mature and their physical energy is at the peak of strength, they are disciplined in matters of convention. When they are old and their physical energy is in decline, they are disciplined in matters of gain."

   The Huainan Masters said, "The eyes, ears, and palate do not know what to take and what to leave; when the mind governs them, they each find their proper place. Seen from this point of view, it is evident that desire cannot be overcome; yet it can be done to the point where insanity does not occur, by any who master themselves and develop their nature, regulate sexual activity and moderate their dining, make their emotions gentle, and act and rest appropriately."

7. The Huainan Masters said, "The harmonious joyfulness and peaceful calm of ancient sages were their nature."

8. The Huainan Masters said, "What sages learn is to return their nature to the beginning and let the mind travel freely in openness. What developed people learn is to link their nature to vast emptiness and become aware of the silent infinite."

Law

1. The Huainan Masters said, "The eyes are fond of color and form, the ears are fond of voice and sound, the palate is fond of flavor: what enjoys contacts without cognizance of their profit and harm is greed. When you eat what doesn't settle in the stomach, what you listen to does not accord with the Way, and what you look at is unsuited to nature, there are battles at these three points of interaction: what uses duty to assert mastery is mind."

Lao-tzu said: "When the courts are very tidy but the fields are very weedy and the granaries are very empty, to wear colorful clothing and carry sharp swords, to eat to satiation and possess excess wealth, is called the arrogance of thieves."

Muhammad the Prophet said, "A believer eats in one gut, while a disbeliever or a hypocrite eats in seven guts."

'Ali said, "Justice puts things in their places, while generosity takes them out of their domains."

Confucius said of a student who was sleeping in the daytime, "Rotten wood cannot be sculpted, a manure wall cannot be plastered."

'Ali said, "How sleep demolishes the resolutions of the day!"

Lao-tzu said, "The sage avoids the extreme, avoids the grandiose, avoids the extravagant."

2. Lao-tzu said, "Wise people wear rough clothing, concealing a treasure."

Confucius said, "A man who aspires to the Way yet is ashamed of poor clothing and poor food is not worth talking to."

3. Muhammad the Prophet said, "The example of one who observes the ordinances of God and one who disparages them is as that of people who draw lots for places on a ship, and some got the higher places while others got the lower places. Whenever those in the lower places wanted to get water to drink, they made their way past those who were above them. So they said, 'Let us make a hole in our part of the ship, so that we will not trouble those above us.' Now then, if the others let them do what they wanted, it would destroy them all. But if they prevented them from doing so, they would save themselves, and would save everyone."

4. Wen-tzu said, "When human leaders determine laws, they should first apply them to themselves, to test and prove them. If a regulation works on the rulers themselves, then it may be enjoined upon the populace. Laws are the plumb lines of the land, the measures used by human leaders, the established rules regulating the unruly."

Self-Destruction

1 and 2. 'Ali said, "Greed motivates without producing, and guarantees without fulfilling. Many a drinker of water chokes before his thirst is quenched, and the greater the importance of that for which one vies, the greater the calamity of losing it. Longing blinds the eye of insight, and good luck comes to the one who does not come after it."

Wen-tzu said, "There are three kinds of death that are not natural passing away. If you drink and eat immoderately and treat the body carelessly and cheaply, then illnesses will kill you. If you are endlessly greedy and ambitious, then penalties will kill you. If you allow small

groups to infringe upon the rights of large masses, and allow the weak to be oppressed by the strong, then weapons will kill you."
3. Lao-tzu said, "Sages want not to want."
4. A Buddhist proverb says, "Bring in a wolf, and it'll crap in the house."

Modesty

1. Lao-tzu said, "Great skillfulness appears clumsy, great surplus is kept out of sight."

    Huanchu Daoren wrote, "To boast of one's work or show off one's literary accomplishment is to base one's person on external things."

    'Ali said, "How many have been lured into destruction by being well treated, have been misled by being protected, have been seduced by being well spoken of!"
2. 'Ali said, "People oppose what they are ignorant about."

    'Ali also said, "Whoever habitually engages in disputation will not see the dawn of his night."
3. 'Ali said, "We are assistants of fate, and our selves are a target of death. So where can you expect permanence when the night and the day do not promote anything without soon turning around and attacking and destroying what they have built, scattering what they have brought together?"
5. 'Ali said, "Whoever gives up saying 'I don't know' has been mortally stricken."
6. Confucius said, "Shall I teach you how to know something? Realize you know it when you know it, and realize you don't know it when you don't."

    Lao-tzu said, "It is excellent to know innocently; it is sick to feign knowledge ignorantly."

Virtue and Action

1. 'Ali said, "Faith is experience by the heart, avowal by the tongue, and action by the limbs."
2. 'Ali said, "Generosity is that which comes from one's own initiative; as for what is given in response to a request, that is either shame or rebuke."
3. Liu I-ming said, "If you cannot even accumulate virtues, how can you presume to imagine realization of the Way?"

    The Huainan Masters said, "There are three dangers in the world. To have many privileges but few virtues is the first danger. To be high in rank but low on ability is the second danger. To receive a large salary without personally accomplishing much is the third danger."

Huanchu Daoren wrote, "Virtue is the master of talent, talent is the servant of virtue. Talent without virtue is like a house where there is no master and the servant manages affairs. How can there be no mischief?"

7. Confucius said, "I have never seen anyone who was firm." Someone named a certain disciple. Confucius said, "He is covetous—how can he be firm?"

'Ali said, "The greedy one is in the shackles of abasement." He also said, "Whoever is full of greed debases himself."

9. 'Ali said, "Understand information you hear with the reasoning of responsibility, not the reasoning of the reporter; for there are many reports of knowledge, but few are responsible."

10. 'Ali said, "Be generous without squandering, appreciate value without being stingy."

Appearance and Reality

1, 2, and 3. 'Ali said, "For those who make their inner thoughts wholesome, God will make their outward manifestations wholesome."

3. 'Ali said, "These hearts weary as the bodies weary, so seek for them rarities of wisdom."

4. 'Ali said, "O God, I take refuge with You from appearing to the public to be better than I am, while my inner mind is repulsive to You for what it conceals."

5. 'Ali said, "There are servants of God whom God favors with blessings for the service of others, and whom God keeps supplied as long as they are generous with what they have." He also said, "Generosity awakens affection more than kinship does."

7. Muhammad the Prophet said, "One who recites the Qur'an is like a citron, whose flavor is good and whose scent is good. One who does not recite the Qur'an is like a date, whose flavor is good but which has no scent. An immoral person who recites the Qur'an is like basil, whose scent is good but whose taste is bitter. An immoral person who does not recite the Qur'an is like the colocynth, whose taste is bitter and which has no scent."

Knowledge and Ignorance

1. 'Ali said, "There is no wealth like intelligence, and no poverty like ignorance." He also said, "You will find the ignorant either remiss or excessive."

6. 'Ali said, "Wisdom stammers in the heart of a hypocrite, until it leaves and comes to rest by its like in the heart of a believer."

Zen Master Fushan said, "The case of those who, while their study has not yet arrived at the Way, still flash their learning and run off at the mouth with intellectual understanding, using eloquence and sharpness of tongue to gain victories, is like outhouses painted vermilion—it only increases the odor."

7. Once Lord Chi Heng was reading a book, when a craftsman said to him, "May I ask what you are reading, sir?" The lord said, "A book of the sages." The craftsman asked, "Are the sages alive?" The lord said, "They are dead." The craftsman remarked, "Then what you are reading is the dregs of the ancients."

Zen Master Huang-po said to a group, "You are all slurping dregs. If you go on like this, where will you have *today?*"

Negativity

1. The *I Ching* says, "Cultivated people eliminate wrath and cupidity." Confucius said, "Petty people are always fretting."

2. 'Ali said, "The greatest wealth is unconcern with people's possessions." He also said, "One who is satisfied with the sustenance God grants him does not grieve over what he has missed."

3. 'Ali said, "Rage is a kind of madness, because the sufferer is regretful; so if he is not regretful, that means his madness is ingrained."

6. 'Ali said, "One who cautions you is as one who brings you good news."

9. Confucius said, "Cultivated people reach upward; petty people reach downward." He also said, "Cultivated people foster what is good in others, not what is bad. Petty people do the opposite."

10. Muhammad the Prophet said, "Good companions and bad companions are like sellers of musk and the furnace of the smithy. You lose nothing from the musk seller, whether you buy some, or smell, or are imbued with its fragrance. The furnace of the smithy, on the other hand, burns your house and your clothes, or you get a noxious odor."

12. 'Ali said, "Words are under your control until you have spoken them; but you come under their control once you have spoken them." He also said, "The heart of the fool is in his mouth."

15. Huanchu Daoren wrote, "Observe people with cool eyes, listen to their words with cool ears. Confront feelings with cool emotions, reflect on principles with a cool mind."

15 and 16. Huanchu Daoren wrote, "When you hear of bad people, don't despise them right away, for their bad repute might be the sputterings of cavilers. When you hear of good people, don't rush to befriend them, because their good repute might have been made up by dishonest people trying to get ahead."

17. 'Ali said, "Forbearance and patience are consonant one with the other; loftiness of aspiration produces them both."

19. 'Ali said, "Anyone who wishes to keep his dignity should give up disputation."

20. The Huainan Masters said, "Praise may cause people trouble; criticism may help them."

Realism

1. 'Ali said, "One who would not receive something anyway would not get it by contrivance." He also said, "Put aside your pride, set down your arrogance, and remember your grave."

2. The *I Ching* says, "Accept others with tolerance, be positive and far-sighted in your endeavors, and you can be impartial and balanced in action."

3 and 4. The Master of Demon Valley said, "Those who speak without seeing what type of person they are talking to will be opposed, and those who speak without finding out the state of mind of the person they are talking to will be denied."

Pleasure

1. The Huainan Masters said, "Those in whom sense overpowers desire flourish, while those in whom desire overpowers sense perish." They also said, "Habitual desires deplete people's energy; likes and dislikes strain people's minds."

2. 'Ali said, "Truth is weighty but wholesome; falsehood is light but poisonous."

3. 'Ali said, "How sleep demolishes the resolutions of the day!"

5. The Huainan Masters said, "The eyes are fond of color and form, the ears are fond of voice and sound, the palate is fond of flavor: what enjoys contacts without cognizance of their profit and harm is greed."

Family and Friends

1. Huanchu Daoren wrote, "There is a true Buddha in family life; there is a real Tao in everyday activities. If people can be sincere and harmonious, promoting communication with a cheerful demeanor and friendly words, that is much better than formal meditation practice."

3. 'Ali said, "Kinship is more in need of friendship than is friendship in need of kinship."

Mind and Matter

1. The Huainan Masters said, "If you set your mind free in tranquillity and relinquish your body in leisure, thereby to await the direction of

nature, spontaneously happy within and free from hurry without, even the magnitude of the universe cannot change you at all; even should the sun and moon be eclipsed, that does not dampen your will. Then you are as if noble even if lowly, and you are as if rich even if poor."

Wen-tzu said, "Those who practiced the Way in ancient times ordered their feelings and nature and governed their mental functions, nurturing them with harmony and keeping them in proportion. Enjoying the Way, they forgot about lowliness; secure in virtue, they forgot about poverty."

2. Wen-tzu said, "Consider the world light, and the spirit is not burdened; consider myriad things slight, and the mind is not confused. Consider life and death equal, and the intellect is not afraid; consider change as sameness, and clarity is not obscured. . . . Those who act justly can be pressed by humanitarianism but cannot be threatened by arms; they can be corrected by righteousness but cannot be hooked by profit. Ideal people will die for justice and cannot be stayed by riches and rank. Those who act justly cannot be intimidated by death."

3. Wen-tzu said, "[Those who practiced the Way in ancient times] considered the world extra and did not try to possess it; they left everyone and everything to themselves and did not seek profit. How could they lose their essential life because of poverty or riches, high or low status?"

4. Wen-tzu said, "The physical body may pass away, but the spirit does not change. Use the unchanging to respond to changes, and there is never any limit. What changes returns to formlessness, while that which does not change lives together with the universe. So what gives birth to life is not itself born; what it gives birth to is what is born. What produces change does not itself change; what it changes is what changes. This is where real people roam, the path of quintessence."

5. The Huainan Masters said, "The vital spirit belongs to heaven, the physical body belongs to earth. When the vital spirit goes home and the physical body returns to its origin, then where is the self?"

6. Wen-tzu said, "The body is the house of life; energy is the basis of life; spirit is the controller of life: if one of these loses its position, all three are injured. Therefore when the spirit is in the lead, the body follows it, with beneficial results; when the body is in the lead, the spirit follows it, with harmful results. Those people whose lives are gluttony and lust are tripped and blinded by power and profit, seduced and charmed by fame and status."

7. 'Ali said, "God has a right in every blessing, and whoever discharges that is given more from it, and whoever shorts that right is in danger of losing the blessing."

8. 'Ali said, "There is no wealth like intelligence."

10. Wen-tzu said, "The physical body may pass away, but the spirit does not change."

Friends and Enemies

1. 'Ali said, "Understanding is what makes relationships."
2. 'Ali said, "How many have been lured into destruction by being well treated, have been misled by being protected, have been seduced by being well spoken of!"
3. Zen Master Yuan-wu said, "In trying to distinguish good people from bad, if you dislike it when they say you are wrong and like it when they follow you, then good and bad cannot be distinguished. Only the wise do not dislike to hear how they are wrong and do not delight in having others go along with them."
4. Zen master Kuei-shan wrote, "Familiarity with the evil increases wrong knowledge and views, day and night creating evil."
5, 6, and 7. Huanchu Daoren wrote, "Flatterers and fawners are like a draft that gets into the flesh; one is harmed unawares."
7. When people praised him to his face, 'Ali said, "O God, You know me better than I do myself, and I know myself better than they do. O God, make us better than they think we are, and forgive us what they do not know."
8 and 9. 'Ali said, "The biggest failures are those who have failed to win friends; but even bigger failures are those who lose what friends they have made." He also said, "One who follows the slanderer loses true friends." He also said, "Friendship is a profitable relationship; and do not trust the disaffected."
10. Asked how he overcame his opponents, 'Ali said, "I never met any man who did not help me against himself."
12. Huanchu Daoren wrote, "When fate slights me in terms of prosperity, I respond by enriching my virtue. When fate belabors me physically, I make up for it by making my mind free. When fate obstructs me by circumstances, I get through by elevating my way of life. What can fate do to me?" He also said, "In adversity, everything that surrounds you is a kind of medicine that helps you refine your conduct."
13. 'Ali said, "Justice is fairness, and goodness is kindness."
14. 'Ali said, "Do not associate with a fool, because he presents his behavior in a favorable light and wishes you would be like him." He also said, "Do not befriend a fool, for he hurts you when he wants to help you. And do not befriend a stingy man, for he will distance himself from you when he is most needed. And do not befriend a profligate, as he will sell you for a trifle. And do not befriend a liar, for he is like a mirage, making the distant seem near to you and the near seem distant."
15. 'Ali said, "Whoever extends wishful thinking spoils action."
16. 'Ali said, "A man's vanity is one of the things that inhibit his intelligence."

Justice

1. Confucius said, "If you would be employed by a just country, it is shameful to be employed by an unjust country." He also said, "Exemplary people understand matters of justice; small people understand matters of profit."

3. The Huainan Masters said, "Humanity and justice are the warp and woof of society; this never changes. If people can assess their abilities and take the time to examine what they do, then even if changes take place daily, that is all right." They also said, "What enables a nation to survive is humanity and justice; what enables people to live is practical virtue. A nation without justice will perish even if it is large; people without good will be wounded even if they are brave."

4. Huanchu Daoren wrote, "Don't be too severe in criticizing people's faults; consider how much they can bear."

Self-Government

1. Zen Master Fo-chih said, "A swift horse can run fast, but does not dare gallop freely because of the bit and halter. When petty people, while obstinate and belligerent, do not indulge their feelings, it is because of punishments and laws. When the flow of consciousness does not dare to cling to objects, this is the power of awareness. If people have no awareness and are unreflective, they are like fast horses with no bit and bridle."

   The Huainan Masters said, "When your spirit rules, your body benefits from obedience to it; when your body is in control, your spirit is harmful by obedience to it."

2. The Huainan Masters said, "Habitual desires deplete people's energy; likes and dislikes strain people's minds. If you don't get rid of them quickly, your will and energy will diminish day by day."

3. Huanchu Daoren said, "When anger or passion boils up, even when we are clearly aware we still go ahead. Who is it that goes ahead? If we can turn our thoughts around in this way, the devil becomes the conscience."

4. The Huainan Masters said, "If you know the vastness of the universe, you cannot be oppressed by death or life. . . . If you know the happiness of the unborn state, you cannot be frightened by death."

5. Zen Master Ming-chiao said, "The study of saints and sages is certainly not fulfilled in one day. When there is not enough time during the day,

continue into the night; accumulate it over the months and years, and it will naturally develop."

6. 'Ali said, "Whoever lets his tongue rule him becomes despicable in his own eyes." He also said, "The heart of the fool is in his mouth, while the tongue of the intelligent man is in his heart."

9. 'Ali said, "Time wears out bodies even as it renews hopes; it brings death nearer and removes aspiration. Whoever takes advantage of it becomes exhausted; whoever lets it slip by toils." He also said, "What a difference there is between two actions: an act whose pleasure departs but whose consequence remains, and an act whose difficulty departs but whose reward remains."

10. The Master of Demon Valley wrote, "The mouth is the door of the mind; the mind is the host of the spirit. Will, intention, joy, desire, thought, worry, knowledge, and planning all go in and out through the door. Therefore they are governed by opening and closing, controlled in their exit and entry."

12. A Zen proverb says, "Once a word enters the public domain, nine horses cannot drag it back."

13. 'Ali said, "This world of yours is more worthless in my eyes than pig entrails in the hand of a leper."

14. 'Ali said, "Endure with the patience of the free, or else forget with the forgetfulness of the ingenuous."

15. 'Ali said, "Do not ask about what does not exist, for there is work for you in what does exist."

16. Huanchu Daoren wrote, "The way to transcend the world is right in the midst of involvement with the world; it is not necessary to cut off human relations to escape society."

18. 'Ali said, "No wealth brings greater return than intelligence. . . . There is no intelligence like good planning, and no high-mindedness like conscience in awe of Truth."

The Life of the World

1. 'Ali said, "One who expects death hastens to good deeds."

2. 'Ali said, "Greed is endless slavery."

4. 'Ali said, "Each breath one takes is a step toward one's destiny." He also said, "The departure is imminent."

5. The Huainan Masters said, "Sages have within them the means to contact higher potential; they do not lose their self-mastery on account of high or low status, poverty or wealth, toil or leisure."

'Ali said, "One who is aggrieved at the world is discontent with the judgment of God, and one who complains about misfortunes that befall him is complaining about his Lord."

Spiritual Perception

2. This allegory attributed to Pythagoras is analogous to the Sufi theme of the King's Son, an archetypal allegory of life in the world as spiritual exile from which the soul can be awakened to seek to return to its origin.

3. Zen Master Tung-shan said, "There is one thing, which supports heaven and earth. It is absolutely black. It is always in the midst of activity, yet activity cannot contain it."

5. 'Ali was asked, "How can God call all creatures to account without being seen by them?" He replied, "Just as God sustains them without being seen by them."

6. The *Qur'an* says, "No vision can comprehend God, but God comprehends all vision. And God is most subtle, perfectly aware."

Political Science

1. Wen-tzu said, "When rulers are wise, they guide and judge fairly; wise and good people are in office, skilled and capable people are at work. Wealth is distributed downward, and all the people are aware of their blessings. When they degenerate, cliques and factions each promote their cronies, discarding public interest for private. With outsiders and insiders overthrowing each other, the positions of power are occupied by the wily and treacherous, while the good and wise remain hidden."

2. 'Ali said, "Whoever sets himself up as a leader of other people should start educating himself before educating others, and let him teach by his conduct before teaching by his tongue."

3. According to the Huainan Masters, a lord asked one of his ministers what made a nation perish. The minister replied, "Numerous victories in numerous wars." The lord said, "A nation is fortunate to win numerous victories in numerous wars—why would it perish thereby?" The minister replied, "When there are repeated wars, the people are weakened; when they score repeated victories, rulers become haughty. Let haughty rulers command weakened people, and rare is the nation that will not perish as a result."

   The Huainan Masters said, "If you indulge desires so much as to lose your essential nature, nothing you do is ever right: to train yourself in this way leads to danger; to govern a nation in this way leads to chaos; to take up arms in this way leads to defeat."

4. The Huainan Masters said, "When the directives of the leadership are ignored because of factionalism, laws are broken out of treachery, intellectuals busy themselves fabricating clever deceits, mettlesome men occupy themselves fighting, administrators monopolize authority, petty bureaucrats hold power, and cliques curry favor to manipulate the leadership. Then, even though the nation may seem to exist, the ancients would have said it has perished."

   The Huainan Masters also said, "When the territory is large because of virtue and the leadership is honored because of virtue, that is best. When the territory is large because of justice and the leadership is honored because of justice, that is next best. When the territory is large because of strength and the leadership is honored because of strength, that is lowest."

6. The Huainan Masters said, "The customs of a decadent society use cunning and deceit to dress up the useless."

8. The Master of Demon Valley said, "When you apprehend people's feelings and states of mind, then you can use your arts masterfully. Applying this method, you can put people off and can bring them in; you can form ties with people, and can separate yourself from them. Therefore, when sages set things up, they use this means to get to know people beforehand and establish solidarity with them. Based on reason, virtue, humanity, justice, courtesy, and culture, they figure out plans."

11. 'Ali said, "When you have overpowered an enemy, show him forgiveness out of gratitude for the ability to overpower him." He also said, "The foremost of people in forgiveness is the most powerful of them in punishment."

12. The Master of the Hidden Storehouse said, "When trust is complete, the world is secure. When trust is lost, the world is dangerous. When the common people labor diligently and yet their money and goods run out, then contentious and antagonistic attitudes arise, and people do not trust each other. When people do not trust each other, this is due to unfairness in government practices. When there is unfairness in government practices, this is the fault of officials. When officials are at fault, penalties and rewards are unequal. When penalties and rewards are unequal, this means the leadership is not conscientious."

13. The Huainan Masters said, "The behavior of sage kings did not hurt the feelings of the people, so even while the kings enjoyed themselves the world was at peace. The evil kings denied the truthful and declared them outlaws, so as the kings enjoyed themselves everything went to ruin."

Speech and Silence

1 and 3. 'Ali said, "Guard your tongue as you guard your gold, for many a word snatches away blessings and brings adversity."

3. The Master of Demon Valley said, "Opening up is to assess people's feelings; shutting down is to make sure of their sincerity."

4. 'Ali said, "Do not say what you do not know, but neither say all of what you do know."

5. Lao-tzu said, "Truthful words are not prettified, prettified words are not truthful." He also said, "Blowhards cannot stand."

Education

1 and 2. Confucius said, "Be an exemplary man of learning, not a trivial pedant."

8. Buddha said, "Whatever knowledge a fool acquires tends to be harmful; it destroys the fool's virtue, going to his head."

Select Bibliography

Glubb, Sir John. *A Short History of the Arab Peoples.* New York: Barnes and Noble, 1995.

Gutas, Dimitri. *Greek Wisdom Literature in Arabic Translation: A Study of the Graeco-Arabic Gnomologia.* New Haven: American Oriental Society, 1975.

Lewis, Bernard. *The Arabs in History.* New York: Harper & Row, 1960.

Maimonides, Moses. *The Guide for the Perplexed.* Translated by M. Friedlander. New York: Dover Publications, 1956.

Maimonides, Obadyah. *The Treatise of the Pool.* Translated by Paul Fenton. London: Octagon Press, 1981.

Palmer, Louis. *Adventures in Afghanistan.* London: Octagon Press, 1990.

Rosenthal, Franz. *Greek Philosophy in the Arab World.* Hampshire, England: Variorum, 1990.

Scott, Ernest. *The People of the Secret.* London: Octagon Press, 1983.

Shah, Idries. *The Sufis.* New York: Doubleday, 1964.

Shah, Ikbal Ali. "Sufism and the Indian Philosophies," in *Sufi Thought and Action.* Assembled by Idries Shah. London: Octagon Press, 1990.

Waddell, Helen. *The Wandering Scholars.* New York, Doubleday, 1955.

THE HUMAN ELEMENT
A Course in Resourceful Thinking

INTRODUCTION

If technology is an embodiment of method, or means, management of human resources can be considered a kind of technology.

From this point of view, it becomes important to look at differences between the technology to be used with machines and the technology to be used with human beings.

Simple as this premise may sound, human beings today are unfortunately found all too often resigned to being treated like machines, if for no other reason than that machines are considered as economically important as human beings.

The deceptive notion that this implies a real and necessary antagonism between technology and humanism, however, is a myth that inhibits the full development of both.

The power of machines seems so great in some areas that it can distract attention from the human elements of their operation, which human elements nevertheless grow *not less* but *more* important in proportion to the power of the machines.

Humanistic arguments against technology, and technological arguments against humanism, are both manifestations of a misplacement of emphasis, and a mistaken belief that the relative importance of these aspects of life rise and fall in an inverse proportion to one another.

Historical processes have resulted in the growth of several bodies of literature dealing with the cultivation of sophistication in recognizing, organizing, and developing human resources. In them are materials that can and do perennially stimulate resourceful thinking in people facing challenging and stressful predicaments.

This literature is about the human element of the total world, the human being as the brain of the material, scientific, and technical body of the world. It is about the evolution and development of the human element in the totality of the life of the world, and how the qualities of these processes are reflected in the experience and ful-fillment of the individual human being.

The humanistic themes of such advanced educational materials, therefore, are not based upon the misconstrued idea of a fundamental antagonism between humanity and technology. This unnecessarily wasteful idea is just a recast of the self-confirming belief that religion and science are doomed, by the very natures of faith and reason, to oppose one another in some way.

In reality, the historical opposition between religion and science, or between humanism and technocracy, has been in the nature of politics and its congeners, not in the inherent essence of what are in reality like brain and body to one another.

Technology is an important, even dominant, element in life today; no sensible humanism can ignore this empirical fact and still hope to fulfill its humanistic aims and ideals in a practical way. Technology is so influential in the whole world today that it affects even those who have never enjoyed its amenities.

Technology is important today, furthermore, not only for today but also for the fact that it will affect all people in the future, both those who do and those who do not enjoy its amenities. This is why the human element in the application and operation of technology does not decrease but increases in importance with the growth of power and sophistication in the technology.

The development and employment of human resources is there-fore of ongoing, increasing, and evolving importance to human soci-ety as technology develops and grows ever more powerful.

When the same technology is used in spite of changing conditions, obsolescence and decline take place. Similarly, when the methods and goals of development and employment of human resources are those of a past no longer producing adequate results for the present and future, the human element begins to lose certain abilities.

One of these abilities is the power to move the evolution of tech-nology forward deliberately, effectively, and meaningfully. Under these conditions, with the gradual dilapidation of that faculty for-merly known in philosophical parlance as free will, the brain eventu-ally begins to lose the ability to keep up with the natural evolution of technology in the laboratory of competitive human behavior.

It has often been assumed that advanced human sciences were al-ways carried out in special milieus such as monasteries or academies, but in reality they were adapted to all walks of life and all sorts of contingencies over centuries of practical application. To the extent that they were subordinated to personal and political ambitions, nevertheless, the human sciences were overexploited but underused.

Nowadays monasteries and academies are largely equivalent to museums. "First establish a firm foothold in daily activities within society," says *The Secret of the Golden Flower*, a textbook of higher psychology written in China at the time of the American Revolution; "only then can you cultivate realization and understand the essence of mind." This new wave of an ancient ocean of teachings heralded the modern dispensation of the perennial Ways.

In America, where the business community is increasingly being asked to assume roles and responsibilities formerly discharged mainly by families, schools, social communities, and governments, it is becoming increasingly imperative to seek the use of whatever may be available to assist the mutual enhancement of individual and group activity, particularly in such a heterogeneous society. The effort required to make the fullest possible use of such materials, furthermore, has in itself the power to develop precisely the sort of constructive versatility that humanity needs to meet the challenges of the twenty-first century.

One of the ironies of history in respect to the great traditions of advanced education is that the potential of their teachings has been regarded as both a blessing and a threat. Just as there have always been individuals and organizations attempting to use the knowledge transmitted in such traditions for the uplift of self and society, there have also been individuals and organizations attempting to use the same knowledge for personal power and control over other people.

This split in the reception of spiritual tradition has often taken place along social and political lines, resulting in what are known as "court" and "field" versions of knowledge and education. Royal and imperial courts of the old world commonly attempted to manipulate philosophy and religion to use for the purpose of consolidation and aggrandizement of their own political power. Workers in the "field" of society at large, in contrast, were more interested in adapting ancient teachings to the needs of contemporary people, both individually and collectively.

This distinction is of critical importance in understanding the different kinds of influence that traditional educational methodologies actually exert in practice. It is also therefore crucial for distinguishing practical applications of those methodologies for the present and future from those belonging to the past.

One of the most significant differences between court and field studies in higher thought is that between the "court" attempt to construct intellectual systems out of ancient classics and the situational "field" use of tested materials to stimulate practical insight and creative thought, fostering pragmatic applications in contemporary life situations and thereby furthering the development of a fertile and resourceful mind.

The literatures on which this course in resourceful thinking draws originated in the ancient Orient, where enormous accomplishments rested on the wealth of human resources. Most of the works cited, furthermore, have been known in the West for more than a century, some for two or more centuries, if often in crude and culturally biased versions. Not only are these literatures therefore naturalized to some degree in the West, but they are also the object today of increasing attention on the part of Western people in all walks of life, including many of those for whom ostensibly ancient or Asian thinking had hitherto seemed irrelevant at best. Each of the four sections draws on a major tradition of practical philosophy; after a general introduction to these ways of thought, actual extracts from important traditional textbooks are translated and interpreted for modern audiences, followed by a brief explanatory bibliography of resources for each tradition.

Confucianism

Confucianism of some sort was the orthodox ideology of China for more than two thousand years. In some forms, Confucianism was tremendously influential in Japan, Korea, and Vietnam as well. Nowadays it is widely recognized in the West that certain aspects of Confucianism subtend the outstanding managerial skills shown by noncommunist Chinese, Japanese, and Koreans.

Ironically, one of the main dicta of Confucianism, that profit is a base motive in comparison with duty and justice, would seem to disqualify it as a useful ideology for business, where it has nevertheless flourished in its own way. While literalistic interpretations of the

Confucian principle may formerly have led Asian governments into disastrously negligent policies toward commerce, nevertheless, the subordination of profit motive to duty and justice does not actually weaken the practicality of Confucianism in the modern world.

This fact can be observed in the exemplary modern Japanese Matsushita business philosophy, formulated on ancient models by the late Matsushita Kōnosuke, who was popularly known as *Keiei no Kamisan*, or "The Genius of Management." His philosophy is based on the idea that industry and business have a duty to fulfill the needs of society, and that profit is legitimate and indeed necessary in that it operates as a means of fulfilling this duty. From such a point of view, to make a fair profit is itself a just duty insofar as it enables an enterprise to continue to serve the public.

In this sense, profit and duty are no longer at odds but even complement one another. The greater the extent to which an enterprise fulfills its just duty of serving the public, the greater its profits; and the greater its profits, the greater the capacity of the enterprise to produce such goods or perform such services as society deems necessary, useful, or desirable.

This sort of "field" Confucianism has always tended to be far more individualistic, varied, pragmatic, and interesting than "court" Confucianism, which relied heavily on authoritarianism and mechanisms of mind control. Communist totalitarianism in China was in fact an extension of this ancient court tradition, even as it pretended to repudiate the past.

Most of the clichés about Confucianism well known in the West come from "court" Confucianism or impressions thereof. This is a result of specific historical conditions, including the remaining force of the very mind-control mechanisms used by ancient courts.

For the purposes pursued in *The Human Element*, sayings of Confucius himself will be taken to stand for the true pulse of this philosophy and the best of what it has to offer any generation that encounters it.

Taoism

Taoism is a general name for the most ancient body of knowledge in East Asia. Legend connects the origins of civilization in Asia to Taoist giants of remote antiquity. Whereas Western scholars following

Chinese court tradition are accustomed to thinking of Taoism as anti-
thetical to Confucianism, orthodox Taoists consider Confucianism to
be an offshoot of an originally unified tradition.

The schism of the ancient tradition into Confucian and Taoist specialties occurred during the first half of the first millennium B.C.E. It
was fostered by pressures mounting along the well-established court/
field division. This split in Chinese culture and society was like a
geological fault along which earthquakes erupted time and again over
the ages.

While Confucianism specialized in social and political studies,
Taoist interests included natural sciences and higher psychology. Although there were many controversies between extremely polarized
factions of Confucians and Taoists, everyone had some exposure to
both traditions, and all people in positions of power studied them
both. In many cases, however, Taoist studies among Confucians and
other secular specialists were kept secret, because the reputation of
Taoist adepts for extraordinary powers was dangerous for lay people
in public life.

Taoism has often been misrepresented as esoteric and otherworldly
because of this secrecy. The political standards of Taoism were so
lofty that they exposed despots of China as the tyrants that they were,
thus also endangering the lives of those who espoused this philosophy. When Confucianism was formally declared the sole orthodox
way of thought by the Chinese government in the second century
B.C.E., the main stream of Taoism went underground until the col-
lapse of the dynasty hundreds of years later.

Taoism reemerged from its privacy into public and political life
near the end of the second century C.E. with unprecedented power. A
secret revolutionary organization led by Taoist healers spread widely
through the countryside, awaiting the moment to overthrow a corrupt and oppressive regime that had been controlling China and
Korea for nearly four hundred years.

Although this movement was betrayed by a traitor and lost its military edge, the shattering force of its residual power played a critical
part in the downfall of the dynasty and the rebirth of a new China.
For a time there was even a separate Taoist state with diplomatic
recognition from the Chinese government.

After the breakup of the Chinese empire in the third century C.E.,
Taoism played several roles in society. Many Chinese Confucian in-

tellectuals, no longer required to maintain the narrow views of the orthodox school of thought, plunged into the broader traditions of Taoism. These thinkers produced vigorous movement in literature and the arts, celebrating a new, more expansive consciousness.

During this period large areas of the old Chinese empire were reconquered or taken anew by smaller nations to the north and west. This political situation allowed for a major influx of shamanistic and Buddhist ideas and practices into China. Taoism played a significant role in absorbing and adapting new currents of thought, developing new institutions and creating new literature to accommodate intellectual and cultural changes.

After China was reunited near the end of the sixth century, Taoism briefly moved to center stage under the resplendent T'ang dynasty (619–905), whose culture amalgamated the results of centuries of international exchange. For a time the Taoist classics were granted the stamp of orthodoxy, and it became possible to qualify for civil service by taking a degree in Taoist studies.

The new official acceptance of Taoism resulted in numerous important findings in researches on ancient Taoism. Less positive was the influence of orthodoxy on the court/field division in Taoist studies. While Taoist churches expanded and Taoist liturgy and literature grew to colossal proportions under royal patronage, the spiritual interest in Taoism drifted away from this formalism. By the end of the T'ang dynasty a new Taoist movement was already emerging in the field, returning to the original principles and practices of ancient Taoism.

After the end of the T'ang dynasty, the next major phase in the development of Chinese culture was the Sung dynasty (960–1278). During the Sung dynasty lively new schools of Confucianism and Taoism emerged with resounding force, championing the ancient classics yet creating radical changes in their exegetical traditions. While these cultural events have puzzled many scholars looking only at Confucianism, there is undeniable evidence that the Sung dynasty revivals of Taoism and Confucianism were both directly stimulated and informed by Ch'an Buddhism.

In spite of its great cultural achievements, Sung dynasty China was ultimately ruined by militarism and overrun by a series of conquerors, culminating in the occupation of the entire country by a dynasty of Mongolian warriors. Although curious and fairly tolerant of different ways of thought, the Mongolian Khans were wary of the political power of organized religion. They destroyed most of the Taoist canon and controlled the Confucians by establishing a radically circumscribed curriculum for the civil service examination system.

These circumstances naturally aggravated the court/field split in both Taoism and Confucianism, with much of the serious spiritual and intellectual activity going underground. In some cases this underground cultural activity was also linked to grass roots liberation movements.

When the Mongolian Khanate was driven from China by the native Ming dynasty in the fourteenth century, the new government repressed these movements as severely as had the Mongols. Far from liberating China from the repressive rule of the Mongolian Khans, the new Ming dynasty focused most of its attention on preserving its own power.

The Ming government continued attempts to control thought, suppressing Buddhism and Taoism and adopting the Khans' measures to restrict the Confucian intelligentsia to a narrow and permanently fixed curriculum. The Manchu Ch'ing dynasty that took over China from the Ming dynasty in the seventeenth century continued these mind-control policies for another three hundred years, all the way into the early twentieth century, leaving an indelible impression on orthodox scholarship in China.

Throughout this difficult history, however, there have always been those who approached the classics without political ambitions but rather for their own personal development, for the improvement of their familial, social, and professional conduct and relationships, for the education and welfare of their communities, and for a sense of connection with a greater reality.

The Book of Change

The *I Ching*, or *The Book of Change*, is one of the oldest and most popular books in the world. Although it is a most ancient sourcebook of both Confucianism and Taoism, antedating both the *Analects* of Confucius and the *Tao Te Ching* of the Taoist ancestor Lao-tzu, *The Book of Change* by itself is so cryptic that these later philosophies are traditionally used to decode it.

The Book of Change in the general form it is known today is approximately three thousand years old. It is the third in a series of such texts, its antecessors supposed by some scholars to have been composed six and twelve hundred years earlier. All three of these *Change* books were associated with the founding of ancient dynasties, whose early kings were tutored by Taoist sages.

The last and most refined of the books of *Change*, which is still in use today, is attributed to the founders of the Chou dynasty, who lived in the twelfth and eleventh centuries B.C.E. These founders, however, were themselves students of a Taoist of towering intellect and colossal knowledge, whose mastery included political and tactical sciences. It is entirely probable, therefore, that *The Book of Change* should really be attributed to the teacher of its reputed authors.

Considered the most profound of the Chinese classics, *The Book of Change* has been interpreted in many different ways, according to each of various schools of thought. Although it has a standard form as a book, there are also numerous traditional systems used for restructuring and reorganizing elements of *The Book of Change* in order to bring out its otherwise hidden dimensions.

Teachings on the Art of War

Because of the attention devoted to social sciences by classical Chinese thinkers, philosophies of conflict and crisis management naturally developed in parallel with the organizational concepts and techniques on which the early successes of civilization were based.

Works on political and military strategy have been traced back to the twelfth century B.C.E., when the original knowledge subtending Taoism, Confucianism, and *The Book of Change* was still preserved in a comprehensive and unified tradition rather than specialized into distinct branches. Focus on political and military strategy naturally sharpened with the decay of the classical Chinese social order from the eighth through the third centuries B.C.E., but the art of war nevertheless remained embedded in one or another framework of broader human science.

Probably the best-known classic on strategic arts is Sun-tzu's *Art of War*, followed by the anonymous mnemonic work *Thirty-six Strategies*. The former text has been known in the West for more than two hundred years and has been translated into several European languages. Both classics have gained widespread attention in the West in recent years. As in their native culture, what is more, both works are understood to relate to other human activities and concerns besides war in a literal sense.

The main difference still existing between Eastern and Western studies of *The Art of War* is that many Westerners omit parallel study of Taoism, Confucianism, and the *I Ching*. This is something unthinkable in the East; it may gradually disappear in the West.

It is for this reason that extracts from *The Art of War* and *Thirty-six Strategies* are included in this workbook in spite of their apparent incongruity. Avoidance of incongruity, both conscious and subconscious, is a universal mental habit that is, unfortunately, regularly targeted for exploitation in strategic warfare. The ability to entertain very different views of reality without mutual interference is therefore not only an avenue to higher intellectual ability but also a prime method of self-defense against the vulnerabilities caused by ignorance, blindness, and sentimental prejudice.

Again, because the commentary throughout the book is intended to stimulate thought rather than delimit meaning, the methodology of the commentary on extracts from *The Art of War* and *Thirty-six Strategies* includes deliberate provocation and radical disillusion. The purpose of this, as with all the commentary in the book, is to extend the horizon of perception and thought by illustrating insights and ideas triggered by contact with perennial observations and ideas.

Confucius

On listening

Confucius said, "Don't promote people just because of what they say. Don't ignore something that is said just because of who says it."

One reason people shouldn't be promoted just because of what they say is that they may be parroting the ideas of others. And yet this is also a reason not to ignore something said just because of who says it. The unifying thread is to focus on ideas rather than personalities.

Conventions

Confucius said, "When everyone dislikes something, examine it. When everyone likes something, examine it."

Spontaneous unanimity is a rare phenomenon. Induced unanimity can conceal latent contradictions and oppositions that may fester and erupt in time. Unanimity may not be the result of an inherent property of the object but may be a result of the desire for confirmation and assurance overriding differences of perception and opinion.

This can turn into an indiscriminate blindness that can be very dangerous; and so both Confucianism and Taoism recommend that when everyone likes or dislikes something, the astute observer should look for the presence of conditioning factors and influences outside the object of approval or disapproval itself. In this way a more objective understanding of the total phenomenon of the trend may be approached. Lao-tzu said, "When 'everyone knows' beauty is beauty, this is ugly; when 'everyone knows' good is good, this is not good."

Talk and Action

Confucius said, "I used to listen to what people said and trusted they would act on their words. Now I listen to what they say and observe whether they act on their words."

A Zen proverb says, "Don't judge others by yourself." It is obviously wrong to project our own shortcomings on others; it is less obviously, but not less actually, wrong to project our own strengths on others. If you unconsciously attribute to others qualities you expect of yourself, this may lead to unreasonable expectations, resulting in failure and disappointment.

Confucius also added to the above remarks, "It was within my power to do this," meaning that he realized he did not have the power to see to it that people did as they said, he had only the power to see for himself whether or not people did as they said. This attitude is not only less of a burden on all concerned, it is more enlightening because less attention is stolen by emotional conflict.

INDIVIDUALISM AND SOCIETY

Confucius said, "Be strict, but not contentious. Associate with others, but do not join factions."

This is a formula for an individualism that is genuinely individualistic without compromising social duty. In this view, to be an individual means to take responsibility for oneself, not to compare oneself with others. Social duty is an acknowledgment of the actual interdependence of all members of society, not the deliberate cooperation of some for their own sake and to the detriment of others.

If it seems extremely difficult to realize these ideals in their pure form, this would be for the basic reason that in this system of thought ideals are conceived to motivate humanity to progress. By reference to ideals, it is believed, people can accustom themselves to a feeling of humility and a sense of inspiration that cannot for all practical purposes be otherwise acquired.

TRUTHFULNESS AND SERIOUSNESS

Confucius said, "When you stand, see truthfulness and seriousness there before you; when you are in a chariot, see truthfulness and seriousness at the reins. Then you can act effectively."

Without truthfulness, seriousness may be little more than an exaggeration of personality or subjective obsession; without seriousness, truthfulness has no way of expression in the world.

Promotions

Confucius said, "Promote the honest over the crooked, and people will go along. Promote the crooked over the honest, and people will not obey."

Confucianism has often been portrayed, from both within and without Chinese tradition, as a philosophy of unquestioning obedience to authority and conformity to the status quo.

Original Confucianism, however, as exemplified by the sayings of Confucius himself, was not like this. Confucius taught thinking people to distinguish natural authority based on moral and mental development from man-made authority based on economic, political, technical, and military development.

It was the cherished vision of Confucius to see natural authority and political authority restored to the original unity in which he believed; therefore he regarded the selection of cabinet members and appointed officials to be the greatest responsibility of the rulership.

Being at the top meant that rulers could actually do very little in the way of seeing to it that things were really done as they were supposed to be; so the empowerment of honest and worthy people to operate a chain of authority was a practical necessity.

This is the crux of the problem of all large organizations, which therefore require the inclusion of human development systems either in their own structures or in their milieus in order to operate successfully in terms of their internal functions and external relations.

Haste and Pettiness

Confucius said, "Do not wish for speed, do not pay heed to small advantages. If you wish for speed you will not succeed, and if you pay heed to small advantages you will not accomplish great things."

This may apply to all sorts of activities and endeavors: creating and maintaining a household, raising children, working at a trade or profession, cultivating the intellectual or artistic sensibilities, pursuing an aim in life. Lao-tzu said, "A great vessel takes a long time to complete."

MAKING MISTAKES

Confucius said, "If you make a mistake and do not correct it, that is called a mistake."

The illustrious Zen master Yuanwu said, "Who makes no mistakes? This is why self-correction is what is valued." Since the mistake is in not correcting a mistake, avoidance mechanisms like self-justification, rationalization, or blaming others turn into worse mistakes than the original mistake. Lao-tzu said, "It is by knowing the sickness of sickness that sages avoid being sick."

SELF-CORRECTION

Confucius said, "If you can correct yourself, what problem would leadership be for you? If you cannot correct yourself, however, what can you do about correcting others?"

Confucius believed, with considerable evidence to back him up, that people tended to disrespect and disobey rulers and officials who did not themselves honor the laws and norms they represented.

On another level, this means that without facing up to your own shortcomings and faults and working out compensation and amendment, you cannot develop the insight into human nature required to be a leader or advisor of others.

WORRY

Confucius said, "Ignoble people are not for positions of authority, because they worry about getting something; and once they have gotten whatever it is they want, then they worry about losing it. As long as they are worried about losing something, there is no telling what they might do."

Please pay particular attention to the conclusion of the argument. According to *The Art of War*, even if you want to defeat opponents, you should not put them in a position where they feel so desperate that they lash out in the blind fury of a cornered or dying beast.

CALMNESS

Confucius said, "Be even-tempered and clear-minded, not always fretting."

Zen masters call this a state of unconcern, or "no-thing." They advise people, furthermore, not to "make a thing of no-thing," for "time and again concern is born of unconcern."

In plain language, evenness of temper and clarity of mind are considered useful states, attained by the practice of calm; but when these states are turned into objects of concern in themselves, this very concern with equanimity and clarity magnifies the influence of disturbance and confusion on the person so concerned.

A BAROMETER

Confucius said, "People make mistakes according to their individual type. When you observe people's errors, you can tell their human character."

This is a particularly useful lesson for people in positions of management and leadership. The least of the benefits of this practice is the transformation of anger and disappointment into knowledge and understanding.

DIFFICULTY AND EASE

Confucius said, "It is better to be easy to work for but hard to please than to be hard to work for but easy to please. To be easy to work for but hard to please means to refuse to be pleased arbitrarily, and to consider individual capacities when delegating tasks. To be hard to work for but easy to please means to be susceptible to being pleased by certain things regardless of whether they are right or wrong, and to expect everything of employees regardless of their individual capacities."

To be exacting without being demanding is a condition of authentic leadership, the mastery of appropriate employment; in everyday terms, choose the right person for the job and it will be done without force or pressure.

To be demanding without being exacting is a symptom of personal intoxication with the power of command; since the attention is mostly on subjective satisfactions, perception of objective realities is unreliable and ineffective.

SERENITY AND ALOOFNESS

Confucius said, "It is better to be serene without aloofness than to be aloof without serenity."

To be serene without aloofness means to be actively involved in the world without being trapped by mundane aggravations; to be aloof without serenity means to aggravate oneself by trying to avoid mundane things.

PEOPLE AND WORDS

Confucius said, "You lose people if you do not talk to those worth talking to; you lose words if you talk to those not worth talking to. The intelligent do not lose people and do not lose words."

It is an interesting exercise to examine oneself in terms of whether one is losing people or losing words. Usually we lose both at one time or another. Something for each individual to note is which kind of loss demands most immediate remedial work. If you find that you tend to lose people, you may need to cultivate the habit of reaching out to what is best in others. If you find that you tend to lose words, you may need to cultivate the habit of silencing impulsiveness in yourself.

GOOD AND BAD

Confucius said, "The best people foster the good in others, not the bad. The worst people foster the bad in others, not the good."

Master this statement and you can dispense with a thousand books on leadership and management.

HUMANNESS

Confucius said, "You are worthy of the name human if you can practice five things in this world: respectfulness, magnanimity, truthfulness, acuity, and generosity."

Confucius regarded humanity, or humaneness, as the cardinal virtue to be practiced in this life, but he found so much depth therein that it was very difficult for him to define his idea of humaneness in all of its particulars. Thus there are many passages in his sayings dealing with this subject but none that go further than this one in specifying those items that distinguish a human from a beast.

JUSTICE

Confucius said, "Avoid both rejection and attachment, and treat people with justice."

Rejection and attachment refer to subjective prejudices, which obstruct the capacity for impartial observation and evaluation. According to a Zen saying, "They are wise who can see what is good about what they dislike and can see what is bad about what they like." But for this impartiality, there is no practical way to treat people justly and without prejudice.

STUDY AND THOUGHT

Confucius said, "Study without thought is blind, thought without study is dangerous."

Without thought, study is not absorbed; without study, thought is uninformed.

INCOMPETENT LEADERSHIP

Confucius said, "If you punish people without having admonished them, this is cruel. If you test them without having instructed them, this is brutal. If you are lax in direction and yet *make deadlines, this is vicious. If you are stingy in giving what is due to others, this is being bureaucratic."*

These remarks are essential reading for people in positions of leadership and command. It is noteworthy that Japanese management of foreign-based branch facilities is often criticized for behavior toward workers contrary to the principles set out here by Confucius. On close examination, this lapse would seem to be due more to Japanese discomfort and reticence in foreign cultural and linguistic milieus than to lack of familiarity with the classical Confucian ideals.

SERIOUSNESS, LOYALTY, AND ENTHUSIASM

Confucius said, "Be dignified, and people will be serious. Be sociable and kind, and people will be loyal. Promote the good, instruct the unskilled, and people will be enthusiastic."

This is a formula for leadership at all levels. Like other such formulas, it is an echo of the central Confucian idea that declarations and regulations are not enough to govern, that leadership needs to embody in itself the conduct it seeks of its people.

DEFERENCE, GENEROSITY, AND JUSTICE

Confucius said, "Be deferential in your own conduct, be respectful in the service of employers, be generous in taking care of people, and be just when employing others."

The communists rejected Confucianism as an ideology of the upper classes. The masses should have been so lucky as to have been ruled by people who really believed in principles of Confucius such as we have here. Confucius directed many of his remarks at the ruling classes because their power made it so urgent that they become civilized and conscientious rather than self-indulgent and rapacious. There are also many remarks, furthermore, that are aimed at helping people do their best in whatever station or walk of life they may be; and this breadth of concern and compassion was indeed one of the marks of leadership in Confucius himself.

HOME, WORK, AND SOCIETY

Confucius said, "Be respectful at home, serious at work, and faithful in human relations."

Any questions?

JUSTICE AND PROFIT

Confucius said, "Superior people understand justice, small people understand profit."

Earlier Chinese classical literature speaks of just profit, or the harmonization of justice and profit: "Justice is the root of profit." By the time of Confucius the alienation of justice and profit had reached the stage illustrated by this statement. The ancient idea was later restored (and expanded) in Chinese Buddhist terminology when the characters for *justice* and *profit* were put together to mean "proper benefit," in reference to the beneficial effects of appropriate practices or actions.

Resources

The Essential Confucius, translated and presented by Thomas Cleary
(San Francisco: Harper San Francisco, 1992). A new collection of
the sayings of Confucius, arranged by topics according to his aphorisms on the I Ching.

I Ching: The Tao of Organization, translated by Thomas Cleary (Boston: Shambhala Publications, 1988). A basic textbook of neo-
Confucianism by Cheng Yi, one of the founders and greatest masters of the neo-Confucian movement.

Worldly Wisdom: Confucian Teachings of the Ming Dynasty, translated and edited by J. C. Cleary (Boston: Shambhala Publications,
1991). A collection of sayings of later neo-Confucian practitioners.

Zen Lessons: The Art of Leadership, translated by Thomas Cleary
(Boston: Shambhala Publications, 1988). A classical compendium
of what might be called Zen Confucianism, writings on parallel
social and spiritual development.

Taoism

DESIRE AND OBSERVATION

Lao-tzu said, "Whenever you are dispassionate, you can thereby observe what is subtle. Whenever you have desires, you can thereby observe what you seek."

Quasi mystics take detachment for a resting place; Taoists use it as a way to see. Quasi mystics regard desire as something to avoid; Taoists use it as a way to see. Both ways of seeing are necessary parts of the operation of the complete mind. It is not possible to attain objective understanding without understanding subjectivity; and it is not possible to evaluate subjectivity truthfully without objective understanding.

BLINDERS OF CONVENTION

Lao-tzu said, "When 'everyone knows' that 'good' is 'good,' this is not good."

This is not good because in practice "everyone knows" actually means "everyone thinks." When there is no room for another view and society's mind is closed on a given subject, it has excluded itself from any further understanding or capacity to deal rapidly and effectively with changes and new realities. This is in fact what often happened in China when official ideology was backed by massive institutional enforcement; and this is why Taoism often had to work outside conventional channels or else invent new modes of expression as yet unshackled by "everybody knows" conservatism.

CONTINUING SUCCESS

Lao-tzu said, "All beings work. If they are not possessive or presumptuous in the way they live and act, and they do not dwell

*on their own successes, then this will ensure continuing suc-
cess."*

Squandering the fruits of success is one way of failure. Personal
wealth is squandered by greed; social wealth is squandered by arrogance.

BLOWHARDS

*Lao-tzu said, "Big talkers reach the end of their wits over and
over again. It is better to remain centered."*

We all know people whose mouths seem to work faster than their
minds. Lao-tzu also says that trust is lost by placing too much faith
in words. Other aspects of effective action may be lost as well if talk
itself becomes the center of attraction.

SURVIVAL AND FULFILLMENT

*Lao-tzu said, "Sages go first by putting themselves last, survive
by disregarding themselves. It is by their selflessness that they
manage to fulfill themselves."*

Lao-tzu's formula for being invulnerable is to avoid contention: "Just
because I contend with no one, no one can contend with me." Far
from being passive and ineffective, as aggressive people are often inclined to believe of it, this Taoist noncontention is a tremendously
powerful and efficient manner of dealing with the world. As Lao-tzu
also says, the flexible are strong, the stiff snap.

FORMS OF GOODNESS

*Lao-tzu said, "Goodness in words means being trustworthy.
Goodness in government means being orderly. Goodness in
work means being capable. Goodness in action means being
timely. Yet extremes are avoided only by not being contentious."*

Among the most popular clichés about so-called philosophical Taoism is that it rejects Confucian morality and preaches habitual disen-
gagement or withdrawal from the affairs of the world. Lao-tzu's

sayings on goodness are enough to dismiss this debilitating misconception, which has taken in many Western scholars since the nineteenth century. The characteristic Taoist stamp on the ideas expressed here is in the last statement about avoiding extremes by not being contentious; this is what maintains the goodness of goodness and preserves it from spoilage.

MODERATION

Lao-tzu said, "It is better to stop than to keep on filling."

This is because to keep on filling leads to overflow, waste, and sorrow. If you haven't observed this already, read some history. It hardly matters what nation or epoch you choose, because the principle is illustrated time and again throughout the human story. For some extra poignancy, however, you might want to read up on the introduction and aftermath of a war of your choice. Often it seems that the question is not one of whether this principle of stopping in time applies but a matter of whether it is realized in time.

ACCUMULATING DEBTS

Lao-tzu said, "When the rich upper classes are haughty, their legacy indicts them."

So if you want to understand today's problems, read in them the indictments of former generations. Lao-tzu suggests that we do more than this, however, and go on to remove the arrogance and extremes from our personality inheritance so that the exaggerated pressures of the situations they create may be taken from the backs of our heirs.

UNDERSTANDING AND INNOCENCE

Lao-tzu said, "Can you remain innocent even as understanding reaches everywhere?"

It is essential to encompass both aspects of this saying, innocence and understanding. Innocence that is equivalent to ignorance or naïveté may be an insecure and perilous condition, dependent upon psychological insulation. The real challenge is to be innocent and unaffected in spite of whatever may confront you. Only thus, in fact, can knowledge be safely extended beyond the boundaries of convention.

It may be difficult, for example, to observe human shortcomings and failures without becoming cynical to a degree; it is only by innocence, inward awareness of the sublime origin and latent potential of humanity, that it is possible to understand human weaknesses intimately without losing the constructive indomitability without which such understanding has no practical meaning except ingratitude and despair.

BALANCE

Lao-tzu said, "Both favor and disgrace are upsetting."

Those who are favored are prone to worry that the favor may lapse, and also suffer from the envy of the envious; those who are disgraced worry that the disgrace may never be cleared, and also suffer from the gloating of gloaters.

There is no end of examples and illustrations of this principle, and anyone can and should conduct an independent survey of what happens to people when they are favored and disgraced.

A successful career may be as hard on the body and mind as an unsuccessful one; then even if the origin of the distress may be different in each case, the effective nature of the stress progressively converges on sameness for all.

A primary reason that alcoholism is generally found in its severest forms in the extreme upper and lower ends of any society may be stated by precisely this observation of Lao-tzu that "both favor and disgrace are upsetting."

The great Japanese Zen master Bunan said that the rich suffer from their riches while the poor suffer from their poverty. This is another reflection of the same principle. Strangely, it would seem that it is no easier for the rich to relieve themselves of their riches than it is for the poor to relieve themselves of their poverty.

If this seems like a conundrum, please remember it and think on it from time to time.

It is for this reason that the ancient Taoists considered a just equilibrium in society to be a matter in the category of health and hygiene, not abstract morality; a matter of natural reason, not philosophical rationale.

Egotism

Lao-tzu said, "The reason we have a lot of trouble is that we have selves."

The trouble to which Lao-tzu refers includes everything from the work involved in upkeep of the physical body to the toilsome vexation of trying to assess whatever happens in terms of its benefit or harm to oneself. Curiously, the solution to the problem is not self-denial or self-mortification as usually understood, because these still revolve around self-concern.

What makes this aspect of Taosim seem vague and remote to Westerners is the Judaeo-Christian tendency to moralize issues that Taoists are inclined to view as pragmatic and strategic matters. Step aside for a moment now and then to behold your self in its various inward and outward guises and roles. See this clearly, as though you were observing other people who concealed nothing, and you may very well find that you now know how to know for yourself whether or not you need to do anything about your self.

Getting the Most for Your Money

Lao-tzu said, "By not wanting fullness, it is possible to use to the full and not have to make anew."

Use it at full blast and it wears out fast: body, mind, matter, machine—all burn in the same furnace. The same can be said for human relationships in themselves: given time, like a fruit-bearing tree growing to natural maturity, a relationship may continue unfolding and renewing its development and satisfaction throughout its lifetime; whereas if pushed, pulled, and squeezed for every possible bit of stimulation and gratification at the maximum possible rate, it does not take an imbecile to tell an idiot what will soon become of it.

The Highest Nobility

Lao-tzu said, "Impartiality is the highest nobility."

The nobility of impartiality is concern for objective truth above subjective inclinations. This is a sine qua non of authentic leadership, a quality whose exercise also tends to precipitate reactions by which the real characteristics of subordinates may be known for what they are.

It is not easy to attain impartiality, no matter how attractive the idea may seem. The nobility of impartiality may be so intellectually appealing, for example, as to lead one into the error of equating equality with sameness, or nondiscrimination with being indiscriminate.

One way to begin cultivating objective impartiality without succumbing to false ideas of its nature is by noticing the good in what you dislike and the flaws in what you like, then putting both to one side for the moment and observing what you neither like nor dislike and thus may scarcely ever notice at all.

PERSPECTIVE

Lao-tzu said, "Knowing the constant gives an impartial perspective."

When you measure things in relation to feelings and trends, which inevitably fluctuate and change, being in their context you regard these measurements as durable qualities of whatever you happen to be evaluating. When you understand how changing feelings and trends affect your perceptions of things, however, you come to understand them in a larger context. Then you need not be limited by perceptions corresponding to temporary subjective conditions, and yet you can take them duly into account and not have to ignore them in order to avoid being swayed into biased attitudes.

MISTRUST

Lao-tzu said, "When faith is insufficient and there is mistrust, it is because of placing too much value on words."

When people know that noble sentiments can be parroted and are parroted, and that fine words can be sold and are sold, then they know that they have to look elsewhere for assurances of truthfulness. Then again, when people are more worried about how things are said than about what things are said, their basis of judgment is no longer substantial and their ability to believe is no longer reliable.

INNER WORK

Lao-tzu said, "See the basic, embrace the unspoiled, lessen self-ishness, diminish desire."

It is extremely important to take these as four steps in a natural sequence. This needs to be stressed even if obvious, because the last item of a series tends to be freshest since it is the one most recently seen or heard; and in this case people see "diminish desire" and start to worry, thus spoiling the whole process.

First see the basic; then you can embrace the unspoiled. When you have embraced the unspoiled, you become less selfish. When you are less selfish, you do not want to consume more than you need.

If you attempt to do this backward, trying to make yourself want less and force yourself not to be so selfish, you will probably find that your sense of the unspoiled and perception of the basic are about as keen as the feeling of scratching an itching foot from the outside of your shoe.

ECONOMICS

Lao-tzu said, "Economy is gain, excess is confusion."

Use less and there's more left over. When there are too many concerns, furthermore, choices come to be made for the sake of time, and judgment becomes fragmented thereby.

SOCIETY

Lao-tzu said, "Be tactful and you remain whole."

Lao-tzu does not suggest dishonesty or flattery, methods that dishonest flatterers may call tact but fall far short of what Taoist thinkers meant by this term. A favorite reminder of the Taoist principle of tact is Chuang-tzu's saying that expert tiger keepers know not to feed tigers with live animals or even with whole carcasses, "for fear of the fury of the killing and the rending."

IDEAL PEOPLE

Lao-tzu said, "Ideal people keep on the move by day without leaving their equipment; though they have a look of prosperity, their resting place is transcendent."

Keeping on the move by day means not stagnating in the course of everyday life; and when you do so without leaving your equipment, this means that you do not move or act at random just for the sake of movement and action but always maintain connection with what is of genuine meaning and value.

The ability to preserve this connection with true meaning and value enables the individual to work in the world successfully, but the real source of this success is not a mundane thing. This is why it is not enough to imitate the outwardness of successful people in order to become successful oneself; it is necessary for each individual to personally tap the very source of success.

SAVE OR WASTE

Lao-tzu said, "It is good to save people, so that no one is wasted. It is good to save things, so that nothing is wasted."

According to the Huainan masters—early followers of Lao-tzu who briefly acted as political advisors to a local king in ancient China—equality means that everyone and everything can find a place in society where their specific capacities are usefully engaged; it does not mean that everyone is supposedly regarded as exactly the same. Equality and sameness are not the same thing and are not equal in effective meaning.

When there is too little real diversity in the choices existing within a society or an organization, there tends to be a polarization of conformists and misfits who take conformity and nonconformity to counterproductive levels, resulting in a secondary tension that is not creative but destructive.

When people who are different all strive to do the same thing, the result is not equality but merely that virtually everything except currently "in" convention is neglected, the independent free will of the individual turns into a vestigial organ, and society loses its ability to adapt to changing needs rapidly enough to avoid massive human suffering.

Curing Sickness

Lao-tzu said, "Remove extremes, remove extravagance, remove arrogance."

Traditional Taoist methods for removing extremes, extravagance, and arrogance are noncontention, stopping at sufficiency, and objective self-understanding.

Effectiveness

Lao-tzu said, "The good are effective, that is all; they do not try to grab power thereby. They are effective but not conceited, effective but not proud, effective but not arrogant. They are effective when they have to be, effective but not coercive."

These beautiful lines describe a critical distinction between efficacy and aggression. The effective can win many allies by their effectiveness; the ambitious, conceited, proud, and arrogant can create many enemies by their ambition, conceit, and pride. This is a way of seeing the difference between real leaders and despots.

On one level of interpretation, this statement also describes a method of discerning truth and falsehood in spiritual teachings and teachers; they are supposed to be effective according to necessity, not to become tyrannical captors of lost souls.

Safety

Lao-tzu said, "By knowing when to stop, you are spared from danger."

One of the ways failure tries you is by tempting you to recoup your losses, including loss of face. One of the ways success tries you is by tempting you to forget your limitations and overreach yourself. Whichever way things are breaking for you, by keeping this perspective of knowing when to stop you can avoid the pitfalls of compulsiveness and thus be spared from its dangers.

KNOWLEDGE

Lao-tzu said, "Those who know others are wise, those who know themselves are enlightened."

In *The Art of War*, the master strategist Sun-tzu says that if you know yourself and others, you will never be endangered in battle; if you know yourself but not others, you will win half your battles and lose half; if you do not know yourself or others, you will be in danger in every single battle.

POWER

Lao-tzu said, "Those who overcome others are powerful, those who overcome themselves are strong."

Defining the word *jihād*, meaning "struggle" but usually translated as "holy war" in Western journals, the prophet Muhammad said that the struggle with oppressors is the lesser *jihād*, and the struggle with the cravings of the ego is the greater *jihād*. He is reported to have said, "We return from the lesser struggle to the greater struggle." This principle is of utmost importance for those who attain to success in the world at some time in their lives.

WEALTH

Lao-tzu said, "Those who are contented are rich."

Is it really any wonder when drug addiction is rife at all levels of a society that embraces a culture of craving?

GOVERNMENT AND SERVICE

Lao-tzu said, "In governing people and serving God, nothing compares to frugality."

The church of the early Taoists was roofed with the sky and floored with the earth, heated by the sun and cooled by the wind. And according to the sayings of the early Taoists, the best of the ancient governments were so minimal that the people only heard of them.

Later reformations in religion and politics throughout the world can be seen to have begun by trying to restore this principle and to have ended by trying to forget it.

CHANGE

Lao-tzu said, "The orthodox also becomes unorthodox, the good also becomes ill."

A great deal of time and energy can be lost defending obsolete ways of thinking and acting just because of familiarity and attachment. We may continue to value what was once useful for no other reason than that we have become accustomed to a particular sense of value. One of the most unfortunate perversions of the democratic system is that politicians can exploit sentimental values beyond the point where they have any useful meaning other than this exploitation potential. A truly successful reformer is not one who mollifies popular illusions with spectacular gestures but one who sees the point where right becomes wrong and good becomes ill, making it possible to break the counterproductive force of habit and switch into a progressive and innovative mode.

GOVERNMENT AND PUBLIC MORALE

Lao-tzu said, "People are pure when government is unobtrusive; people are wanting when government is invasive."

Ancient Taoist political theory held that otherwise innocent people would tend to become corrupt when consistently burdened with demands that were extremely difficult for them to fulfill. Confucius also believed that if people were ruled solely by regulations and penalties, they would come to feel no compunction about trying to avoid them, whereas if they were ruled by example, they would obey their leaders without being ordered around.

OBSERVATION

Lao-tzu said, "Observe yourself by yourself, observe the home by the home, observe the region by the region, observe the nation by the nation, observe the world by the world."

To observe yourself by yourself is to understand your own capacities and know the extent to which you are fulfilling them; it is not measuring yourself against an arbitrary standard set up by others for yet others.

To observe the home by the home is to understand the workings of a family in terms of the effective interaction of individuals with each other and with the group as a whole; again, not as compared with what other families could be and do with their resources but with what this particular family could be and do with its own resources.

To observe the region, nation, and world by the region, nation, and world follows the model of the family, involving understanding and appreciation of groups on successively larger scales. To observe each grouping in itself means, for example, to see a society or culture in terms of how it meets its own needs and requirements rather than how its individual elements or mechanisms subjectively compare with isolated elements of other societies or cultures.

One of the most useful but more subtle points of this exercise is to understand how evolutionary development can be deliberately induced without need for competition or contention.

CRIMES, CALAMITIES, AND FAULTS

Lao-tzu said, "No crime is greater than approving of greed, no calamity is greater than being discontent, no fault is greater than being possessive."

Approving of greed is worse than greed itself, because it nullifies the innate sense of unworthiness mature people feel toward greed. Since greed is an exaggeration of desire, which occurs as a natural impulse in all living beings, anyone might be susceptible to greedy thoughts. It is only the recognition of its unworthiness in humanity that prevents greed from turning into rapacity. Discontent breeds when greediness is accepted as a way of life. Possessiveness is an attempt to soothe the discomfort and insecurity of chronic discontent.

For modern Western people born into a mass society, perhaps the most difficult aspect of understanding these Taoist ideas is not the so-called culture gap between East and West; it is simply to give up thinking of these principles as moral sentiments and realize they are just practicalities.

TRUSTWORTHINESS

Lao-tzu said, "The wise keep their faith and do not pressure others."

If you pressure others without keeping your own promises, this will undermine your reputation and make you ineffective as a leader of others.

OVERCOMING THE ADAMANT AND FORCEFUL

Lao-tzu said, "The flexible overcome the adamant, the yielding overcome the forceful."

Rigidity inhibits successful adaptation to changing circumstances; excessive excitement consumes itself and burns itself out.

OPPOSITE WAYS

Lao-tzu said, "The way of heaven is to reduce excess and fill need. The way of men is otherwise, stripping the needy to serve the excessive."

This passage is an illustration of Taoist ideas of good and bad government and taxation.

STIFFNESS AND FLEXIBILITY

Lao-tzu said, "Stiffness is an associate of death, flexibility an associate of life."

If you fail to adapt to changes in the current of trends and events, the consequences can be catastrophic. This is true whether you are concerned with ultimate reality, social reality, or material reality.

SELF-TREATMENT

Lao-tzu said, "The wise know themselves but do not see themselves; they take care of themselves but do not exalt themselves."

In this sense, to know oneself means to understand oneself objectively; not to see oneself means not to regard oneself as the center of attention. To take care of oneself means to attend to the requirements of existence; not to exalt oneself means not to consider this maintenance of oneself an end in itself. One might add, from Zen teaching, that the wise use themselves and are not used by themselves.

THE SICKNESS OF PRESUMPTION

Lao-tzu said, "To presume to know what you do not know is sick. It is possible to avoid sickness only by recognizing the sickness of sickness."

In modern times, criticism has so often degenerated into an instrument of destruction that sight is lost of the constructive aim of authentic criticism. Eventually criticism becomes almost an end in itself, with its other main function being to elevate the opinions of critics to the status of objective facts in the minds of the consuming public.

UNDERESTIMATING OPPONENTS

Lao-tzu said, "No disaster is worse than to underestimate your opponents."

Never believe that what you consider a stupid or unworthy idea cannot dominate the minds of large numbers of people, or that far-reaching power cannot come into the hands of someone you consider a stupid or unworthy person.

VICTORY

Lao-tzu said, "When opposing armies clash, the compassionate are the ones who win."

To get the most out of this statement, think about what it means to win. Think about what it means to win in general, and what it means in each instance where the question of winning or losing arises.

THE EASY WAY

Lao-tzu said, "The most difficult things must be done while they are easy; the greatest things must be done while they are small."

Those who are too big for small things eventually find themselves too small for big things. Those who want to achieve dramatic successes may thereby fail to accomplish what is inconspicuous but necessary.

SHALLOWNESS

Lao-tzu said, "If you agree too easily, you will be little trusted."

Try to please everyone and you wind up pleasing no one. Try to be all things to all people and you wind up able to be nothing to anyone. Treasures are hidden because of their value.

Resources

Back to Beginnings, by Huanchu Daoren, translated by Thomas Cleary (in this volume). Accessible reflections for lay people, re-combining the essences of pristine Taoism and Confucianism.

The Book of Leadership and Strategy, translated and edited by Thomas Cleary (Boston: Shambhala Publications, 1992). Selections from *Huainan-tzu*, one of the most comprehensive works of early Taoism, connecting the development of the individual with that of the family, state, and world.

The Essential Tao, translated and presented by Thomas Cleary (San Francisco: Harper San Francisco, 1992). Taoist translations of *Tao Te Ching* and the essential *Chuang-tzu*, two primary texts of Tao-ism, covering the basic range of classical concepts and practices.

Vitality, Energy, Spirit: A Taoist Sourcebook, translated and edited by Thomas Cleary (Boston: Shambhala Publications, 1991). An exten-sive collection of Taoist materials covering a wide spectrum of de-velopments from the original tradition up to modern times.

Wen-tzu, translated by Thomas Cleary (Boston: Shambhala Publica-tions, 1992). Attributed to Lao-tzu, reputed author of the *Tao Te Ching*, this is one of the last of the classics of the old Taoist tradition, elucidating the principles and practices found in its predecessors.

The Book of Change

Don't deploy a concealed dragon.

In other words, don't deploy a power when it should be hidden. A power should be hidden as long as it is itself immature and insufficient to affect a situation constructively. A power should also be hidden when the time and circumstances are not meet for positive action.

Then again, there is a power that cannot be deliberately used, and yet it is power; therefore it is called a concealed dragon, lying coiled at the root of things.

If power is used too soon, or if there is a deliberate attempt to employ power that can only emerge spontaneously without selfish will, in either case the power is vitiated and may even wane away altogether.

Go back before you have gone too far, and you will have good luck.

When you stray from your path or your purpose, the sooner you wake up to the fact and return to your course, the easier it will become to be successful in your endeavors.

Because errant action derives from errant thought, it is most critical to observe your mental state as the basis of your activities. Then it is much easier to "go back before you have gone too far." A Zen proverb says, "When thinking is sick, stopping is medicine."

It is good to be sensitive, as long as you are sensitive in the right way; you will be lucky if your intentions and your actions are upright.

Sensitivity can mean vulnerability. Then it is important to be carefully aware of the nature and quality of the influences to which you expose yourself or allow yourself to be exposed.

Sensitivity also means the ability to put your energy at the disposal of a source of stimulus or motivation. Here again it is imperative to consider the inward and outward character of the forces to which you make yourself available.

It is the reality of your intention that attunes you to specific influences or forces that affect your action. The test of uprightness, or correctness, is in the objective effect, not the subjective definition.

When you are successful, be modest and do not make an ostentatious display of your achievement. While you are pursuing your aim, furthermore, you should avoid attachment to the means you employ in hopes of attaining the desired end. You should be aware, however, that modesty and detachment will be criticized by petty people.

There is a Zen saying that goes, "The spoils of war are ruined by celebration," meaning that self-congratulation and complacency can easily turn into the dark lining inside a silver cloud.

Addictive behaviors and wild mood swings are specialized manifestations of susceptibility to external influences, being heightened by elation through immodest indulgence in what is sensed as a pleasant experience, followed by depression through the removal of the stimulus or the vitiation of its effect.

You are alarmed when there is a stir, but the effect is good if you use that as a stimulus to bring about improvement.

Because things cannot remain the same forever and must eventually change, it is important to understand the implications of how we react to change. When our sense of security is based entirely on the status quo, on a particular state of affairs external to ourselves, then we can hardly avoid upset when changes take place. Understanding this reaction, we have the option to develop a relationship with the world at large that is more flexible and adaptive, and an inner trust in the power and resourcefulness of the will to live.

Rather than blunt ourselves by trying to control our sensitivity to shock in itself, we can develop sensitivity even further to enhance the educational or inspirational value of slight changes. In this way the evolution of human character and institutions can proceed more smoothly and consciously, without building up unbearable tensions through denial and neglect to a degree where they are liable to burst out so violently as to compromise the future value of the inevitable reaction and adjustment.

Whatever you do, in whatever work you strive, there will always be times when you do not attain your will. This may disturb you, but it will not cripple you as long as you use that disturbance in its proper place as a catalyst for self-understanding and adaptive reaction.

In any relationship, for example, there may be upsets and changes along the way. As in the case of a fevered body, this does not simply mean there is a flaw or malfunction in the system; it also means the system is working to adapt to crises.

Be upright and true, steady and in control.

When you start out on a basis of strength, the orientation of strength is all-important. It is best to master yourself and not to be impulsive in the use of strength.

It is bad luck to ignore what you already have and look for something else.

A Zen proverb says, "Gazing at the moon in the sky, you lose the pearl in your hands." People may overlook their own strengths and capacities at the stage where these endowments are still subtle and as yet undeveloped. Yet it is precisely this stage of dormancy that should be examined if the full potential of the individual is ever to be brought into play. Unless there is an awakening from within, nothing added from outside can complete a human being, as emphasized in the oft-forgotten second half of the famous biblical saying, "You are the salt of the earth: if the salt loses its flavor, what can salt it?"

It bodes well to work together for progress.

Collective effort is especially important when individual power is at a low level. Inwardly, working together means using your own inner resources in a concentrated and directed way; outwardly, it means people cooperating to carry out an undertaking or achieve an aim. When both inward and outward cooperation and coordination are achieved, maximum performance can be realized on both individual and group levels at the same time, in the same endeavor.

It bodes well to be constant in dedication.

Except for unusual cases of grace or inspiration, in most of human life nothing of importance can be achieved without steady application to its accomplishment. When people work faithfully and consistently at a worthy aim over a long period of time, seldom do they fail to attain success; and the entire process also affects the development of human character itself.

You can avoid error if you know when to refrain from action.

Progress and success are not just matters of doing the right thing at the right time. It is not only important to act when it is necessary to do so; it is also important not to act when action is useless or counterindicated. In particular, it is best not to use what strengths you have compulsively as long as they are still immature or unfocused.

When people less capable than you are in need, it is not blameworthy to drop what you happen to be doing in order to help them out; but it is imperative to determine proper measure and avoid excess.

Whatever you are doing may seem to be the most important thing to you at the moment, but in a larger context there may be a greater need for you to help others who are not in a position to help themselves. Since people at home and in society are interdependent upon one another, it is important to consider the balance of self-help and helping others; it is necessary to take care of one's own responsibilities, and it is also essential to do what one can to look after the interests of others. If the one is taken too far, it becomes selfishness and solipsism; if the other is taken too far, it becomes meddling and interference.

When two people have similar qualities but are not developed to the same degree, if they work together as equals it is possible to raise the level of the less-developed partner.

A Zen proverb says, "When water is level, it does not flow." If you see people only in terms of their similarity, you cannot fully appreciate their differences and learn from them; but if you see people only as different, you cannot make full use of the feelings of sympathy and communality that draw people together and make the interaction of their different qualities a constructive force in their mutual evolution.

If you want to achieve your end without error, be careful of how you begin.

Lao-tzu says, "The journey of ten thousand miles begins at the first step." It is not only a matter of having the energy and determination to take a step; it is also crucial to consider the questions of how, when, and where to take that step.

Work on yourself first; take responsibility for your own progress.

At the outset of an undertaking, when there is potential but no momentum, it may be that all you can do at first is to marshal your own resources and try to develop the capacities and qualities you will need along the way. Without a developed framework of support at this stage, you will need to manage yourself and do your own work, under your own steam. If you rely on others before you have consolidated your own strength and awakened your own faculties, you may tend to become dependent and weak.

As standards change, it is imperative to choose wisely. You can be effective at this if you communicate with other people.

Standards of conduct and procedure are originally adopted, then adapted, to answer the needs of specific times and circumstances. Eventually they become customary; then they are taken for granted. Finally they are turned into objects of proprietary interest. At that point, the process of adaptation to change is blocked by conservative sentiments, which cling to the forms of established standards but forget their original meaning and purpose.

As society and environmental conditions nevertheless change, therefore, as they inevitably do, standards must also change. Thus it is important to exercise good judgment in adopting new standards to suit new situations. The most efficient way to accomplish this is through understanding the special needs of the group or the community in the process of evolving new ways of life.

If trouble is stopped at once, there is nothing wrong.

It is unrealistic to imagine that anything will go exactly as you wish or that you will encounter no problems in your activities and undertakings. It may often happen that too much time is spent looking for someone to blame when things unexpectedly go wrong. The important thing in such a case is to stop the problem itself as soon as possible. When it is stopped at once, a problem is no longer a problem; but if the reaction is more emotional than practical, continued recriminations will only make more trouble.

It may be beneficial to undertake a great work, but you will only avoid blame if it turns out very well.

When you have personal power and capacity but lack rank or authority, you may want to do something that is commensurate with your own ability but for which you have no outside support, encouragement, or authorization. In such a case you may well attempt something great, but you should be aware that in the absence of organized backing you will be criticized unless you are unusually successful.

It is unlucky to act on power impetuously.

The greater your personal power, the greater your need and responsibility to yourself and others to keep your self-control and enhance the inner qualities that give meaning and direction to power.

When the time is not yet ripe to act, and you are waiting on the fringes of a situation, you will not go wrong if you remain steady and avoid giving in to impulse.

Timing is an essential ingredient of success, and the successful person is one who knows how to wait for the right time before acting. If your acts are impelled by involvement in a situation you are not ready to handle, or by inward impulses you cannot control, then it will be easy to go wrong.

When there is danger, it is best to desist.

Success depends on acting at the right time and desisting at the right time. When it becomes apparent early on that a course of action will lead into danger, it is better to desist at once than to proceed with vague hopes for the best.

Enjoyment in harmony with others is auspicious.

If you are enjoying yourself while others around you are in distress, or if you delight in what displeases others, your enjoyment is not likely to continue long. Enjoyment in harmony with others means that there is no selfishness, no envy, and no resentment to mar your happiness. Confucius said, "What you do not like yourself, do not pass on to others."

You should not mull over the past. If you feel you have lost yourself, still you should not pursue a false image: then you can recover spontaneously. Seeing evil people, be blameless yourself.

Regret over the past is useless unless it is transformed into knowledge for the future. If you find you have strayed from your real nature or lost your true aim, do not let anxiety impel you to seek at random for something to fill that void. Pursuing a false image will only lead you further astray.

It is good to be prepared. Distractions will make you uneasy.

In any undertaking, intention and effort need to be grounded on a solid foundation before they can be sustained with effect. The groundwork or preparation of intention is self-examination and self-understanding. What are the underlying motives, what are the immediate and final goals? Knowing what you are doing and why you are doing it also forms part of the groundwork of effort, preparing to carry out an undertaking by marshaling and coordinating the necessary psychological, physical, and environmental conditions for success.

This calls for concentration and direct focus on the purpose and process of your endeavor. During this time, concern with extraneous matters saps your energy and causes you to deviate from your purpose. This results in a state of internal discomfort caused by the disparity between your intention and your attention.

Be centered and harmonious.

Being centered means not leaning toward extremes, not becoming unbalanced by an overwhelming predominance of one quality over others. In this way it is possible to achieve inward harmony within the self as well as outward harmony with the world at large. Inward harmony means your own faculties are working together; outward harmony means people are working together. Both of these are essential ingredients of success.

When you are mixed up, be careful, and you can avoid fault.

Sometimes situations are too confused to admit of any positive progress at a given time; under these circumstances, the most that can be hoped for is to avoid error. It is best to recognize such conditions for what they are and to concentrate the attention on preventing mishaps rather than attempt to forge blindly ahead.

There is no regret when you guard the home.

The home is the basis, both metaphorically and literally. External conditions may be unpredictable and unreliable, so guard the home, keeping your inner resources intact, and you have nothing to regret even when things do not go your way.

    Even in the midst of a chaotic society, a stable home can safeguard the sanity and well-being of the people of the family. Similarly, self-mastery can safeguard the integrity and viability of the individual even in the midst of uncertain conditions.

You will be lucky if you proceed without error.

Luck is not something that the successful wait for passively. The successful person is one who beckons luck by meaningful, well-directed effort. When undertakings accurately reflect the needs and demands of the time and circumstances, good luck is nothing mysterious but simply a manifestation of the natural order of things.

Impulsive actions resulting in failure are faulty.

Successful endeavors are the result of strategic planning, adequate preparation, and appropriate timing. An arrow that is loosed before the bow is fully drawn will not likely reach the target; an arrow that is loosed before the aim is made certain will surely fly wide of the mark. When things go wrong, it is easy to blame other people or external conditions; but when failure is due to one's own impulsiveness, the responsibility belongs to oneself alone.

You will be faultless if you avoid association with what is harmful. You will be blameless if you realize the danger and struggle against it.

It is naive to underestimate the influence of the outside world on our character and way of life. Becoming impeccable is not simply a matter of inward cultivation; it also calls for good judgment in respect to the environment within which one chooses to live and work. It is important to be alert and learn to recognize what is harmful in order to be able to take intelligent and effective steps to avoid contact with it if possible or to counteract its negative influences in cases where it cannot be completely avoided.

You will be lucky if you use the appropriate means to return to normalcy, for what blame can there be then?

Sometimes intensity of concentration and effort can lead to an exaggeration or warp in the way you look at things in the course of everyday affairs. Without an overall perspective, therefore, early intimations of success can actually lead you astray from your purpose in life. It is auspicious if you are able to take note of any one-sidedness developing in your character and take appropriate measures to restore a sense of balance and proportion. Then you can be blameless in attitude and conduct.

There is no blame when you act plainly.

Much that is awry in our actions comes from artificiality. When excessive emphasis is placed on appearances at the expense of substance, the ability to act directly from our inner selves is diminished. The result of too much concern with superficials is a kind of alienation that makes it difficult to get down to real issues and to deal meaningfully with underlying realities. The advantage of simplicity is in its directness, enabling us to lay hold of essentials and to avoid being confused by extraneous matters.

You will be blameless if you are impartial toward others.

Many faults and errors derive from subjective biases that prejudice relationships, attitudes, and actions. Likes and dislikes can blind us to what is good in people we dislike as well as to what is bad in people we like. When we cannot deal with people fairly and objectively, we lose contact with the real potential of human interaction and wind up blundering because of our own failure to appreciate the true qualities of the people we encounter in the course of living and working.

If there is no error at the central core, that is auspicious.

External propriety does not compare to inner uprightness. An outward facade of correctness that is not supported by truth in the heart will ultimately prove to be of no lasting worth. A Zen proverb says, "Falsehoods are hard to uphold."

Sensitivity in overseeing is good, beneficial all around.

When overseeing a project, it is essential to be consciously aware of all its requirements and to be sensitive to the quality of work in progress. When it involves overseeing others, it is also important to be sensitive to the individual skills, capacities, and personalities of the workers. In this way sensitivity benefits everyone concerned, leading to success in the task at hand.

You will be blameless if you communicate with sincerity.

Faulty communications result in inefficiency and error. Because of the confusion caused by lack of accurate communication, blame may be assigned arbitrarily, so the real cause of the problem may go undetected. If you communicate sincerely, you can clarify the situation at the outset, thereby avoiding fault and blame in the end.

Balance is correct and brings good fortune.

Extremist tendencies are not found only in political arenas; they generally beckon disaster in any field of endeavor. By maintaining balance and avoiding exaggeration, it is possible to mitigate the effect of negative influences and to avoid backlash against progressive action.

Only small gains can be made in a dangerous position.

Even if you have knowledge and capacity, environmental circumstances, whether human or natural, may limit your practical ability to achieve your goals. Under such conditions, it is better to content yourself with small gains for the time being rather than imperil future possibilities by rash or impetuous undertakings at an inopportune time.

Compassion and cooperation lead to future success.

If those who have greater abilities or are more developed do not make common cause with those of lesser ability or lesser maturity, the group or society cannot make progress as a whole. It is by the sympathetic interaction and sharing of people with different qualities and characteristics that collective development can take place with greatest effect.

Accept others with tolerance, be positive and farsighted in your endeavors, and you can be impartial and balanced in action.

Overall progress in a group, an organization, or a society cannot take place through the actions of an elite acting alone, even if the elite really has superior capacities. It is essential to include the less powerful and less talented so that all can develop through the energy of pooled abilities.

This can only work if solidarity is expressed in understanding and action, in practical undertakings based on a long view. Thus by enlarging the context of understanding what is to be done over time and how it can be accomplished through cooperative effort, inequalities can be transcended and extreme polarization can be avoided.

It is beneficial to be singleminded and reserved.

For successful achievement of an aim, it is helpful to concentrate your attention and husband your energy. When attention is scattered among various concerns and energy is expended on extraneous matters, it is difficult to develop effective degrees of will power and creative vitality.

You will be unlucky if you are too withdrawn.

If you are too passive, or if you are too narrow in your preoccupations or ideas, you will miss opportunities. There may be possibilities of which you cannot avail yourself, simply because of limited perspective and unwillingness to reach forward toward new perceptions of untapped potential.

When action would lead to bad luck, it is beneficial to be firm and abstain, remaining evenminded.

Sometimes excitement or restlessness may lead one into a course of action that reason would indicate inadvisable. It may be that subjective considerations lend compelling appeal to what would appear undesirable to the objective observer. In such cases it is best to be steadfast and not give in to impulse, keeping a level head to avoid unfortunate mistakes.

When isolated, seek support, and regrets disappear.

As social beings, people cannot be completely effective alone. When you are thwarted by isolation and lack of support, you need to find some way of relating with others usefully. As individual beings, people seek inner security in their souls; this is why they search for truth and also why they sometimes accept assurance instead of truth.

Hardship ennobles you. It is beneficial to communicate true sincerity. It is unlucky to be aggressive. If you suffer misfortune because of having been aggressive, you have no one to blame but yourself.

It is easy to resent hardship, but if it is faced squarely with calm determination to overcome it, then it can be a positive experience that helps you grow. If you complain and expect others to take responsibility for what you have to do yourself, you are not dealing with the situation in a truly honest manner. If you react to hardships vengefully, you will run into even more trouble. In that case you may blame others, but it is really your own fault.

When the situation requires gentleness and flexibility, it will not do to be adamant.

A tree that cannot bend in the wind gets broken down or rooted up in a gale. When you are strong, you may unconsciously assume that you can accomplish everything you need to do by means of strength. But there is always a limit to the power of an individual, and there are always situations too delicate to handle with force.

Unless you develop yourself, you cannot be of much help to others.

Good intentions may turn out to be ineffective if you do not have the means to personally see them through. Compassion impels us to try to help our fellow human beings when we see them in need; wisdom tells us what we can do and what we could do, what we need in ourselves in order to be able to really help others.

If you are strong, you will do nothing regrettable as long as you are flexible and balanced.

Power or energy of any kind can lull and intoxicate the unwary, leading to indulgence in the experience of power and energy for the sake of the experience itself. This indulgence can result in a blind and aggressive quest for power and exercise of power, without regard for the rights and feelings of others. The greater the power, the greater the need to temper it with harmony and balance.

Rectitude is auspicious.

When handling power, it is important to avoid becoming so fascinated by it that you begin to feel you can do anything you want without suffering any negative consequences. The more power you command, the more critical the question of how you put it to work. Power without control simply begs the question and creates its own blind momentum. When power is balanced with self-mastery, only then can it be properly directed; power is then the servant and not the master.

When you are on the brink of a difficult situation, people will talk a little, but if you remain centered and relaxed, it will turn out well in the end.

When problems arise, people who are strong and energetic may address them too hastily because of eagerness to effect speedy resolutions. Immediate action may be contraindicated, however, when to become embroiled in a difficult situation would vitiate strength and energy before anything positive can be effectively accomplished.

When you remain for a time on the periphery of such a situation, awaiting the right time to act, it will appear to others that you are doing nothing; and thus they will be inclined to criticize you for negligence or timidity. All will be well in the end, however, if you keep your balance, remain calm and objective, and do not let such complaints impel you into acting prematurely.

Strength should not be used impulsively.

When personal power is in balance, it is stabilized and controlled so that it cannot act out in compulsive behavior. Used flexibly, without adamant aggressiveness, strength is adaptable and responsive, therefore able to harmonize with the needs of the time rather than operate as a self-propelling impulse.

The joy of truthfulness is auspicious; it makes regret vanish.

To please others merely as a ploy to attain personal ends is to play a dangerous game, making your security depend upon deception. The constant effort to maintain deception diverts creative energy and robs the will of freedom. Conversely, to take pleasure in being the recipient of false flattery undermines the conscience and makes the individual dependent upon an unrealistic idea of the self.

You can be impeccable if you see the truth in all situations.

When personal biases and emotional judgments color perceptions, this can result in an unrealistic response that is out of harmony with real needs and thus ineffective or even counterproductive. When the first concern is to see the truth of a situation, whatever it may be, then it becomes possible to address problems or needs in a manner that is accurate and to the point, not distorted by subjective expectations or wishful thinking.

Even if you are not given recognition, keep working sincerely and your heart's desire will come to you. When you are fulfilled, you share with others spontaneously.

Do not be discouraged if others do not understand or acknowledge what you are doing, as long as you are clear about your own purpose. If you continue to make an honest effort, you will surely be rewarded for it. Take care of the cause, and you need not worry about the effect. When you finally succeed in your aim, the results of your efforts will naturally become part of the experience of your associates and other people around you.

An old and enfeebled organization benefits from an infusion of fresh life.

When the inspiration and energy of an enterprise have waned, it may be impossible to regenerate it fully from within. In that case, there is profit in absorbing new inputs, such as fresh ideas and new personnel, in order to revitalize the operation.

If you are inwardly secure, even if people are jealous, luckily they cannot affect you.

When you are insecure in yourself, you may look to others for direction and support. This may be flattering to them, but it increases your inner weakness by habituating you to dependency. When you are inwardly secure, in contrast, people may be resentful and jealous of your independence, but this cannot influence you. Then it is possible to bring forth your abilities to the full without worrying about being resented and ostracized by those who are envious of your success.

When you are in a position of subordinate responsibility, it is good to keep up frequent and honest communications.

In a position of subordinate responsibility, on the one hand you are in charge of those under you, while on the other hand you are answerable to those above you. It is therefore imperative to maintain good relationships with both subordinates and superiors in order that the entire organization or operation run smoothly, with all involved doing their part in a continuum of efficiency.

The key to good relationships is regular communication, and the key to communication is sincerity. By frequent communications it is possible to keep up with changes in conditions, and by sincere honesty it is possible to connect effectively with the minds and hearts of associates.

When you have been thwarted, you will escape calamity if you go back home and live unobtrusively.

It is impossible to win every time, to succeed in all your undertakings, or to have everything your own way. If you are unsuccessful in something and yet adamantly refuse to acknowledge failure or defeat, or if you take on more than you can handle and are unwilling to recognize situations where you cannot prevail, and instead you arrogantly insist on pressing your suit and contending for victory, you may bring disaster on yourself. If you know when you have had enough and accept your limitations honestly and gracefully, resting content with your lot and living within your means, then you can avoid unnecessary trouble and will not be crushed even in defeat.

It is lucky for people to lead each other back to normalcy.

When some aspect of your life has become exaggerated, this in itself will bias any attempts you may make to restore your own balance. It is therefore important to maintain communicative relationships with other people so that through your association you may help each other to rectify your errors and recover normalcy. You will be particularly fortunate in this respect if you can find people who are wiser and more experienced than you are, for their example and influence can be of inestimable value to you in your own development.

If the course of action you have taken turns out to be smooth, you will be lucky only if you are steadfast and inwardly undisturbed by external things.

Whenever the going is easy, you may become prone to complacency. This can lead to carelessness, which in turn makes you susceptible to outside influences. When you are relaxed and unwary, you may be distracted and deflected from your course by the appearance of unforeseen events. Everyone knows the importance of steadfastness and inward fortitude in the midst of difficulty; these qualities are even more important to remember in times of ease, for the very fact that they are readily forgotten in the absence of abrasive conditions. Therefore, when you are on a smooth course you will ultimately be fortunate only if you are careful to avoid being deceived by ease, remaining steady and aloof from outward distractions.

There is nothing wrong with working on yourself alone when necessary, but it does not help those around you just then.

You cannot do for others what you cannot do for yourself, so it is necessary to develop yourself before you can be of genuine help to others. To work on your own development may therefore be in fact altruistic when it appears to be selfish; but at the stage when you are concentrating on self-work, the benefit this may have for others in the future has not yet materialized and is therefore not yet apparent to those around you.

When in an unsettled state, it is well to practice moderation.

If you exercise strength immoderately while in an unsettled condition, you are likely to lose balance and go too far. Even if you have the energy to act, if the situation is uncertain you may misapply your efforts and thereby increase confusion. Therefore it is best to control yourself under such conditions and to avoid acting impulsively.

When inner power begins to manifest outwardly, it is beneficial to be exposed to enlightened guidance.

Power without meaningful direction is worse than weakness, inasmuch as it poses the danger of arbitrary and uncontrolled exercise of force. When energy is built up within you and begins to appear in your outer life, it is especially important to look to worthy exemplars to guide you in its useful employment.

Humble workers who accomplish their end will be lucky.

Humility is a useful quality insofar as it reduces friction. It smooths the path of human relationships and enables you to derive maximum benefit from association with others, freeing you from the baggage of egotistical contentiousness. Humility also allows you to pursue a goal patiently, without being inhibited by making unrealistic demands on yourself.

Elevated to the status of a virtue of value in itself, humility turns into its opposite and becomes a vice. Taking pride in humility cancels its beneficial effects. Therefore effective humility is not that contrived modesty in which one secretly takes pride but is, rather, transcendence of the ego whereby environmental resistance is minimized and undertakings are facilitated. Thus true humility is known by effect, not by appearance.

When it is nearly time to emerge from concealment, do not attempt to effect a hasty correction of affairs.

When reason and justice are suppressed by the brutality of tyrants (be they human, conceptual, or material tyrants), and conditions are such that there is no present possibility of bringing about improvement by overt action, it may be prudent or even necessary to go into hiding.

To go into hiding may mean removing oneself from the thick of things, or it may simply mean keeping one's ideas to oneself. Depending on conditions, it may also mean intelligent dissimulation. In any event, nothing can last forever, including the oppressive power of tyranny; eventually a time must come when the tide turns and there is potential for positive action.

Eagerness for change, however, added to the force of suppressed feelings, may provoke hasty action before the time is quite right. According to a Zen saying, "What has been long neglected cannot be restored immediately; ills that have been accumulating for a long time cannot be cleared away immediately."

If there is no resistance, there is no questioning.

When everything seems to be going your way, you may become complacent and act arbitrarily without feeling any need to question your motives and actions. According to a Zen saying, "Calamity can produce fortune" if one becomes earnest and sincere when faced with difficulties, and "fortune can produce calamity" if one becomes complacent and presumptuous when everything is going smoothly. Thus it is said that "sages have worries all their lives and thus never any trouble."

When you are in the ascendancy, you will be attacked if you do not take precautions; that is unfortunate.

An everyday Japanese proverb says, "The nail that stands out gets hit." This is often used to illustrate the attitude and mechanism of conformism in Japanese society, but it can also be used more generally to illustrate the workings of envy and jealousy. Whenever anyone succeeds at something, or rises to a position of eminence, unfortunately there always seem to be those who attack the successful and strive to encompass their downfall. Understanding this aspect of human psychology, the prudent will be wary of attracting the envy of others. It was for this very reason that ancient Zen masters spoke of eschewing fame and embracing humility.

Turn back on seeing danger.

Ancient Taoist philosophy places great value on knowing when to stop. If you see that a course of action will lead to perilous situations, it is much better to stop and turn back than to proceed blindly ahead hoping for the best. To be safe, therefore, it is important to be able to foresee danger while it is still possible to avert it. This is one of the primary functions of *The Book of Change* itself—honing insight into the nature of events as the working out of predictable processes.

Inflexibility is fatal, too much ambition is dangerous.

If you cannot adapt to changes, you eventually lose contact with the realities of the times. If you are unable to put yourself in others' positions you cannot understand them or communicate with them effectively. Thus inflexibility puts you at a disadvantage in both professional and social life.

This is especially true when you are inflexible in the sense of being adamant about your personal ambitions, insisting on achieving predetermined goals regardless of anything or anyone else. In such a case your ambitions will imperil you because you have no way to avoid head-on confrontations with people or situations that seem to stand in your way.

You cannot be comfortable forever; when hard times come, be steadfast.

Everything is in a state of flux; the fact of life that does not change is change itself. In an unpleasant state of affairs this realization can bring joy; in a pleasant situation this awareness can bring sorrow. It is particularly important to remember the reality of change when things are going well, in order to head off the consequences of the complacency, arrogance, and presumption that can readily develop under such conditions.

There is an ancient maxim of martial artists and strategists that applies just as well to other fields of endeavor: "When you have won, behave as if you had not." When you are successful, if you remember that change comes like the wind and thus consciously avoid falling into routine expectations, then you can be steadfast when hardship and difficulty arise. In this way you will be able to survive well under any circumstances.

It is counterproductive to employ too much strength.

Everything has its proper measure, anything short of which will not do the job and anything beyond which may spoil the result. To use force in a situation that calls for tact ruins harmony; to use strength instead of skill brings on many blunders. The fundamental teaching of *The Book of Change* hinges on the need to temper strength with yielding, moderating firmness with flexibility to achieve an effective balance of complementary qualities.

Use the best of yourself to overcome negative influences.

When you are beset by frustrating problems, it is important to avoid letting them have a decisive influence on your mood, because the frame of mind thus created will tend to beckon its own kind in the form of further frustrations and problems. You will have a better chance of surviving well under negative conditions, and even of ultimately thriving, if you are able to reach into your inner reserves and draw forth your most positive qualities. If you can discover hidden strength untouched by external influences, by nurturing and fostering that strength you may overcome conditions that would otherwise thwart you and inhibit you from fulfillment.

It is good to always be upright when successful.

When success leads to complacency, inflation of the ego, and disregard for others' problems and concerns, then it will eventually turn into failure through loss of the qualities necessary to renew and maintain successful undertakings. Therefore rectitude and honesty are all the more necessary when one becomes successful, to avoid being spoiled by the fruits of success.

As long as you are really alert, there is no worry even if people try to take you unawares.

You cannot necessarily prevent people from behaving in aggressive ways toward you, and you cannot necessarily make yourself invulnerable to attack; but if you are watchful, you can foresee such problems and avoid them by removing yourself from the line of fire before anything serious happens.

When you have great capacity for bearing responsibility, if you have an aim you will be impeccable.

Someone may have a goal without having the means to achieve it; another may have the power to achieve great things without the direction to guide it. The one who has the goal but lacks the means may become an idle dreamer or an embittered failure; the one who has the power but lacks direction may become a bully or a pawn. Only when you have both the capacity to accomplish works and a worthy aim to guide it can you be impeccable in your actions.

Immature people exploit power; mature people do not.

Power is one of the severest tests of character. If it goes to your head, you may become an egotistical tyrant. Power employed to aggrandize individual personalities cannot be used effectively for the benefit of society as a whole. Mature people are those able to master themselves and avoid abuse of power.

Resources

The Buddhist I Ching, by Chih-hsu Ou-i, translated by Thomas
Cleary (Boston: Shambhala Publications, 1987). An analytic interpretation and commentary on the classic from political, social, religious, philosophical, and psychological viewpoints.

I Ching: The Book of Change, translated by Thomas Cleary (Boston:
Shambhala Publications, 1992). A unique translation of the core
text of the classic, with essential commentary and explanation traditionally attributed to Confucius himself. In pocket-book format.

I Ching Mandalas, translated by Thomas Cleary (Boston: Shambhala
Publications, 1988). A set of programs for organizing, analyzing,
reading, and consulting the classic to yield a highly intensified sys-
tems-generating core.

The Taoist I Ching, by Liu I-ming, translated by Thomas Cleary. (Boston: Shambhala Publications, 1986). An in-depth elucidation of the
classic from a pragmatic neo-Taoist point of view. Also includes
"The Confucian Changes," a neo-Taoist explanation of key commentaries attributed to Confucius.

Teachings on the Art of War

Sun-tzu

Flexibility

Sun-tzu said, "Structure your forces strategically, according to what will be beneficial or advantageous."

Keep flexibility in the mechanism of organizational structuring and operation so that setups can shift and regroup with maximum efficiency in response to changes or special needs that arise with time.

Deception

Sun-tzu said, "Warfare involves deception."

In struggle, appear to be as you are not, so that you cannot be pinned down or figured out. Then you deprive opponents of the advantage of knowing what they are facing and what to expect.

Are things as you yourself figure them to be, or do the projections of others enter into the picture? Try to assess what you are projecting as well as what others are projecting.

Does anyone "have your number?" Does anyone *think* they "have your number"? Do you play to that role, that expectation? Do you use that image as a cover, a camouflage? What for? What else could be accomplished in the room left by people who are dealing with an image of you that is only a projection of their expectations?

Suckers Are Made

Sun-tzu said, "Seduce opponents with the prospect of gain, take them by causing confusion."

Here is a general tactic to think about: Make everyone believe there is more to gain by maximum reliance on foreign trade and currency than by maximum self-sufficiency supplemented by foreign trade in essential items lacking in the domestic economy. Compare your ideas of the results and future consequences of the former tactic and the latter policy.

Here are some questions to think about: Do Americans believe it is better to individually pay less for a better foreign product, if by doing so the domestic industry becomes that much less viable? Should the citizens support domestic industry, if it means greater destruction of the environment through backwardness of local standards and technologies?

Considering the fact that there is a price to pay for everything, a minus for every plus, how can issues become confused by isolating one gain or one loss from its total context and magnifying it out of proportion?

ANGER AND DISARRAY

Sun-tzu said, "Anger opponents so as to throw them into disarray."

Making opponents "lose their heads" may be an effective way to diffuse the energy of aggressive people who cannot be successfully met head-on. It may be an effective way to encompass the downfall of the arrogant and complacent.

Consider the energy expended in America on Japan-bashing. This is often an empty and ineffective gesture of frustration. If the same energy were funneled into seeking constructive solutions, there would be a more harmonious situation. A lot of impotent emotion is accepted, nevertheless, because it is useful to politicians as a sideshow for their constituents, in lieu of promising answers to America's loss of face as an industrial power.

Japan would probably rather see America blow off steam consoling itself by Japan-bashing than become more truly competitive. If America is busy enough being angry at others for its own plight, that may well prevent the focus and concentration necessary for genuine solutions from ever developing in the American consciousness.

So when Americans indulge in anger at Japan, they should watch out to see if they are not thereby shooting themselves in the foot with this attitude.

To observe the effects anger has on perceptions, try to cultivate the ability to call up an angry mood at will. There is usually something past or present that you can use to annoy yourself if you think about it. Then use the mood of anger as a lens through which to view other things, and see how they look when you feel this way.

Mastering anger does not necessarily mean suppressing your feelings. Mastering anger first involves understanding how it affects you, learning to take this influence into account, and learning to step aside. By seeing it as a guest and not identifying with it as the host, you can learn to leave anger unused even when it occurs or to divert it to positive inspiration, without losing your effectiveness by expending excess energy on trying to control emotion.

HUMILITY

Sun-tzu said, "Feign humility toward opponents to make them arrogant."

When Japan is self-assertive, America gets furious. When Japan is meek, America becomes arrogant. If Japan does not seem to want to take up a position of political leadership in the world, as America often complains, it might be for the reason that nonassertion seems to the Japanese to be a better method of getting their own way.

FATIGUE

Sun-tzu said, "Tire out opponents by running away from them."

Endless discussions and negotiations in which one side appears to give way but little to nothing actually gets done—this has almost been the norm of U.S.–Japan trade talks.

It probably happens all over the place, a lot of the time. When you see some action, try to determine whether the action is taking place to fulfill its overt function or to make it impossible to do anything else with the time and resources involved.

If it is an interaction, try to find out if all parties see it the same way. If one side thinks the overt aim is the real agenda while the other assumes otherwise, the result can be some fairly comical tragedies and tragic comedies. There again, it depends on the vantage point of the observer.

THIRTY-SIX STRATEGIES

Sneak over the ocean in plain view.

This strategy involves cultivating a facade to the point where it is taken for granted and thus can be used as a cover to accomplish an ulterior purpose.

The contemporary image of Japan as a peaceful, pacifistic country and the image of Japan as a lightweight in international politics are seldom examined for the value they could have to neo-fascists and militarists.

Because of the peaceful, political-lightweight image, it is possible that contrary tendencies in Japanese government and society could be effectively overlooked, or not taken seriously, until they have grown to proportions that are perceptibly difficult to control.

Besiege one party in order to rescue another.

This is a ploy whereby a group enters into a dispute on one side, ostensibly as a defender of a beleaguered party, but really to extend its own sphere of influence.

If a nation can actually contribute to the resolution of socioeconomic problems in foreign locales, it can in effect increase its "territory" with impunity.

If Japan became more independent of the United States in global politics and then went to the aid (as the USSR used to do) of small nations feeling put-upon or exploited by U.S. power, it could increase its sphere of influence under the guise of moral probity.

This is exactly what Japan tried to do with its "Greater East Asia Co-Prosperity Sphere" idea, which was in reality nothing more than a front for Japanese imperialism.

Unlikely as a repeat of the same scheme in the same form may seem to be, the assumption of the impossibility of the unlikely is one of the first omens of defeat in the art of war.

Borrow another's weapon to kill your own enemy.

This means getting someone else to do your fighting for you. When the United States accuses Japan of being a political lightweight, what this often really means is that Japan will not "lend its sword" to the

United States in the arena of global politics to the degree that the United States would like, in view of the actual material power of that sword.

The idea of Japan "accepting its share of the defense burden" could be seen by Japan as an attempt to use it as a "borrowed sword" against enemies of the United States. Japan, however, does not want to be drawn into the middle of political struggles perceived as being in the interests of other nations.

A nation whose economy relies heavily on arms production, on the other hand, might be willing to take up the role of the "borrowed sword" if its military technology has advanced to the point where it feels confident of a favorable cost/benefit ratio.

Confront those who are tired while you yourself are comfortable.

This means that it is advantageous to see to your own security while getting competitors to run themselves ragged.

Compare education and industry in Japan and in the United States, not only from the point of view of what they are accomplishing but also in terms of the relevant moods and attitudes within those concerns themselves as well as in society at large.

Take particular note of the implications inherent in the claim that Japan is securing world leadership in high technology, finance, and management skills.

Confucius said that one should not fret about not being in a position of power but rather worry about how to become actually competent and qualified to handle power usefully. When you are in the position of the weary and others are in the position of ease, it makes no sense to attack; the advice of Confucius is the indicated remedy for this situation.

Observe others' problems from a safe vantage point.

This means to look on from a distance when competitors become embroiled in their own internal problems, waiting for them to fall into such a state of dilapidation that they turn into easy pickings for raiders and scavengers.

It would be interesting, in light of this strategy, to make a comparison of how much economic influence Japan wields in the United

States vis-à-vis how much Japan contributes to the resolution of socioeconomic problems in the United States.

In more general, global terms, how much do nations take advantage of the resources of other nations, how much do nations take advantage of the problems of other nations, and how much do nations contribute to the welfare of other nations?

Conceal aggressive intentions behind an ingratiating facade.

An example of this is the Japanese cultural front as it exists on the level sponsored by nationalistic Japanese interests on the premise that Westerners will not feel so much antipathy toward Japan if they have more knowledge and appreciation of Japanese culture, and presumably will therefore resent Japanese economic power to a lesser extent.

This doesn't always work that well, because Americans are not necessarily thrilled by traditional Japanese high culture, and because Americans are not schooled to think of other cultures as even equal to their own, much less superior and more worthy of a position of global leadership.

Another example of this is found in the Americans who learn some Japanese on the premise that it will be of advantage to them in dealing with Japan. This does not always work very well either, because the Japanese do not necessarily regard gestures made for motives of personal profit to reflect authentic interest in any part of their culture except the financial; and if they cannot discern an individual's motives, they will take steps to find out, or if they haven't time for this, simply shun that person (in reality, if not appearance) just for good measure.

Yet another example is the counterpart of ultranationalist-inspired Japanese studies abroad: the cliché financed by the foreign interest who wishes to appear to be interested in and even sympathetic to Japanese culture while covertly fostering cultural clashes through promotion of less noticeable if no less influential unrealities and biases.

One tree is felled for the sake of another.

One of the organizational strengths the Japanese are often able to muster is represented by this stratagem, which basically means the willingness, or recognition of the necessity, for an individual to make a personal sacrifice in the interests of the group. Although self-sacrifice is a Christian virtue in theory, post-Renaissance individualism and the vast possibilities of territorial expansion in a seemingly endless New World have made it difficult for Westerners, particularly Americans, to muster this particular strength to the degree attained in much older civilizations. This, however, may be expected to change in the future.

Make temporary use of a dead body in order to revive a spirit.

An example of this in Japan is the revival of traditional culture as a focus of national pride, in spite of the fact that traditional culture actually has relatively little to do with everyday life in modern Japan, except for some token observances. This use of fossilized traditional high culture as a pacifier or a decoy to capture or divert the attention of factions within the organizations of political and economic rivals would be another example of this stratagem.

Steal a beam from another's structure to replace a pillar in your own.

This is a classic description of what we call head-hunting. This is not practiced as much within Japanese society as it is within American society, but it is definitely practiced by the Japanese on an international level. Numerous high-ranking persons from among U.S. trade negotiators and the U.S. federal bank system have been very profitably head-hunted by Japanese concerns involved in foreign trade.

Let opponents climb up onto the roof, then take the ladder out from under them.

An example of this would be Japan and other countries taking over the manufacturing sector while the United States turns to the service sector. If service and management are viewed as resting on a foundation and support structure of primary and secondary production (agriculture and industry), the metaphor traditionally used for this stratagem fits so well that it is chilling to contemplate in its actual reality.

Let your fortress appear to be empty.

This refers to feigning weakness or inability so as to mislead opponents as to the nature of the threat against them. An example of this is Japan's apparent acceptance of the political-lightweight role, even focusing attention on this itself by public displays of self-excoriation over its supposed passivity in global politics, all the while wielding vast economic power that cannot in reality be separated from political power.

Employ double agents in your schemes.

Although for some reason this is not formally regarded as employment of double agents, it is well known that powerful Japanese businesses regularly hire Americans formerly employed in critical offices in order to obtain the sensitive information, contacts, and influence necessary to strike deep Japanese roots into the structure of the American economy.

Resources

The Art of War, by Sun-tzu, translated by Thomas Cleary. In: *Classics of Strategy and Counsel*, vol. I (Boston: Shambhala Publications, 2000). Includes eleven classic commentaries, with Taoist introductory material. Also available, abridged, in pocketbook and audiotape formats.

The Book of Five Rings, by Miyamoto Musashi, translated by Thomas Cleary. In: *Classics of Strategy and Counsel*, vol. II (Boston: Shambhala Publications, 2000). A classic on the practice of confrontation and victory, written by the famed seventeenth century duelist and undefeated samurai. Also included is Yagyu Munenori's *Book of Family Traditions on the Art of War*, which emphasizes the spiritual and ethical dimensions of the way of the warrior.

The Japanese Art of War, by Thomas Cleary. In: *Classics of Strategy and Counsel*, vol. II (Boston: Shambhala Publications, 2000). An account of the distinctive peculiarities of martial/strategic traditions in Japan as they developed under the prolonged domination of the military caste.

Mastering the Art of War, by Zhuge Liang and Liu Ji, translated and edited by Thomas Cleary. In: *Classics of Strategy and Counsel*, vol. I (Boston: Shambhala Publications, 2000). Writings on the martial tradition of Sun-tzu by two of the greatest strategist generals in Chinese history, Zhuge Liang and Liu Ji. Includes discussion of organizational principles as well as war stories illustrating the application of strategic concepts.

Thunder in the Sky: Secrets on the Acquisition and Exercise of Power, translated by Thomas Cleary. In: *Classics of Strategy and Counsel*, vol. II Boston: Shambhala Publications, 2000). Presents two secret classics from ancient China on the arts of strategy and leadership, with commentary on the application of these teachings.

BACK TO BEGINNINGS
Reflections on the Tao

Huanchu Daoren

TRANSLATOR'S PREFACE

Back to Beginnings is a collection of meditations on fundamental things in human life. It was written around 1600 by a retired Chinese scholar, Hong Yingming, whose Taoist name, Huanchu Daoren, means "A Wayfarer Back to Beginnings." In it can be seen a form of lay Taoism dating many centuries further back into history, in which the historical and sociological insights of pristine Confucianism were combined with the advanced educational and psychological knowledges and methodologies of Buddhism and Taoism.

Nothing is really known of Huanchu Daoren, except that he wrote the present volume of meditations, which was originally entitled "Vegetable Root Talks," and compiled a collection of stories on the extraordinary deeds of Taoist and Buddhist adepts. He identifies himself as a Confucian, which means that he is a layman; his Taoist epithet, "Back to Beginnings," says in calendrical symbolism that he has passed the age of sixty, has retired from public affairs, and has started a new cycle of life. These are his thoughts on the secrets of serenity and wisdom in a changing world, reflections on the four seasons of a lifetime.

Back to Beginnings

Those who live virtuously may be desolate for a time, but those who depend on flattering the powerful are destitute forever. Awakened people observe what is beyond things and think about life after death, so they would rather experience temporary desolation than permanent destitution.

, , ,

When you are but slightly involved in the world, the effect the world has on you is also slight. When you are deeply enmeshed in affairs, your machinations also deepen. So for enlightened people simplicity is better than refinement, and freedom is better than punctiliousness.

, , ,

The mentality of enlightened people, like the blue of the sky and the light of the sun, is not to be concealed from others. The talents of enlightened people, as gems to be hidden, are not to be easily made known to others.

, , ,

People are considered pure of heart when they do not approach power and pomp; but those who can be near without being affected are the purest of all. People are considered high-minded when they do not know how to plot and contrive; but those who know how yet do not do so are the highest of all.

, , ,

When you are constantly hearing offensive words and always have some irritating matter in mind, only then do you have a whetstone for character development. If you hear only what pleases you, and deal only with what thrills you, then you are burying your life in deadly poison.

, , ,

Even the birds are sad in a violent storm; even the plants are happy on a sunny day. Obviously, heaven and earth cannot do without a moderating force for even a day; the human mind cannot do without a joyful spirit for even a day.

˹ ˌ ˌ

Strong drink, fat meat, and spicy dishes are not really flavorful; true flavor is delicate. Marvels and oddities are not characteristic of completed people; complete people are simply normal.

˹ ˌ ˌ

The universe is silent and unmoving, but the workings of energy never rest, even for a while. The sun and moon are in motion day and night, but their light never changes. So enlightened people should have a sense of urgency when at leisure and a mood of relaxation when they're busy.

˹ ˌ ˌ

Late at night, when everyone is quiet, sit alone and gaze into the mind; then you will notice illusion ending and reality appearing. You gain a great sense of potential in this every time. Once you have noticed reality appearing yet find that illusion is hard to escape, you also find yourself greatly humbled.

˹ ˌ ˌ

Blessings often give rise to injury, so be careful when things are going your way. Success may be achieved after failure, so don't just give up when you've been disappointed.

˹ ˌ ˌ

Those who live simply are often pure, while those who live luxuriously may be slavish and servile. It seems that the will is clarified by plainness, while conduct is ruined by indulgence.

˹ ˌ ˌ

Be open and broad-minded in this life, so that none may bear a complaint against you. Let your generosity continue long after your death, so that people may be satisfied.

, , ,

Where the road is narrow, stop for a moment to let others pass; when there is good food, leave a third of your portion for others to enjoy. This is one good way to live in the world in peace and happiness.

, , ,

There is a true Buddha in family life; there is a real Tao in everyday activities. If people can be sincere and harmonious, promoting communication with a cheerful demeanor and friendly words, that is much better than formal meditation practice.

, , ,

People who are compulsively active are unstable, while those who are addicted to quietude are indifferent. One should have a lively spirit while in the midst of tranquillity; this is the mentality of the enlightened.

, , ,

Don't be too severe in criticizing people's faults; consider how much they can bear. Don't be too lofty in enjoining virtue, so people may be able to follow.

, , ,

A grub in filth is dirty, but it changes into a cicada and sips dew in the autumn breeze. Rotting plants have no luster, but they turn into foxfire and glow in the summer moonlight. So we know that purity emerges from impurity, and light is born from darkness.

, , ,

Conceit and arrogance are acquired states of mind. Conquer acquired states of mind, and basic sanity can unfold. Passion and willfulness are part of false consciousness; erase false consciousness, and true consciousness will appear.

, , ,

Think about food on a full stomach, and you find you don't care about taste. Think of lust after making love, and you find you don't care about sex. Therefore, if people always reflect on the regret they will feel afterward to forestall folly at the moment, they will be stable and will not err in action.

, , ,

When in an important position, do not lose the mood of retirement in the countryside. When at leisure in retreat, keep the affairs of state in mind.

, , ,

One need not necessarily seek success in the world; avoiding mistakes is itself a success. Do not seek gratitude from other people; it is a favor not to be resented.

, , ,

Conscientious diligence is a virtue, but if it is too harsh, it does not bring comfort and joy. Frugality and plainness are noble, but if they are too austere, there is no way to help others.

, , ,

Those who have come to an impasse should examine their original intentions; those who have succeeded should note where they are heading.

, , ,

When the rich and well-established, who should be generous, are instead spiteful and cruel, they make their behavior wretched and base in spite of their wealth and position. When the intellectually brilliant, who should be reserved, instead show off, they are ignorant and foolish in their weakness in spite of their brilliance.

, , ,

After one has been in a lowly position, one knows how dangerous it is to climb to a high place. Once one has been in the dark, one knows how revealing it is to go into the light. Having maintained quietude, one knows how tiring compulsive activity is. Having nurtured silence, one knows how disturbing much talk is.

, , ,

One can shed worldliness after putting down mundane ambitions. One can enter sagehood after putting down spiritual ambitions.

› › ›

Desires do not hurt the mind as much as opinions do. The senses do not hinder enlightenment as much as the intellect does.

› › ›

Human feelings are fickle; the world is full of hazards. When at an impasse, know how to step back. When things are going smoothly, strive to remain deferential.

› › ›

In dealing with petty people, it is easy to be severe with them but hard to avoid despising them. In dealing with superior people, it is easy to be respectful to them but hard to be courteous to them.

› › ›

It is better to be simple and reject intellectualism, to retain one's sanity and return it to the universe. It is better to decline extravagance and be content with plainness, to leave a good name in the world.

› › ›

To conquer demons, first conquer your mind. When the mind is subdued, demons withdraw obediently. To control knaves, first control your own mood. When your mood is balanced, scoundrels cannot get at you.

› › ›

Teaching students is like bringing up a chaste daughter; it is necessary to be strict about where they go and to be careful about who they see. Once they get in with the wrong people, it is like planting bad seed in a clear field; it will be hard to grow a good crop.

› › ›

In matters of desire, don't get hastily involved because of easy availability; once you get involved, you will sink in deeply. In matters of principle, don't back off for fear of difficulty; once you back down, you will lose your ground entirely.

, , ,

Those who are careful take good care of themselves and others as well, careful in every situation. Those who are careless slight themselves and others too, careless in everything. Enlightened people make it a point to be neither too concerned nor too indifferent.

, , ,

To those who approach you with riches, respond with humanity. To those who approach you with rank, respond with justice. Enlightened people are not prisoners of rulers. When people are determined, they can overcome fate; when the will is unified, it can mobilize energy. Enlightened people do not even let nature put them in a set mold.

, , ,

In establishing yourself in society, if you are without nobility of character, it will be like brushing your clothes in the dust or washing your feet in the mud. How can you be free? In your dealings with the world, if you are not deferential, it will be a moth flying into a flame or a ram butting a fence. How can you be at peace?

, , ,

Students need to gather in their vital spirit and set it wholly on one path. If you cultivate personal qualities with your mind focused on success and honor, you will make no real progress. If you read with your interest focused on enjoyment of literary aesthetics, you will not deepen your mind.

, , ,

There is great compassion in everyone; a Buddha and a butcher do not have different minds. There is real enjoyment everywhere, whether in a gilded mansion or in a reed hut. It is just that when one is shrouded by desires and locked up in feelings, one misses what is really there; and that makes all the difference in the world.

, , ,

To develop strength of character and cultivate enlightenment require a degree of aloofness. Once there is fascination, you pursue objects of desire. To help the world or run a state requires a sense of detachment. Once there is attachment, you fall into danger.

, , ,

Good people are calm not only in action; their spirits are gentle even in dreams. Bad people are perverse not only in their deeds; even their voices and laughter are vicious.

, , ,

When the liver is diseased, the eyesight fails; when the kidneys are diseased, the hearing is adversely affected. The disease is not visible, but its effects are. Therefore, enlightened people, wishing to be free from obvious faults, first get rid of hidden faults.

, , ,

There is no greater fortune than having few concerns, no greater misfortune than having many worries. Only those who have suffered over their concerns know the blessing of having few concerns. Only those who have calmed their minds know the misfortune of having many worries.

, , ,

In an orderly era one should be punctilious; in a turbulent era one should be flexible. In a degenerate era one should combine punctiliousness and flexibility. In dealing with good people one should be magnanimous; in dealing with bad people one should be strict. In dealing with average people one should combine magnanimity and strictness.

, , ,

Do not think about whatever service you may have done for others; think about what you may have done to offend them. Don't forget what others have done for you; forget what others have done to offend you.

, , ,

When those who give charity do so without any sense of self-satisfaction and without any thought of reward, even a small gift is great. When those who aid others calculate their own sacrifice and demand gratitude and recompense, even a great gift is small.

, , ,

People's circumstances may be settled or unsettled; how can you guarantee that you alone are settled? Your own feelings may be reasonable or unreasonable; how can you expect others to always be reasonable? It is useful to see things in this light and thereby correct the contradictions in your expectations for yourself and others.

, , ,

Only when your mind is clean are you in a suitable state to read books and study the ancients. Otherwise, when you read of a good deed, you will try to claim it as your own; and when you hear a good saying, you will borrow it to cover your shortcomings. This is like lending weapons to a rebel, or giving supplies to a thief.

, , ,

The extravagant who are rich yet unsatisfied are not as good as the frugal who have more than enough even though they be poor. The talented who work hard and become targets of resentment cannot compare with the inept who take it easy and keep their real nature whole.

, , ,

Those who read books but do not see the wisdom of the sages are slaves of the letter. Those in public office who do not love the people are thieves stealing salaries. Those who teach but do not themselves practice what they teach are mere talkers. Those who try to do successful work without considering development of character will find it insubstantial.

, , ,

In the human mind there is a real book, but it is locked up in fragmentary editions. There is a real melody, but it is obscured by weird songs and ostentatious dances. Students should sweep away externals and directly seek the original; only then will they be really able to experience it and use it.

, , ,

In the mind engaged in struggling with hardship, one always finds something delightful. The sorrow of disappointment arises in the complacency of satisfaction.

, , ,

Wealth, status, honor, and praise that come from enlightened qualities are like flowers in the mountains, growing and blossoming naturally. Those that come from achievements in one's career are like flowers in pots, being moved about, removed, replanted. Those that are gained by temporal power are like flowers in vases, without roots, soon to wilt.

, , ,

When spring comes and the weather warms, the flowers beautify the land and the birds chirp pleasantly. If people who are lucky enough to obtain official positions and be well fed and housed do not make it their concern to establish good education and do good works, even if they live a hundred years, it is as if they had never lived at all.

, , ,

The learned should be vigorous and diligent, but they should also be free-spirited. If they are too rigorous and austere, they have the death-dealing quality of autumn but lack the life-giving quality of spring. How can they develop people then?

, , ,

Those who are really virtuous have no reputation for virtue. Those who establish such a reputation do so for selfish motives. Those who are really skillful have no cunning artifices. Those who employ cunning artifice are inept because of it.

, , ,

There is a kind of vessel that tips over when it is full. A piggy bank is not broken as long as it is empty. So for enlightened people it is better to dwell in nonbeing than in being, better to be lacking than replete.

❜ ❜ ❜

As long as people have not gotten rid of the desire for fame, even if they scorn princehood and content themselves with poverty, they are still captives of the senses. As long as people have not shed impetuous adventurism, even if they help the nation, it is just an exploit.

❜ ❜ ❜

If the mind is illumined, there is clear blue sky in a dark room. If the thoughts are muddled, there are malevolent ghosts in broad daylight.

❜ ❜ ❜

People know that fame and position are pleasant, but they do not know that the pleasure of anonymity is most real. People know that hunger and cold are distressing, but they do not know that the distress of not experiencing cold or hunger is greater.

❜ ❜ ❜

If you fear that people will know if you do something bad, then there is something good in bad. If you are eager for people to know when you do something good, then there is something bad in good.

❜ ❜ ❜

The workings of heaven are unfathomable—sometimes encouraging, sometimes suppressing. All this makes sport of heroes and tumbles the great. Enlightened people take adversity in stride and are prepared for trouble even when at ease; therefore, they are not at the mercy of fate.

❜ ❜ ❜

Those who are harsh and aggressive are like fire, burning whatever they touch. Those who are ungrateful are like ice, chilling whomever they encounter. Those who are obsessive and inflexible are like stagnant water or rotten wood, already void of life. All such people have trouble accomplishing works and extending welfare.

❜ ❜ ❜

One should not seek happiness, just nurture the spirit of joy as the basis of summoning happiness. One should not try to escape misfortune, just get rid of viciousness as a means of avoiding misfortune.

, , ,

If ninety percent of what you say hits the mark, you will not necessarily be praised as exceptional; but if one statement misses the mark, you will be blamed by everyone for this mistake. If nine out of ten plans work, you will not necessarily be considered successful; but when one plan fails, you will be heaped with abuse. Therefore enlightened people prefer silence to impetuosity and ineptitude to cleverness.

, , ,

When the air is warm, there is growth; when it is cold, there is death. Similarly, those who are by nature cold receive little happiness, while those who are warm of heart are richly blessed.

, , ,

The road of truth is broad; set the mind on it, and you feel expansive openness and broad clarity. The road of human desires is narrow; set foot on it, and you see brambles and mire before you.

, , ,

Happiness lasts only for those who achieve it by using both hardship and ease as means of self-cultivation. Knowledge is real only in those who achieve it by investigation in which both doubt and faith play a part.

, , ,

The mind should be emptied, for when it is emptied, truth comes to it. The mind should be fulfilled, for when it is fulfilled, desire for things doesn't enter it.

, , ,

Soil with a lot of manure in it produces abundant crops; water that is too clear has no fish. Therefore, enlightened people should maintain the capacity to accept impurities and should not be solitary perfectionists.

, , ,

Even a wild horse can be tamed; even metal that is difficult to work eventually goes into a mold. If you just take it easy and do not stir yourself, you will never make any progress. It has been said, "It is no disgrace to have many afflictions; I would worry if there never were any afflictions."

, , ,

Even a little greed and selfishness turn strength into weakness, knowledge into ignorance, care into cruelty, and purity into defilement, thus ruining one's character. Therefore, people of old deemed freedom from greed precious, and this is how they got beyond the world.

, , ,

The eyes and ears, seeing and hearing, are external plunderers; emotions, desires, and opinions are internal plunderers. But if the inner mind is awake and alert, sitting aloof in the middle of it all, then these plunderers change and become members of the household.

, , ,

To count on success as yet unattained is not as good as preserving work already accomplished. To regret past mistakes is not as good as preventing future errors.

, , ,

One should be high-minded, but not unrealistic; punctilious, but not picayune. Tastes should be simple, but not too austere; behavior should be strict and clear, but not too severe.

, , ,

When the wind comes to sparse bamboo, the bamboo doesn't keep the sound after the wind has passed. When geese cross a cold pond, the pond doesn't retain their reflection after the geese have gone. Similarly, the minds of enlightened people become manifest when events occur and then become empty when the events are over.

, , ,

Even if you do no work that is particularly lofty or far-reaching, if you can shed mundane feelings, that is a great achievement. Even if you do not strive much for progress in learning, if you can minimize the influence things have on you, you will soar into the realm of sages.

> , , ,

Be chivalrous in dealing with acquaintances; be pure of heart in being yourself.

> , , ,

Do not claim precedence over others for favor or gain; do not lag behind others in doing good works. Do not take more than your share; do not do less than your duty.

> , , ,

Be deferential in dealing with the world; deference is the starting line of progress. Be generous in your treatment of others; helping others is really the basis on which you help yourself.

> , , ,

Shame and disgrace should not be attributed completely to others but should be taken upon oneself as well, so as to conceal one's light and nourish virtue.

> , , ,

In whatever you do, if you leave a sense of incompleteness, then Creation cannot resent you, ghosts and spirits cannot harm you. If you insist on fulfillment in your work and perfection in achievement, you will become either inwardly deranged or outwardly unsettled.

> , , ,

Be pure yet tolerant, benevolent yet decisive, observant yet not intrusive, straightforward yet not stiff. As it is said, the best candy is not too sweet; the best seafood is not too salty.

> , , ,

If a poor house is well kept, or a poor girl well groomed, there is elegance if not beauty. If good people should come upon hard times, why should they immediately give up on themselves?

> , , ,

If you are not lax when at leisure, you will be effective when busy. If you are not absentminded in tranquillity, that will be useful in action. If you are not hypocritical in private, that will show up in public.

, , ,

When thoughts arise, as soon as you sense them heading on the road of desire, bring them right back onto the road of reason. Once they arise, notice them; once you notice them, you can change them. This is the key to turning calamity into fortune, rising from death and returning to life. Don't be careless and indulgent.

, , ,

When your thoughts are perfectly clear in quietude, you see the real substance of the mind. When your mood is serene at leisure, you perceive the real workings of the mind. When you are profoundly calm and aloof, you find the real taste of the mind. Nothing compares to these three ways of observing the mind and realizing enlightenment.

, , ,

Calmness in quietude is not real calm; when you can be calm in the midst of activity, this is the true state of nature. Happiness in comfort is not real happiness; when you can be happy in the midst of hardship, then you see the true potential of the mind.

, , ,

When you sacrifice yourself, do not hesitate; if you keep hesitating, your intention in sacrificing yourself will be disgraced. When you give to others, don't expect any reward; if you expect a reward, your intention in giving will be wrong.

, , ,

When fate slights me in terms of prosperity, I respond by enriching my virtue. When fate belabors me physically, I make up for it by making my mind free. When fate obstructs me by circumstances, I get through by elevating my way of life. What can fate do to me?

, , ,

Upright people have no thought of seeking prosperity; heaven then guides their sincerity through their innocence. Devious people are intent on avoiding misfortune; heaven then takes away their spirit through their obsession. So we can see the workings of heaven are most marvelous; human cleverness is helpless in this regard.

, , ,

If a playgirl becomes a good wife in her later years, her early indiscretions don't matter. If a chaste wife loses her virtue in her later years, that cancels out her former purity. Truly it is well said, "When you observe people, just observe the second half of their lives."

, , ,

If you want to know the bequest of your ancestors, it is what you are enjoying now. You should think about how hard it was to build this up. If you want to know about the welfare of your descendants, it is what you leave them. You should think about how easy it is to lose this.

, , ,

If ordinary people will plant virtues and exercise generosity, they are nobles without rank. If grandees just hanker after power and sell favor, after all they become beggars with titles.

, , ,

Gentlemen who feign goodness are no different from petty people who indulge in evil. Gentlemen who compromise their morals are not as good as lesser people who reform themselves.

, , ,

When a family member has made a mistake, one should neither become enraged nor set it aside lightly. If something is hard to say, hint at it indirectly. If they do not understand today, admonish them again tomorrow. The model for family life is to be like the spring breeze melting ice.

, , ,

If one sees complete fulfillment always in one's heart, there will be nothing defective in all the world. If the mind is kept open and equanimous, there will be no warped feelings in all the world.

, , ,

People who are aloof will always be doubted by those who are obsessive. People who are strict will always be disliked by those who are indulgent. In such situations, enlightened people should never compromise their conduct, yet they should not reveal their sharpness too much either.

, , ,

In adversity, everything that surrounds you is a kind of medicine that helps you refine your conduct, yet you are unaware of it. In pleasant situations, you are faced with weapons that will tear you apart, yet you do not realize it.

, , ,

Those born and raised amid wealth and privilege have desires like a roaring fire, ambitions like fierce flames; if they do not keep some clarity and coolness, that fire and those flames will either burn other people or consume themselves.

, , ,

Once people's hearts are genuine, they can affect the world positively. People who are false have no real self; they are detestable to others and a disgrace to themselves.

, , ,

Culture at its best has nothing extraordinary, just what is appropriate. Personality at its best has nothing unusual, just what is natural.

, , ,

In terms of ephemeral manifestations, even the body passes away, to say nothing of success, fame, wealth, and rank. In terms of reality, all beings are oneself, to say nothing of family members. If people can see through the ephemeral and recognize the real, then they can bear great social responsibilities and at the same time be free from the bonds of the world.

, , ,

Delicious foods are drugs that will inflame the gut and rot the bones, but there is no harm if one eats moderately. Delightful things are all purveyors of destruction and decadence, but there is no regret if one enjoys them moderately.

➤ ➤ ➤

Do not criticize people for minor faults; do not reveal people's secrets; do not remember people's past wrongs. These three things can build character and prevent harm.

➤ ➤ ➤

People should not take self-control lightly, because if they do, things can disturb them, and they have no sense of tranquil stability. People should not be obsessive in attending to affairs, because if they are, they will get bogged down by things and lack freedom and lively vigor.

➤ ➤ ➤

The universe may exist indefinitely, but this body is not obtained a second time; human life only lasts a hundred years at most, and these days slip by easily. Those who would live happily know the joy of having life and remember the sorrow of wasting life.

➤ ➤ ➤

Resentment becomes manifest because of goodwill; so rather than try to get people to exercise goodwill toward you, it is better to forget about both resentment and goodwill. Enmity is based on favor; so rather than try to get people's gratitude, it is better to forget about both enmity and favor.

➤ ➤ ➤

The sicknesses of old age are brought on during one's youth; the troubles of one's declining years are created during one's prime. Therefore, people should be very careful when in full bloom.

➤ ➤ ➤

Selling personal favor is not as good as assisting public consensus. Making new acquaintances is not as good as warming up old friendships. Establishing a glorious reputation is not as good as planting hidden virtues. Valuing unusual conduct is not as good as being care-ful about ordinary actions.

, , ,

One should not oppose what is fair and just. If one does so, it will leave a legacy of shame. One should not enter in among power bro-kers. If ones does so, the stain will last all one's life.

, , ,

Compromise to please others is not as good as integrity that annoys others. Rather than be praised without being good, it is better to be slandered without being bad.

, , ,

When there is trouble among relatives, one should remain calm and not get excited. When friends are in error, one should be stern and not gloss over it lightly.

, , ,

When one is not slipshod in small matters, not hypocritical in secret, and not reckless in disappointment, only then is one a true hero.

, , ,

A thousand pieces of gold may hardly bring a moment's happiness, but a small favor can cause a lifetime's gratitude. Too much love can turn into enmity, while aloofness can produce joy.

, , ,

Hide cleverness in clumsiness; act ignorant but be bright; use re-straint to expand. These are three hiding places for dealing effectively with life.

, , ,

Decline is inherent in prosperity, the potential for development is in destitution. So when at ease one should take care to think about trou-ble, and when in trouble one should be infinitely patient so as to eventually succeed.

, , ,

Those who are amazed at wonders and delight in the extraordinary do not have great knowledge. Solitary ascetics do not have enduring discipline.

> , , ,

When anger or passion boils up, even when we are clearly aware we still go ahead. Who is it that is aware? Who is it that goes ahead? If we can turn our thoughts around in this way, the devil becomes the conscience.

> , , ,

Don't be biased in belief and let yourself be deceived by the dishonest. Don't rely on yourself too much and let yourself be compelled by moods. Don't use your own strengths to bring out others' short-comings. Don't resent others' abilities on account of your own in-competence.

> , , ,

People's shortcomings should be treated with tact; if you expose them crudely, this is attacking weaknesses with a weakness. When people are stubborn, it requires skill to influence them; if you treat them with anger and spite, this is treating stubbornness with stub-bornness.

> , , ,

When you meet silent and inscrutable people, don't tell them what you are thinking. When you meet irritable and self-serving people, be careful what you say.

> , , ,

When your thoughts are muddled or distracted, you should know how to alert yourself. When your thoughts are tense, you should know how to let them go. Otherwise, once you get rid of torpor you may bring on excitement.

> , , ,

A clear sunny day can suddenly shift to thunder and lightning, a rag-ing storm can suddenly give way to a bright moonlit night. The

weather may be inconstant, but the sky remains the same. The substance of the human mind should also be like this.

, , ,

Regarding the work of self-mastery and control of desires, some say
that if you do not perceive immediately, it will be hard to muster
sufficient strength; some say that even with penetrating perception,
forbearance is insufficient. Perception is a clear jewel that shows up
demons; strength is a sword of wisdom that cuts down demons. Both
are necessary.

, , ,

To notice people's deceptions yet not reveal it in words, to bear people's insults without showing any change of attitude—there is endless meaning in this, and also endless function.

, , ,

Unexpected hardship refines people; if you can accept it, both mind
and body will benefit. If you cannot accept it, on the other hand, both
mind and body will be harmed.

, , ,

Our body is a small universe; to regulate emotions and feelings is a
way of harmonization. The universe is a great set of parents; to cause
people to be without enmity and things to be without affliction is a
sign of warmth.

, , ,

"One should have no intention to harm others, but should not lack
the awareness to avoid being harmed by others." This is a warning
against carelessness. "It is better to be deceived by people than to be
on the lookout for deception." This is a warning against paranoia. If
one can keep both of these sayings in mind, one can be precise and
clear yet simple and friendly.

, , ,

When parents are kind and children obedient, elder siblings friendly
and younger siblings respectful, even if this is carried out to the fullest possible extent, it is all as it should be and is nothing to be consid-

ered impressive. If those who give are conscious of their own generosity and those who receive feel indebted, they are no longer family but rather strangers doing business.

, , ,

When there is beauty, there is inevitably ugliness in contrast. If you do not take pride in your own beauty, who can consider you ugly? When there is purity, there must be defilement as its opposite. If you do not crave purity, who can defile you?

, , ,

When it comes to changes of attitude, warm and cold, the rich are more extreme than the poor. When it comes to envy and resentment, relatives are worse than strangers. If you do not deal with such situations coolly and calmly, you will rarely avoid vexation.

, , ,

Don't let the doubts of the crowd interfere with an individual view, but don't reject the words of others because of faith in your own opinion. Don't miss the larger reality by taking a little kindness personally; don't use public opinion to please yourself.

, , ,

If you cannot become familiar with good people right away, it is not advisable to praise them beforehand, lest that incite slanderers. If you cannot easily get rid of bad people, it is not advisable to criticize them at first, lest that invite troublemakers.

, , ,

Public behavior is nurtured in private; earthshaking measures come from careful steps.

, , ,

Merit and fault do not admit of the slightest mixup; if you mix them up, people will become lazy. Gratitude and enmity should not be too clear; if you make them too clear, people will be alienated.

, , ,

When salary and rank are very great, there is danger. When skills are exerted to the utmost, there is decline. When manners are too dignified, there is criticism.

, , ,

Darkness is bad for evil, light is bad for good. When evil is apparent, its harm is little; but when it is hidden its harm is great. When good is apparent, its merit is little; but when it is hidden its merit is great.

, , ,

Virtue is the master of talent, talent is the servant of virtue. Talent without virtue is like a house where there is no master and the servant manages its affairs. How can there be no mischief?

, , ,

To get rid of villains and knaves, it is necessary to give them a way out. If you don't give them any leeway at all, they will be like trapped rats. If every way out is closed to them, they will chew up everything good.

, , ,

Share people's mistakes, but don't try to share in their achievements, for that will lead to resentment. Share people's troubles, but don't try to get a share of their happiness, for that will lead to enmity.

, , ,

When enlightened people are so poor that they cannot help others, if they speak a word to awaken the confused or to resolve a problem, there is also boundless merit in that.

, , ,

One of the common troubles of human sentiments is that people cleave to others when they are hungry and thus drift off when they are filled; they go to those who are in comfortable circumstances and abandon those who have fallen on hard times. Enlightened people should clarify their perception and see coolly, being careful to remain firm-hearted and not be easily shaken.

, , ,

Virtue evolves according to capacity; capacity grows through perception. Therefore, if you would enrich your virtue, you must broaden your capacity; and if you would broaden your capacity, you must increase your perception.

, , ,

When a lone lamp burns faintly and everything is silent, this is the time we enter quiet repose. When we have just awakened from dawn dreams and nothing is yet stirring, this is where we emerge from the undifferentiated. If you can take advantage of these moments to turn your attention around to inner awareness, then you will realize that senses and desires are all fetters.

, , ,

For those who reflect on themselves, everything they encounter is medicine. For those who attack others, every thought is a weapon. One is the way to initiate all good, one is a way to deepen all evil. They are as far apart as sky and earth.

, , ,

Business and scholarship pass away with the person, but the soul is forever like new. Fame and fortune change with the generations, but the spirit is always the same. Enlightened people surely should not exchange the lasting for the ephemeral.

, , ,

A net set up to catch fish may snare a duck; a mantis hunting an insect may itself be set upon by a sparrow. Machinations are hidden within machinations; changes arise beyond changes. So how can wit and cleverness be relied upon?

, , ,

If you are not at all truthful or sincere in your thoughts, you are useless to society, and everything you do is vain. If you have no roundness and liveliness in your way of life, you are a manikin and are inhibited everywhere.

, , ,

When water isn't rippled, it is naturally still. When a mirror isn't clouded, it is clear of itself. So the mind is not to be cleared; get rid of what muddles it, and its clarity will spontaneously appear. Pleasure need not be sought; get rid of what pains you, and pleasure is naturally there.

, , ,

It is possible to transgress upon the taboo realm of ghosts and spirits with a single thought, to injure the harmony of heaven and earth with a single remark, and to brew trouble for your posterity with a single deed. Best beware.

, , ,

There are some things that do not get cleared up by rushing them but may clarify themselves if given room to do so; in such cases, do not be hasty, lest that make people quick to anger. There are some people who are not made obedient by attempting to control them, but may civilize themselves if given the freedom to do so; in such cases, do not try to manipulate them rigorously, lest that increase their stubbornness.

, , ,

Even if you have lofty ideals and write high-minded essays, if you do not form them by means of the essence of virtue, they will end up as personal mettle and spin-offs of technical ability.

, , ,

When you retire from office, you should do so at the peak of your career. As for where to place yourself in society, you should live in the state of a survivor.

, , ,

As you attend to your virtue, you should attend to it even in the minutest things. When you give charity, strive to give to those who cannot repay.

, , ,

Association with city people is not as good as friendship with elderly peasants. Calling on upper-class mansions is not as good as getting to know peasant homes. Listening to the talk of the streets and alleys is not as good as hearing the songs of the woodcutters and shepherds. Talking about the moral failures and professional blunders of people today is not as good as retelling the fine words and noble deeds of people of old.

᾽ ᾽ ᾽

Your virtue is the foundation of your professional work; no house frame ever lasted without a solid foundation. Your mentality is the root of your prosperity; no branches and leaves ever flourished without a well-planted root.

᾽ ᾽ ᾽

One of our predecessors said, "Throwing away the inexhaustible treasury of your own home, you go with your bowl from door to door, acting like a beggar." He also said, "Let the poor who've made a windfall stop talking of dreams; in whose house has the hearth fire no smoke?" One saying cautions those who blind themselves to what they have; one cautions those who pride themselves in what they have. They can be taken as urgent warnings in the domain of education.

᾽ ᾽ ᾽

The Way is something public, into which people should be led according to the individual. Learning is an everyday affair, in which caution should be exercised in each situation.

᾽ ᾽ ᾽

Those who trust others will find that not everyone is necessarily sincere, but they will be sincere themselves. Those who suspect others will find that not everyone is necessarily deceiving them, but they have already become deceivers themselves.

᾽ ᾽ ᾽

Those who are broad-minded and considerate are like the spring breeze, warm and nurturing, at whose touch all beings grow. Those who are envious and cruel are like the snow of the northlands, stilling and freezing, at whose touch all beings die.

> , , ,

When you do good but do not see its benefit, it is like a squash growing in the grasses; it should naturally grow unknown. When you do
evil but do not see its harm, it is like spring snow in the yard; it will
inevitably sink in or evaporate.

> , , ,

When you meet old friends, your spirits should be all the more fresh.
When you deal with private matters, your intentions should be all
the more open. When you are treating people in their decline, your
generosity and courtesy should be all the more magnanimous.

> , , ,

Diligence means to be keen in matters of virtue and justice, but
worldly people use diligence to solve their economic difficulties. Frugality means to have little desire for material goods, but worldly people use frugality as a cover for stinginess. Thus do watchwords of
enlightened life turn into tools for the private business of small people. What a pity!

> , , ,

Those who act on excitement act intermittently; this is hardly the
way to avoid regression. Those whose understanding comes from
emotional perceptions are as confused as they are enlightened; this is
not a lamp that is constantly bright.

> , , ,

You should be forgiving when others make mistakes, but not when
the mistakes are in you. You should be patient under duress yourself,
but not when it affects others.

> , , ,

Generosity should begin lightly and deepen later, for when it is first
rich and then lessens, people forget the kindness. Authority should
begin strictly and loosen up later, for if it is loose first and then strict,
people will resent the severity.

> , , ,

If you can be free of conventions, that is extraordinary; if you intentionally value the unusual, that is not extraordinary but weird. If you do not join the polluted, then you are pure; if you reject society in search of purity, that is not purity but fanaticism.

, , ,

When the mind is empty, its essence appears. Trying to see the essence without stopping the mind is like stirring up waves looking for the moon. When the will is clean, the heart is pure. Seeking to clarify the heart without understanding the will is like obtaining a mirror and piling dust on it.

, , ,

When you are in a high position and people serve you, they are serving your regalia of office. When you are in a humble position and people despise you, they are despising your simple attire. So since they are not serving you, why should you be glad? And since they are not despising you, why should you be angry?

, , ,

"Always leave some food for the mice; pity the moths and don't light the lamp." Thoughts like these that the ancients had are the living, life-giving mechanism of us humans. Without this, we are no more than statues or manikins.

, , ,

The substance of mind is the substance of heaven. A joyful thought is an auspicious star or a felicitous cloud. An angry thought is a thunderstorm or a violent rain. A kind thought is a gentle breeze or sweet dew. A stern thought is a fierce sun or an autumn frost. Which of these can be eliminated? Just let them pass away as they arise, open and unresisting, and your mind merges with the spacious sky.

, , ,

When unoccupied, the mind is easily dimmed; best be very calm yet radiantly alert. When occupied, the mind easily runs wild; best be alert yet very calmly in control.

, , ,

When people are in positions of power and occupy important offices, their behavior should be strict and clear, while their state of mind should be gentle and easy. Don't let a little accommodation bring you close to cliques of self-seekers; and don't let excessive intensity run you afoul of the poison of the vicious.

> , , ,

Those who make a show of morality are inevitably slandered on moral grounds; those who make a show of learning are always blamed on account of learning. Therefore, enlightened people neither approach evil nor establish a good repute. Only an integrated mood of harmony is of value in social life.

> , , ,

When you meet dishonest people, move them with sincerity. When you meet violent people, affect them with gentility. When you meet warped people, inspire them with justice. Then the whole world enters your forge.

> , , ,

A moment of kindness can produce a mood of harmony between heaven and earth. Purity of heart can leave a fine example for a hundred generations.

> , , ,

Hidden schemes, weird arts, strange practices, and unusual abilities are all sources of calamity in social and professional life. Only by normal qualities and normal actions can one keep natural wholeness and bring peace.

> , , ,

There is a saying that goes, "Climbing a mountain, you endure steep pathways; walking in snow, you endure dangerous bridges." There is much meaning in the word *endure*. For example, when dealing with unstable human feelings and uneven pathways in life, without endurance to hold you up, you may fall into a pit in the brush.

> , , ,

To boast of one's work or show off one's literary accomplishments is to base one's person on external things. People who do this do not know that the substance of mind is bright as it is, and as long as it is not lost, one may completely lack skills and learning yet still be a fine upstanding person.

> , , ,

If you would "snatch some leisure in the midst of hurry," you must first get a grip on it when you are already at leisure. If you would "grab some quiet in the midst of the hubbub," you must first establish self-mastery from quietude. Otherwise, anyone would be influenced by situations and overwhelmed by the course of events.

> , , ,

Don't obscure your own mind; don't exhaust people's emotions; don't use up material powers. With these three things, it is possible to establish a mind with universal perspective, establish meaningful ways of life for people in general, and create prosperity for descendants.

> , , ,

Here are two sayings for people in public office: "Only impartiality gives rise to clarity," and "Only honesty produces dignity." Here are two sayings for home life: "Only by forgiveness are feelings evened," and "Only by frugality are necessities sufficient."

> , , ,

When you are in positions of wealth and status, you should know the miseries of those who are poor and lowly. When you are young and strong, you should remember the pains of the old and feeble.

> , , ,

You should not be too much of a purist in your way of life, for you need to be able to accept all that is foul. You should not be too clear in making distinctions in social interactions, for you need to accept everyone whether they are good or bad, wise or foolish.

> , , ,

Give up antagonism to small people, for small people have their own peers. Give up trying to flatter and charm enlightened people, for enlightened people don't do personal favors.

, , ,

The sickness of indulging desires can be treated, but the sickness of clinging to abstract principles is hard to treat. Obstacles presented by events and objects can be removed, but obstacles presented by social principles are hard to remove.

, , ,

Polish what you polish until it is like gold that has been refined a hundred times; anything that is done in a hurry is not deeply developed. Do what you do like a thousand-pound catapult; one who pops off too easily does not accomplish much.

, , ,

It is better to be reviled by petty people than to be flattered by them. It is better to be rebuked by enlightened people than to be indulged by them.

, , ,

When those who like to gain something for themselves exceed the bounds of reason and right, the harm is obvious and therefore shallow. When those who are interested in their own reputation weasel their way into reason and right, the harm is hidden and therefore deep.

, , ,

To accept people's favors yet not repay them no matter how serious they are, to take revenge on those with whom you have any grievances no matter how slight they are, to give credence to anything bad you hear about others even if it is not evident, to doubt whatever good you hear even if it is obvious: this is all extremely cruel and heartless. Best beware.

, , ,

Cavilers and calumniators are like flecks of cloud temporarily blocking the sun; it will be clear again before long. Flatterers and fawners are like a draft that gets into the flesh; one is harmed unawares.

, , ,

There are no trees on the high mountain crags; plants and trees grow in profusion in the valley bowls. There are no fish in the rapids; fish and turtles gather in the still depths. Thus, enlightened people are wary of impractical actions and fanatical attitudes.

, , ,

Most people who are successful in their work are open-minded and well rounded. Those who fail in their undertakings and lose opportunities are the obstinate and inflexible.

, , ,

In social life, it is not good to be a conformist, yet it is not good to be a nonconformist either. In doing things, it is not good to cause people aversion, yet it is not good to try to gain their favor either.

, , ,

At dusk the sunset is beautifully bright; at year's end the tangerines are even more fragrant. Therefore, at the end of their road, in their later years, enlightened people should be a hundred times more vital in spirit.

, , ,

A hawk stands as though dozing, a tiger walks as though ill; these are ploys by which they claw and bite. So enlightened people should not show their brilliance and talent, for only thus have they the power to bear great responsibilities.

, , ,

Frugality is an excellent quality, but if excessive it becomes stinginess and miserliness, which instead damage the good life. Deference is fine conduct, but if excessive it becomes servility and cautiousness, which often come from a scheming mind.

, , ,

Don't worry about what offends you; don't take a liking to what pleases you. Don't count on a prolonged state of ease; don't shrink in fear at the first difficulty.

, , ,

Those who drink and party are not good neighbors. Those who are addicted to vanities of repute are not good citizens. Those who think much of fame and status are not good public officials.

, , ,

Worldly people enjoy what agrees with them, then are pulled by enjoyment into misery. Enlightened people enjoy what offends them, as ultimately they gain happiness for their pains.

, , ,

Those who dwell in fullness are like water about to overflow; don't add another drop. Those who are in urgent danger are like wood that is about to snap; don't add any more pressure.

, , ,

Observe people with cool eyes, listen to their words with cool ears. Confront feelings with cool emotions, reflect on principles with a cool mind.

, , ,

Humane people are broad-minded, so they are richly blessed and have lasting happiness; everything they do makes an atmosphere of relaxation. Base men are fussy, so they are less fortunate and their good times are short; everything they do is a model of fussiness.

, , ,

When you hear of bad people, don't despise them right away, for their bad repute might be the sputterings of cavilers. When you hear of good people, don't rush to befriend them, because their good repute might have been made up by dishonest people trying to get ahead.

, , ,

The reckless and crude-minded accomplish nothing whatever. To those who are gentle-hearted and even-minded, a hundred blessings accrue of themselves.

, , ,

When you employ people, don't be harsh, for if you are harsh, even the earnest workers will leave. When you make friends, it is not good to be promiscuous, for if you are promiscuous, then flatterers will come to you.

> , , ,

In a blasting wind and driving rain, it is necessary to stand fast. In the midst of finery and glamour, it is necessary to set one's sights on high. Where the road is perilous and the pathway steep, it is necessary to turn back early.

> , , ,

If conservative and moralistic people complement this with harmony and balance, only then will they avoid anger and contention. If successful and famous people bear this with modesty and virtue, only then will they avoid inspiring envy and jealousy.

> , , ,

When prominent people are in public office, they should not write letters without restraint. It is necessary to be inscrutable to others, to prevent opportunists from taking advantage. When in private life, on the other hand, it will not do to be remote and aloof. It is essential to be easily visible to others, to deepen old friendships.

> , , ,

You should fear important people, for if you do so, you will not be heedless. You should also fear small people, for if you do so, you will not be known for acting like a thug.

> , , ,

When things are not going your way, then think of those who are worse off than you, and resentment will naturally disappear. When your mind lazes off, then think of those who are better than you, and your vital spirit will be naturally aroused.

> , , ,

Don't get so carried away by delight that you agree too easily; don't get so drunk that you give rise to anger. Don't get so high-spirited that you take on too many things; don't let fatigue reduce your achievements.

> , , ,

To be good at reading the classics, you must read to the point where your hands and feet dance, for only thus do you avoid getting caught in literalism. To be good at observing things, you must observe to the point where your mind merges with them, for only thus do you avoid getting mired in the forms they leave behind.

> , , ,

Heaven makes individuals intelligent so that they may instruct the ignorant, but in society those individuals flaunt their talents to show up people's shortcomings. Heaven enriches individuals so that they may help the destitute, but in society those individuals cling to their possessions to lord over the poor. Such individuals are truly capital criminals against heaven.

> , , ,

Complete people have no thoughts or worries, while ignorant people have no knowledge; both can be partners in study or business. It is only the mediocre intellectuals who think too much and have too much information, so that they also do too much thinking and doubting; as a result it is hard to do anything at all with them.

> , , ,

Speech is the gate of the heart; if you do not guard your speech closely, you divulge all the real workings of your mind. Attention is the mind's feet; if you do not control your attention strictly, it runs into misleading pathways.

> , , ,

When you take others to task, if you look for where they are faultless in spite of having other faults, then feelings will be equanimous. When you take yourself to task, if you look for where there are flaws in your impeccability, then virtue will progress.

> , , ,

Children are embryos of adults; intellectuals are embryos of grandees. If the power of the development process at that time is not complete and the molding is impure, on another day, when they are members of society and government officials, it will turn out to be virtually impossible for them to function well.

, , ,

Enlightened people in trouble still do not worry, yet in merriment are still cautious. They are not cowed when they meet socially prominent people, but they are moved by the plight of the orphaned.

, , ,

Although peach and plum blossoms are beautiful, how do they compare with the constancy of the green in the pine and cedar? Although pears and apricots are sweet, how do they compare with the intensely fragrant coolness of the oranges and tangerines? How true it is that a short life of luxury is not as good as a simple life that is long, that early blooming and fruitage are not as good as late perfection.

, , ,

When the wind is still and the waves are quiet, you see the true realm of human life. When flavor is light and sound is rare, you know the original state of the body of mind.

, , ,

Those who talk about the pleasures of mountains and forests have not necessarily really attained the pleasures of mountains and forests. Those who disdain talk of fame and fortune have not necessarily completely forgotten feelings for fame and fortune.

, , ,

Fishing is just a pastime, but even so one holds the handle of life and death. Chess is just a game, but even so it stirs the warlike mind. Obviously, it is more comfortable to minimize occupations than to avidly seek them; and it is more wholesome to be simple than to be clever.

, , ,

When nightingales and flowers are abundant and the mountains and valleys are steeped in luxuriant beauty, this is all an illusory state of heaven and earth. When the waters dry, the leaves fall, the rocks are bared, and the cliffs withered, then you see the real self of heaven and earth.

, , ,

The months and years are originally long, but people in a hurry themselves shorten them. Heaven and earth are originally wide, but base people make them narrow. The four seasons are originally serene, but people who fuss and worry make them a bother.

, , ,

It doesn't take much for some atmosphere—a bit of haze and mist over a little pond and a few rocks, and that's enough. One needn't go far for scenery—the breeze and the moon at a rustic window are naturally serene.

, , ,

Listening to the sound of a bell on a still night awakens one from a dream in a dream; watching the reflection of the moon in a clear pool, one espies a body beyond the body.

, , ,

The speech of the birds and the voices of the insects are all the secret of transmitting mind; the brilliance of the flowers and colors of the grasses are all writings on seeing the Way. To learn, it is necessary to have your higher potential clarified thoroughly and your heart clear as crystal. Then you will find understanding of mind whatever you encounter.

, , ,

People know how to read books with writing in them, but they do not know how to read unwritten books. They know how to play a harp with strings, but they do not know how to play a stringless harp. If you work through traces and not through spirit, how can you get the aim of music and literature?

, , ,

When there are no material desires in the mind, it is like a clear sea under the autumn sky. If you have a harp and some books at your side, they make an immortal abode in a mountain fastness.

, , ,

When guests and friends gather in great numbers and drink heavily, they enjoy themselves with abandon. Suddenly, the night is spent, the candles burn low; the incense is gone, the tea is cold. Unawares, people find themselves gagging and choking, making them feel desolate and taking away the fun. Just about everything in the world is like this, so why don't people wake up sooner?

, , ,

When you understand the sense of the here and now, the misty moonlight of the scenic lakes will enter your heart. When you break through the machinations before your eyes, the heroics of the ages will all wind up in the palm of your hand.

, , ,

Mountains, rivers, and continents are already just atoms, and we are but particles within those atoms. The physical body will presently turn out to be a bubble, a shadow, and so will all the other shadows outside your shadow. If you do not have the highest knowledge, you do not have the clearest mind.

, , ,

Life passes by in a flash, yet people vie and compete with each other. How much time do we have? There is very little room, yet people contest and debate with each other. How big is the world?

, , ,

A cold lamp without flame, a worn leather coat without warmth—both are but shadows of themselves. Similarly, if your body is like a withered tree and your mind is like dead ashes, you unavoidably fall into stupid vacantness.

, , ,

If people are willing to stop at once, then they finish at once. If you insist on seeking a place of rest, then "even though you've married off all your children, there are no fewer things to do; even though monkhood is fine, you still haven't understood your heart." An ancient said, "If you stop now, then stop; if you seek an ending, there is no ending." This is highly perceptive.

, , ,

When you look upon fervor from coolness, then you know the vanity of frenetic activity in fervor. When you enter from hurry into leisure, then you notice how the flavor in quietude lasts longest.

, , ,

There is a way to look upon wealth and status as like floating clouds without having to live in a mountain cave. One need not be addicted to springs and rocks to be always drinking by oneself and lost in poetry.

, , ,

Let people compete if they will, but do not despise them for all being intoxicated. Be calm and aloof to suit yourself, but do not be proud of being the only one who is sober. This is what Buddhists call not being bound by religion, not being bound by voidness, body and mind both free.

, , ,

Length and brevity of time depend on a thought; breadth or narrowness of space depend on the heart. So for one whose mind is free, a day is longer than a thousand ages; for one whose mind is broad, a small room is wider than heaven and earth.

, , ,

Whatever meets the eye is the realm of immortals for the contented, the realm of mortals for the discontented. All the bases of activity in society have life-giving potential if used well and death-dealing potential if not used well.

, , ,

The calamities brought about by cleaving to the powerful are very severe, and also very swift. The savor of a simple life is most delicate, and most enduring.

, , ,

I walk alone with my staff by a valley stream among the pines; where I stand, clouds rise about my ragged patchwork robe. I sleep aloof with a book for my pillow under a window framed with bamboo; when I wake, the moon's gotten into the worn felt.

> , , ,

Sexual desire may burn like fire, but when you give a thought to when you are ill, then your excitement dies down. Fame and fortune may be as sweet as candy, but when you give a thought to when you die, then their flavor is like chewing wax. Therefore, if people are usually concerned about death and illness, this can also dissolve unreal activities and develop longing for the Way.

> , , ,

The road of contention for precedence is narrow; take a step back, and it broadens a step. The rich flavor of intense beauty is short-lived; dilute it with a measure of pure clarity, and it will naturally last that much longer.

> , , ,

If you will have your nature undisturbed in busy situations, it is necessary that mind and spirit be nurtured to pure clarity when at leisure.

> , , ,

In the forest of hidden aloofness, there is neither glory nor disgrace. On the road of enlightened justice, there is neither heat nor cool.

> , , ,

Even if you can't get rid of the heat, as long as you can get rid of bother with the heat, your body is always on a cool terrace. Even if you can't get rid of poverty, as long as you can get rid of the sadness of poverty, your mind always lives in a comfortable abode.

> , , ,

If you immediately think about stepping back whenever you step ahead, you may avoid the calamity of bumping into fences. If you plan to detach yourself beforehand whenever you start a project, only then will you escape the danger of mounting a tiger.

, , ,

When greedy people are given gold, they are bitter that they haven't gotten jewels; when they are made barons they are resentful that they haven't been made lords. Though powerful and rich, their attitude is that of beggars. For those who know how to be content, simple fare is more delicious than rich delicacies, a cloth coat is warmer than fox fur, and an ordinary citizen does not defer to a king or a lord.

, , ,

Taking pride in fame is not as interesting as avoiding it. Cultivating hobbies is not as peaceful as minimizing interests.

, , ,

Those who enjoy silence understand mysteries as they watch white clouds and recondite rocks. Those who head for glory forget weariness when they see fine singing and dancing. Only for those who are masters of themselves is there no noise or silence, no flourishing or withering, nowhere that is not a spontaneously comfortable heaven.

, , ,

A lone cloud emerges from a mountain cave, with nothing at all to keep it from going or staying. A bright mirror hangs in the sky, unaffected by either quiet or uproar.

, , ,

The sense of eternity is found not in fine wine but in eating beans and drinking water. The mood of lament comes not from loneliness but from flutes and harps. So we know that the flavor of intense experience is always short-lived, while the charm of subtle experience alone is real.

, , ,

Chan Buddhism says, "When hungry, eat; when tired, sleep." A work on the essence of poetry says, "The scene before the eyes is expressed in everyday sayings." Generally speaking, that which is most lofty dwells in that which is most ordinary; that which is most difficult emerges from that which is most easy. Those with subjective ideas are farthest away, while those who are mindless are naturally close.

, , ,

When there is no sound even as the stream flows, you are able to perceive the mood of quiet in the midst of clamor. When the clouds are unobstructed in spite of the height of the mountains, you realize the way to leave being and enter nonbeing.

, , ,

Mountain forests are beautiful places, but once you become attached to them, they become cities. Calligraphy and painting are elegant pastimes, but once you get greedy they become commercialized. In general, when the mind is unattached, then the realm of desire is the capital of immortals; when the mind is attached, then objects of pleasure become an ocean of suffering.

, , ,

The way to transcend the world is right in the midst of involvement with the world; it is not necessary to cut off human relations to escape society. The work of understanding the mind is right in the midst of full use of the mind; it is not necessary to exterminate desire to make the mind like ashes.

, , ,

Always put yourself in a position where there is room; then who can manipulate you by glory or disgrace, gain or loss? Always rest your mind in tranquillity; then who can fool you about right and wrong or advantage and disadvantage?

, , ,

If I do not seek prosperity, how can I be bothered by the fragrant bait of profitable emolument? If I do not compete to get ahead, why should I fear the crises of officialdom?

, , ,

In times of clamor and confusion, one tends to forget what one ordinarily remembers; in a state of clarity and calm, one tends to glimpse what one had forgotten long ago. So we can see that as soon as stillness and business are divided, darkness and light suddenly diverge.

᾽ ᾽ ᾽

Lying in the snow, sleeping in the clouds, under a reed-flower quilt, I keep a room of night breath whole. In a cup of wine I sing with the breeze, enjoying the moon, having sidestepped tidal waves of red dust.

᾽ ᾽ ᾽

When an entourage of aristocrats includes a mountain man, it has a more lofty air. When a leather-clothed courtier is on a road traveled by fisherfolk and woodcutters, it adds so much vulgarity. So we know that richness is not superior to austerity, vulgarity is not as good as refinement.

᾽ ᾽ ᾽

When you roam in the mountain forests, among the springs and rocks, the materialistic mentality gradually ceases. When you steep yourself in poetry, writing, and painting, the mood of worldliness fades away. So even though enlightened people do not amuse themselves with objects to the point where they lose their will, yet they ordinarily use the environment as a means of tuning the mind.

᾽ ᾽ ᾽

The atmosphere of spring makes people's hearts and spirits relax, but that is not as good as the white of the clouds and clarity of the wind in autumn, the fragrance of the orchids and cassia, the water and sky one color, above and below empty and bright, making people's spirits and bones both pure.

᾽ ᾽ ᾽

Those who have poetic ideas even though they are illiterate attain the true enjoyment of poets. Those who have the taste of Chan even though they haven't studied it understand the mysterious devices of Chan Buddhism.

᾽ ᾽ ᾽

When the workings of the mind are stirred, a reflection of a bow may be mistaken for a serpent, a large rock in the underbrush may be seen as a crouching lion; here is all killing energy. When thoughts cease, even the violent can become gentle, the ordinary can be elegant; everywhere you see true potential.

> , , ,

When the body is like an unmoored boat, it may go with the flow or come to a stop. When the mind is like wood reduced to ashes, what does it matter whether one is cut by swords or painted with perfume?

> , , ,

To delight in listening to the call of the nightingale, to weary of hearing the croaking of frogs, to want to cultivate flowers on seeing them, to wish to remove weeds on finding them: these are human sentiments, and this is just acting on form and mood. If you look upon beings in terms of the essential creative power in them, are they not all spontaneously expressing their natural potential and sense of aliveness?

> , , ,

When your hair falls out and you lose your teeth, you let the chiseling and fading of the illusory form go. When the birds sing and the flowers bloom, you know the real likeness of inherent nature.

> , , ,

If you fill your heart with desires, waves boil even on a cold pool, and you do not experience tranquillity even if you are in a mountain forest. If you empty your heart, coolness arises even in scorching heat, and you do not notice the hubbub even if you are in a city.

> , , ,

The more people possess, the greater their losses; so the rich are not as carefree as the poor. The higher people rise, the faster they fall, so the upper classes are not as secure as the common people.

> , , ,

It is just because people take themselves too seriously that they develop all sorts of addictions and passions. An ancient said, "If you do not even recognize the existence of self, how can you recognize value in things?" Also, "If you know the body is not the self, how can passions afflict you?" These sayings really hit the target.

, , ,

Looking upon youth from the perspective of old age can melt away ambition and contentiousness. Looking upon success from the point of view of dereliction can stop thoughts of glamour.

, , ,

Human feelings and social conditions are very mercurial and should not be taken too seriously. A philosopher said, "What you called your self before is now already another. I wonder who today's self will belong to later?" If people make this observation from time to time, they can unclog their hearts.

, , ,

Open a cool eye in the midst of intense activity, and you save yourself that much bitter thought. Keep an enthusiastic attitude in hard times, and you gain that much true enjoyment.

, , ,

When there is a pleasant state, there is an unpleasant state in contrast. When there is a good situation, there is one that is not good to replace it. Only an ordinary, simple life is a comfortable nest.

, , ,

If you know that whatever is made inevitably breaks down, you needn't seek too hard for achievement. If you know that all living beings inevitably die, you needn't work too hard on health lore.

, , ,

An ancient saint said, "As bamboo shadows sweep the stairs, no dust is stirred; as the moonlight penetrates the pond, no ripple is made on the water." A Confucian said, "Rapid as the flow of the river may be, the surroundings are always calm; though the flowers fall again and again, the mood is naturally relaxed." If people can keep these attitudes to deal with events and interact with others, how free they are in body and mind!

, , ,

The rhymes of the pines in the forest, the murmuring of a spring in the rocks—listen to them in quietude, and you know the natural music of sky and earth. The glow of mist in the meadows, the reflections of clouds in the river—gaze on them calmly, and you see the highest art of the universe.

, , ,

Even if people see wastelands in the wake of war, they still take pride in their weapons. Even though people are to be eaten by the animals of the graveyards, they still cling to material goods. There is a saying that goes, "It is easier to tame wild beasts than to conquer the human mind; it is easier to fill up a canyon than to satisfy the human mind."

, , ,

When there are no wind and waves in your mind, then wherever you are is all green mountains and trees. When there is evolutionary development in your nature, then everywhere you go you see fish leap and birds fly.

, , ,

As fish dart through water, they are forgetful of the water; as birds fly on the breeze, they are not conscious that there is a breeze. Discern this, and you can transcend the burden of things and enjoy natural potential.

, , ,

Foxes sleep on broken steps, rabbits run on overgrown terraces; all are former sites of song and dance. Dew lies cold on yellow flowers, mist meanders through wilting grasses; all are old battlegrounds of past wars. Where is there any constancy in flourishing and decline? Where are the strong and the weak? It cools people's minds down to think of this.

, , ,

Undisturbed by favor or disgrace, at leisure I watch the flowers in the garden bloom and then drop. With no intention of either going or staying, casually I follow the receding and spreading of the clouds.

, , ,

In a clear sky with a bright moon, what heaven cannot be roamed in flight? Yet the moths cast themselves into the night lamplight. Where there are pure springs and green grass, what creatures cannot eat and drink? Yet the owls like rotting rats. How many people in the world are there who do not act like moths or owls?

, , ,

Only those who think of giving up a raft as soon as they have gotten on it are really unobsessed wayfarers. Those who mount an ass and then go looking for an ass turn out to be unenlightened meditation instructors.

, , ,

The powerful and prominent soar like dragons, the heroic and valiant fight like tigers: but if you look upon them with cool eyes, they are like ants gathering on rancid meat, like flies swarming on blood. Judgments of right and wrong arise like hornets, gain and loss bristle like porcupine quills: but if you meet them with cool feelings, that is like a forge melting metal, like hot water dissolving snow.

, , ,

When you are fettered by material desires, you feel that your life is pathetic; but when you immerse yourself in essential reality, you feel that your life is enjoyable. When you know life is pathetic, material senses are immediately seen through; when you know life is enjoyable, the realm of sages comes of itself.

, , ,

When there are no longer any material desires in your heart, they are like snow melted in the flames of a furnace, like ice melted in the sun. When there is a single open clarity spontaneously before your eyes, then you see that the moon is in the blue sky and its reflection is in the waves.

, , ,

What has been kept down for a long time will surely soar to the heights when it flies. What has bloomed first will be the soonest to fade. If you know this, you can avoid the trouble of becoming worn out on the way, and you can dissolve thoughts of impulsive hurry.

, , ,

When deciduous trees go bare, then you know the vain glory of flowers and leaves; when people are sealed in their coffins, you know that children and wealth are no help.

, , ,

True emptiness is not empty; clinging to appearances is not reality, nor is denying appearances. How did Buddha communicate this? "Be in the world, yet beyond the world." Pursuing desires is painful, but so is stopping desire altogether. It is up to us to cultivate ourselves skillfully.

, , ,

A just person will defer a whole state, a greedy person will fight over a coin. Their personalities are vastly different, yet fondness for honor is no different from fondness for gain. An emperor runs a country, a beggar cries for a meal. Their ranks are vastly different, but how is feverish thinking different from feverish talking?

, , ,

When you've had your fill of the flavors of the world and know them intimately, then whatever may happen, you are not terribly concerned. When you understand human feelings completely, then whatever people may call you, you just nod.

, , ,

People today concentrate on the quest to have no thoughts but find that their thoughts ultimately cannot be annihilated. Just don't linger on the preceding thought, don't greet the following thought; if you can just use the present adaptation to circumstances to break through, you will naturally enter nothingness in a gradual manner.

, , ,

Whatever spontaneously occurs to your mind is fine. When things come out naturally, only then do you see their real potential. If you add any adjustment or arrangement, grace is lost. One of the immortal poets said, "The mind is comfortable whenever free of concerns; the breeze is clear as it blows along with nature."

                     ,   ,   ,

When your essential nature is thoroughly pure, then even eating when hungry and drinking when thirsty strengthen and help body and mind. When your mind is sunk in confusion, even if you talk about meditation and expound verses, all of it is mental gymnastics.

                     ,   ,   ,

There is a real state in the human mind that is naturally calm and pleasant even without music, naturally clear and fragrant even without incense and tea. You can swim in it only when the mind is clean and objects are empty, when worries are forgotten and the body is at ease.

                     ,   ,   ,

Gold comes from ore, jade comes from stone. If not for illusion, there would be no way to seek reality. The Way is found in wine, immortals are met among the flowers. Even if refined, one cannot leave the ordinary world.

                     ,   ,   ,

The myriad beings in sky and earth, the myriad feelings in human relations, the myriad affairs of the social world: when you look upon them with the ordinary eye, they are each different; but when you look upon them with the eye of the Way, all of them are normal. Why bother to discriminate? What's the use of grasping and rejecting?

                     ,   ,   ,

When the spirit is ecstatic, one finds the mellowing energy of heaven and earth even in humble circumstances. When you savor things to the full, after simple fare you know the reality of plainness in human life.

                     ,   ,   ,

Whether you are bound up or free is all in your own mind. When the mind is perfectly understood, even the profane world is a pure land as it is. Otherwise, even if you take up classical culture and have elegant hobbies, bedevilments are still there. It is said, "If you can stop, the realms of the senses become the realm of reality. If you don't understand, you are a worldling, even if a priest." How true!

, , ,

When you suddenly hear a bird warbling in the midst of utter silence, it calls up so many mysterious feelings. When you suddenly see a lone branch bearing a flower after all the plants have withered away, it touches off unlimited living potential. So it can be seen that the sky of nature never withers permanently, and the spirit of potential is best touched off.

, , ,

One poet said, "Better let body and mind be free, tacitly leaving them up to Creation." Another said, "Better collect body and mind, stabilize them, and return them to tranquil poise." Now "letting be free" can deteriorate into wildness, while "collecting" can get into quietism. Only those who skillfully control body and mind, and who can deliberately exercise mastery, can collect and let free autonomously.

, , ,

On a winter night when the land is covered with snow and the moon is in the sky, your state of mind is clarified simply and spontaneously. When you feel the gentle energy of the spring breeze, your psychological realm is also naturally harmonized. Creation and the human mind merge intimately without separation.

, , ,

Those who turn things around by themselves do not rejoice at gain or grieve over loss; the whole world is the range they roam. Those who are themselves used by things hate it when events go against them and love it when they go their way; the slightest thing can create binding entanglements.

, , ,

When reason is calm, things are calm, so to avoid things in order to hold to reason is like trying to get rid of the shadow but keep the form. When mind is empty, objects are empty, so to keep away from objects in order to maintain the mind is like shooing away insects while gathering raw meat.

, , ,

Try to think of what you were like before you were born, and also what you will be like after you die. Then myriad thoughts cool down, leaving your whole essence calm; you are thus spontaneously able to transcend things and live in a state prior to formalization.

, , ,

If you treasure strength only after having gotten sick, or value peace only after having experienced turmoil, that is not being quick-witted. If you run into good fortune but realize already that it can be the basis of calamity, or if in your eagerness for life you realize beforehand that it is the cause of death, that would seem to be a lofty view.

, , ,

Performers put on makeup and portray beauty and ugliness; but when the play is over, where are beauty and ugliness then? Chess players vie for precedence and seek to better each other in their moves; but when the game is over and the pieces are put away, where is the contest then?

, , ,

When mind is mindless, what is there to contemplate? When Buddhists talk about contemplating mind, they increase their obstacles. Things are originally one thing; what need have they of equalization? When Taoists talk about equalizing things, they themselves split their sameness.

, , ,

As long as your self-mastery is uncertain, it is best to be aloof of the mundane world, causing the mind not to see anything desirable and so not to be disturbed, thus to clarify your state of tranquillity. Once your discipline is firm, you should get involved in the mundane world again, causing the mind not to be disturbed even on seeing desirable things, thus to nurture your rounded capacity.

, , ,

Those who like tranquillity and dislike clamor tend to avoid people to seek quietude. They do not know that when one wishes there were no one around, that is egotism; and when the mind is attached to quietude, that is the root of disturbance. How can they reach the state where others and oneself are seen as one, where disturbance and quietude are both forgotten?

, , ,

When I get into a happy mood and walk barefoot in the fragrant grass, sometimes wild birds forget their wariness and accompany me. When the scenery suits my mind and I open my collar and sit still under falling flowers, white clouds slowly gather without saying a word.

, , ,

The realms of good fortune and calamity in human life are all made of thoughts and imaginings. Therefore Buddhists say that the burning of desire for gain is itself a pit of fire, while drowning in greedy love is itself a bitter sea. The moment thoughts are pure, fierce flames become a pond; the moment you become aware, the boat has arrived on the further shore. If your thoughts vary at all, your world will immediately differ; so can we not be careful?

, , ,

Chafing rope can cut through wood, dripping water can pierce stone; those who study the Way need to seek it with extra effort. Where water reaches a channel forms, when a melon is ripe the stem falls off; those who attain the Way entrust everything to the workings of nature.

, , ,

When machinations cease, then the moon is there and the breeze comes; so one needn't experience the world as an ocean of misery. When the mind is aloof, there are no dust and tracks from the rat race; so why get addicted to mountains?

, , ,

As soon as the plants and trees have withered, they show sprouts at the roots. Even though the order of the seasons brings freezing cold, eventually it brings back sunny energy. In the midst of purging and killing, the sense of continually renewing life is always in control. Thereby one can see the heart of heaven and earth.

> , , ,

When you gaze on the colors of the mountains after a rain, the scenery seems freshly beautiful. When you listen to the sound of a bell on a still night, the tone is most sublimely clear.

> , , ,

Climbing a high mountain makes people's hearts broad; gazing into a stream makes people's minds aloof. Reading books on a rainy or snowy night makes people's spirits clear; relaxing and humming a tune on top of a knoll makes people's feelings soar.

> , , ,

Without the wind and moon, flowers and willows, there wouldn't be Creation; without sensual desires and likings, there wouldn't be the substance of mind. As long as you operate things by yourself and do not let things use you, then likes and desires are all celestial mechanisms, senses and feelings are themselves the realm of principle.

> , , ,

When you understand yourself as an individual, only then can you entrust all things to all things. When you return the world to the world, only then can you transcend the mundane while in the mundane.

> , , ,

If a person's life is too leisurely, extraneous thoughts arise insidiously; but if one is too busy, true essence does not appear. Therefore, enlightened people should not fail to embrace the concerns of body and mind, yet they still should not fail to steep themselves in aesthetic delights.

> , , ,

The human mind often loses reality through movement. If you sit in a state of clear serenity without a single thought born, then as clouds arise, you calmly go off into the distance with them; as raindrops patter, you coolly share in their purity. As the birds call, you joyfully sense communication; as flowers fall, you have a profound understanding of yourself. Where is not the realm of reality, what is not the working of reality?

, , ,

When a child is born, the mother is endangered; when money piles up, robbers look in: so what joy is not a worry? When you are poor, you are willing to economize; if you are sick you are willing to take care of your body: so what worry is not a joy? Therefore, people of attainment should look upon ups and downs as one, and let both joy and sorrow be forgotten.

, , ,

When the ear is like a valley, through which whirlwinds pass casting echoes, letting them go through and not keeping them, then "right" and "wrong" both disappear. When the mind is like a pond reflecting the moon, open and unattached to the forms in it, then things and self are both forgotten.

, , ,

When worldly people get tangled and bound by prestige and profit, they are apt to call the material world a sea of misery. They are not aware of the white of the clouds or the green of the mountains, the flow of the river or the lay of the rocks, the response of the valleys to the songs of the woodcutters. The world is not material, the sea of life is not misery—they just make their own minds materialistic and miserable.

, , ,

Flowers should be viewed when half open, wine should be drunk only to subtle intoxication; there is great fun in this. If you view flowers in full bloom and drink to drunkenness, it becomes a bad experience. Those who are living to the full should think about this.

, , ,

Wild vegetables are not irrigated by people, wild animals are not raised by people; their taste is flavorful and clear. If we can avoid being stained by things of the world, will our smell not be vastly different?

⸲ ⸲ ⸲

If you are going to raise flowers, grow bamboo, enjoy the birds, and watch fish, you do need to have some self-mastery. If you are just passing the time as a sightseer or aesthete, this is what Confucians call superficiality and what Buddhists call insensitive openness. What refined sense is there in that?

⸲ ⸲ ⸲

Educated people who live in the mountains and forests are poor because of their high ethical standards, but the delights of freedom are plenty in themselves. Farmers in the fields lead rustic and simple lives, but their natural reality is all there. If you might lose yourself to merchants in the cities, it would be better to fall and die in a ditch or a ravine with your spirit and character still clean.

⸲ ⸲ ⸲

Fortune you don't deserve and gains gotten for no reason are either Creation's hook and bait or traps of the human world. If your perception is not highly developed here, you will rarely avoid falling for their devices.

⸲ ⸲ ⸲

Human life is like a puppet. Just keep the root and stem in hand, so that not a single string gets tangled up, and you can reel in and reel out freely, action and response being up to you, not subject to the slightest control by anyone else. Then you transcend this stage play.

⸲ ⸲ ⸲

When something happens, some harm is done. This is why everyone usually considers it lucky when life is uneventful. I read a poem by someone who lived in the past that said, "I urge you not to talk about the affairs of entitlement as a lord; for a single general's success, ten thousand skeletons dry in the sun." Also, "If everything were always peaceful, swords might well rust in their scabbards for a thousand years." Even though I had a heroic heart and a fierce spirit, unawares they turned to ice and hail.

⸲ ⸲ ⸲

Promiscuous women may become nuns to feign reform, while obsessive men may enter religion due to some stimulus or excitement. This is why the "schools of clear purity" are always hotbeds of promiscuous and perverted people.

, , ,

The people in a boat on rough water don't know to fear, while bystanders are frozen with terror; the people in a group being reviled by a madman do not know to be alarmed, while onlookers bite their tongues. Therefore, enlightened people may be physically in the world, but their minds must transcend the world.

, , ,

Human life is made freer by minimization. For example, if you party less, you avoid that much more frenzy, and if you speak less, you avoid that much more resentment. If you think less, your vital spirit doesn't get worn out, and if you are less clever, your wholeness can be preserved. Those who seek not to lessen daily but to increase daily are really fettering their lives.

, , ,

The cold and heat of the climate are easy to avoid, compared with the difficulty of eliminating the fevers and chills of human society. But the fevers and chills of human society are easy to eliminate, compared with the difficulty of getting rid of the ice and embers in one's mind. If you can get rid of the ice and embers inside you, your whole body will be filled with harmonious energy and the spring breeze will naturally be there wherever you are.

, , ,

The Buddhist teaching of adapting to conditions and the Confucian teaching of plain living are rafts to cross the ocean. This is because the ways of the world are uncertain, and a single thought of seeking to have everything leads to myriad complications. If you make yourself comfortable wherever you happen to be, you can go anywhere.

Sources

The Art of Wealth: Strategies for Success, translated by Thomas Cleary. Deerfield Beach, Florida: Health Communications, Inc., 1998. Copyright © 1998 by Thomas Cleary.

Living a Good Life: Advice on Virtue, Love, and Action from the Ancient Greek Masters, translated by Thomas Cleary. Boston: Shambhala Publications, 1997. Copyright © 1997 by Thomas Cleary.

The Human Element: A Course in Resourceful Thinking, by Thomas Cleary. Boston: Shambhala Publications, 1994. Copyright © 1994 by Thomas Cleary.

Back to Beginnings: Reflections on the Tao, by Huanchu Daoren, translated by Thomas Cleary. Boston: Shambhala Publications, 1990. Copyright © 1990 by Thomas Cleary.